THE PATH TO ZERO

1—

THE PATH TO
ZERO

Dialogues on

Nuclear Dangers

For dear Nancy
Peace!

RICHARD FALK &
DAVID KRIEGER

Love,
David

PARADIGM PUBLISHERS

Boulder & London

Copyright © 2012 Paradigm Publishers

Published in the United States by Paradigm Publishers, 2845 Wilderness Place, Boulder, CO 80301 USA.

Paradigm Publishers is the trade name of Birkenkamp & Company, LLC, Dean Birkenkamp, President and Publisher.

Falk, Richard A.
The path to zero : dialogues on nuclear dangers /
by Richard Falk and David Krieger.
p. cm.
Includes index.
ISBN 978-1-61205-214-4 (pbk. ; alk. paper) 1. Nuclear nonproliferation.
2. Nuclear disarmament. 3. Nuclear arms control. I. Krieger, David, 1942–
II. Title.
JZ5675.F35 2012
327.1'747—dc23

2011048268

Printed and bound in the United States of America on acid free paper that meets the standards of the American National Standard for Permanence of Paper for Printed Library Materials.

Designed and typeset in Adobe Caslon by Straight Creek Bookmakers.

16 15 14 13 12   1 2 3 4 5

Dedicated to

Sarah, Matthew, and Juliet

Ryan, Eric, Zachary, Andrew, Alyse, Nat, Addie, and Alice

And the children of the future

Contents

9 Nuclear Weapons and Democracy 167

10 The Path to Zero 191

Acknowledgments

We thank the pioneers in seeking a world free of nuclear weapons, including Albert Camus, John Hersey, Albert Einstein, Joseph Rotblat, Bertrand Russell, E. P. Thompson, Albert Schweitzer, Kenzaburo Oe, Norman Cousins, Robert Jay Lifton, Jonathan Schell, James Yamazaki, Daniel Ellsberg, and Helen Caldicott for their illuminating writings and activities exhibiting understanding, conscience, commitment, and courage.

We thank also the *hibakusha*, the survivors of Hiroshima and Nagasaki, for their forgiveness, firmness, and perseverance in insisting that no one else on the planet should suffer their fate.

We extend our deep appreciation to our many colleagues who work for a world without nuclear weapons. Among these, we would mention particularly the board, advisors, associates, and staff of the Nuclear Age Peace Foundation, a dedicated group, many of whom have been our ongoing partners in dialogue.

Our special appreciation to Carol Warner for her help in preparing the manuscript for publication and for her helpful suggestions, and to Jennifer Knerr at Paradigm Publishers for her enthusiastic engagement with the entire substantive and editorial process of producing our book on an accelerated schedule.

We thank Plato for his seminal dialogues and all those seekers of truth and justice over the centuries who have kept the art of dialogue alive.

We also thank our wives, Hilal and Carolee, for the long continuity of their love and encouragement.

It is our hope that those who read this book will act on these issues, which are certain to affect the lives of countless future generations and could constrain and even foreclose them. It is in this spirit of an engaged concern for the future that we dedicate this book to our grandchildren.

The views expressed in these dialogues have been developed through our relations over many decades with colleagues near and far. They represent, however, our personal perspectives and not those of any of our institutional affiliations. We hope that these dialogues will be a stimulus to greater action toward achieving a world without nuclear weapons.

Key Reference Documents

These documents can be accessed on the Paradigm Publishers Web page for *The Path to Zero*, available at http://www.paradigmpublishers.com/ Books/BookDetail.aspx?productID=298814

Ban Ki-moon. "The United Nations and security in a nuclear-weapon-free world." Address to the East West Institute, New York, October 24, 2008. http://www.un.org/apps/news/infocus/sgspeeches/search_full .asp?statID=351

Green, Robert. "Breaking Free from Nuclear Deterrence." Santa Barbara: Nuclear Age Peace Foundation, Tenth Annual Frank K. Kelly Lecture on Humanity's Future, 2011. http://wagingpeace.org/menu/ programs/public-events/frank-kelly-lecture/10th-annual-lecture/ kelly_lecture_2011.pdf

"Legality of the Threat or Use of Nuclear Weapons." Advisory Opinion of the International Court of Justice, The Hague, July 8, 1996. http://www .icj-cij.org/docket/index.php?p1=3&p2=4&k=e1&p3=4& case=95

McCloy-Zorin Accords. "Joint Statement of Agreed Principles for Disarmament Negotiations," signed on September 20, 1961, unanimously adopted by the United Nations General Assembly on December 20, 1961. http:// nuclearfiles.org/menu/key-issues/nuclear-weapons/issues/arms-control -disarmament/mccloy-zorin-accords_1961-09-20.htm

Model Nuclear Weapons Convention. "Convention on the Prohibition of the Development, Testing, Production, Stockpiling, Transfer, Use and Threat of Use of Nuclear weapons and on Their Elimination, April 2007." United Nations General Assembly A/62/650, January 18, 2008. http://inesap.org/sites/default/files/inesap_old/mNWC_2007_ Unversion_English_N0821377.pdf

Obama, Barack. Remarks of President Barack Obama, Hradčany Square, Prague, Czech Republic, April 5, 2009. http://prague.usembassy.gov/obama.html

Rotblat, Joseph. "Remember Your Humanity." Nobel Lecture, Oslo, Norway, December 10, 1995. http://www.nobelprize.org/nobel_prizes/peace/laureates/1995/rotblat-lecture.html

Russell-Einstein Manifesto, issued in London, July 9, 1955. http://www.pugwash.org/about/manifesto.htm

Santa Barbara Declaration. "Reject Nuclear Deterrence: An Urgent Call to Action," Santa Barbara, CA, February 17, 2011. http://www.wagingpeace.org/articles/db_article.php?article_id=209

Treaty on the Non-Proliferation of Nuclear Weapons, entered into force on March 5, 1970. http://www.state.gov/www/global/arms/treaties/npt1.html#2

Vancouver Declaration. "Law's Imperative for the Urgent Achievement of a Nuclear-Weapon-Free World," Vancouver, Canada, March 23, 2011. http://www.lcnp.org/wcourt/Feb2011VancouverConference/declarationmediarelease.pdf

Introduction

Nuclear weapons are not currently a subject of intense public discussion and debate, but they should be. They are weapons that define an era, the Nuclear Age, and they define it by their immense and unprecedented power of destruction. Nuclear weapons are the result of scientific discoveries that opened the door to the splitting of heavy atoms and, with thermonuclear weapons, to even greater releases of power by the fusion of light atoms. The scientific discoveries and engineering feats that created nuclear weapons prior to and during the World War II Manhattan Project were only the beginning of an era in which the future of the human species and most life on earth would be put in danger of annihilation.

The questions for humankind are: How will we respond to these immensely powerful weapons? Are we capable of eliminating their threat? Can civilization make the leap to survival in a world with thousands of nuclear weapons? Will humankind become the victim of its own cleverness? These are daunting questions, not to be swept aside or trivialized.

This book was conceived as a way to explore many of the dangers of nuclear weapons, to dig beneath the surreal surface tranquility that has largely surrounded their existence. The means by which we have undertaken this exploration is a series of dialogues in which we exchange ideas about various aspects of the nuclear weapons dilemma confronting humanity. We have both spent many decades thinking, writing, and speaking about nuclear weapons. We have both written books and articles about nuclear weapons, their relation to international law, and the need to abolish these weapons. We both believe that continuing on the path of reliance on nuclear weapons is a recipe for disaster.

Although we agree on much, our thoughts diverge in many areas, including with regard to the value of the Non-Proliferation Treaty and President Barack Obama's level of commitment to abolishing nuclear weapons. We favor a new international treaty, a nuclear weapons convention for the phased, verifiable, irreversible, and transparent elimination of nuclear weapons. While we see this path as the way to escape the overriding dangers of the Nuclear Age, we realize that achieving this new treaty will not be easy and will require global cooperation on a vast new scale. We explore in our dialogues ways to move forward.

We hope that the dialogues will be a catalyst to broader societal discussion of nuclear dangers. This is not a subject to be left only to experts. In the field of nuclear survival, there are no true experts. There is only reason, intelligence, values, and emotional response. We humans are all potential victims of nuclear annihilation, and therefore we all have a right and responsibility to address the issue. We also share a responsibility for the lives and well-being of future generations, those who lack a voice to speak for themselves yet. The so-called experts and their political allies have brought us to the brink of the nuclear precipice, where we must tread lightly due to the risk of slipping over into the abyss below.

We hope that this book will lead readers to think more deeply about the dangers nuclear weapons pose to humanity and about the limits of our human capacities to control such dangers. We do not claim to have all the answers, but we hope that we have raised enough of the right questions and explored enough facets of the nuclear dilemma so that readers will be sufficiently challenged to become a force for a world without nuclear weapons.

None of us has the power to bring about global change alone, but acting together we are immensely powerful. In fact, in cooperative solidarity we have a power far greater than the arsenals of nuclear weapons that currently endanger us. Will we recognize the nuclear dilemma that confronts us in the twenty-first century? Will we be able also to recognize and mobilize our power, when acting together, to become a force for change? Will we act soon enough and effectively enough to assure civilization's survival?

There is no simple way to bring the nuclear weapons era to an end, and there are many among us who believe it cannot happen. Abolishing nuclear weapons will not occur as a matter of either logic or magic. Like all great social and political endeavors, it must be a common enterprise that encompasses our highest ideals and our most determined efforts. If our dialogues encourage deeper thought and stimulate collective action toward achieving a world without nuclear weapons, we will count our efforts as worthwhile beyond the satisfactions of this intensive dialogic learning experience.

The Nuclear Age

Krieger: There are many ways in which our time can be defined, depending upon what one feels are its most important characteristics. Some think of our time as an information age, others as an age of expanding inequities, others as a postcolonial age, and still others as an age of terror. Any of these concepts—and I'm sure there are many other possibilities—could arguably define the period in which we live. The one that seems most relevant to me, though, is the Nuclear Age. This description of our time focuses on our most powerful technology, just as the labels "Stone Age," "Bronze Age," and "Iron Age" described earlier times. What is unique about the Nuclear Age is that we humans have created a technology powerful enough to destroy ourselves along with most, if not all, other complex forms of life on the planet.

The Nuclear Age may be said to have begun with the first nuclear weapon test on July 16, 1945. Three weeks later the power of the new weapon was revealed to the world when the United States used a nuclear weapon to destroy the city of Hiroshima. Three days later, the United States bombed the city of Nagasaki with another nuclear weapon. Many of the scientists who worked on the Manhattan Project to create nuclear weapons tried to stop them from being used on Japanese cities. They argued instead in favor of a harmless demonstration of the power of the weapons for a select group of Japanese leaders, but U.S. leaders rejected this idea. Thus, with the devastation of Hiroshima and Nagasaki, the bomb literally burst into the consciousness of people throughout the world. People discovered not only that a single bomb could destroy a city, but that there were leaders in possession of these weapons who were not inhibited by law or morality from using their enormous destructive power on civilians. The opening salvos of the Nuclear Age set the tone for the arms races and nuclear recklessness that have followed.

The Challenge of the Nuclear Age

Krieger: In a sense, the Nuclear Age has pitted humans against their most destructive technological creations. In the past, tribes have fought against tribes and nations have fought against nations, but now humans are confronted by the dangers of their own technological creations. The challenge of the Nuclear Age is to control and eliminate these weapons of nearly unlimited destructive power. The survivors of Hiroshima and Nagasaki, called *hibakusha* in Japanese, have fought to ensure that their past does not become someone else's future. They have argued that nuclear weapons and human beings cannot coexist and that we must eliminate the weapons before they eliminate us. Their perspective is very different from that of the theorists who have developed elaborate strategies for possessing and threatening to use nuclear weapons to "prevent" war. The Nuclear Age has been characterized by the differing perspectives of those who have viewed nuclear weapons as valuable for maintaining the peace, those who have viewed nuclear weapons as a potential threat capable of destroying humanity, and those who for various reasons have remained largely ignorant of and indifferent to the weapons.

Many people in the Nuclear Age live in denial of the threat posed by these weapons, but many others believe the weapons are so powerful that they have prevented wars between major powers. Still others see the weapons as a great threat to humanity but feel helpless to effect change with regard to national or international policies. Since nuclear weapons were first created and used, humans have struggled with their meaning for our lives and for the future of humanity. It seems clear to me that nuclear weapons pose an intolerable threat to the human future. They bring us to the edge of a precipice where we can see into the abyss below; but, seemingly paralyzed by fear, we have hesitated to move away from the danger to ourselves, our children, and our grandchildren.

Those who argue that nuclear weapons make the world safer have a relatively short time frame in which to show signs of this "benefit." Over the course of only six and a half decades, which is barely a tick on the geological clock, there have actually been many serious mishaps and near catastrophes. There were also many proxy wars during the Cold War. And we are not yet out of the Nuclear Age; it did not end with the end of the Cold War. Today there are new sets of dangers, and even the old dangers did not completely recede with the end of the Cold War. Whereas once the Cold War dominated the nuclear threat to humanity, today the threats are more diverse. India and Pakistan, both nuclear armed, have fought many battles over Kashmir. Future wars between these antagonistic countries could trigger a nuclear exchange. North Korea has shown the "value" of nuclear weapons as "military equalizers" and "bargaining chips," but it pursues a dangerous strategy. Despite its threats of retaliation if attacked, it could be inviting the annihilation of its people. Israel's nuclear arsenal could trigger a nuclear arms race in the Middle East, with even greater uncertainties and dangers for the region than currently exist. There is also the threat of nonstate extremists obtaining nuclear weapons or the materials to construct them. The possibility of nuclear terrorism cannot be dismissed.

The Human Future Endangered

Krieger: Many issues in the Nuclear Age deserve our attention and the attention of humanity. Nuclear weapons and nuclear arsenals are a starting point. There are also issues of nuclear strategies and their reliability, particularly the reliability of deterrence theory, which has been central to the nuclear enterprise. There are issues of the "peaceful" uses of nuclear energy and the relationship of these uses to the proliferation of nuclear weapons. There are issues of law and morality and of the relationship of nuclear weapons to democracy. The Nuclear Age is not just a critical time for humanity; it is also our time on earth. Those of us alive today are responsible not only for the dangers that nuclear weapons pose to vast numbers of people but also for assuring that there is a future. In the Nuclear Age, a future for humanity can no longer be assumed.

Falk: My initial response is to think it may be diversionary to discuss whether it is appropriate to label our historical present as the Nuclear Age. There is no doubt that you approach the challenges of our time from this angle, placing stress on this infernal capability to destroy human civilization and to rest the security of peoples on the willingness to use such destructive might against the civilian population of an enemy state, especially should it launch or even threaten to use nuclear weaponry. I believe it was true that the shock effect of the bombs dropped on Hiroshima and Nagasaki at the end of World War II did give rise to a human-generated apocalyptic fear that had not existed before and made it sensible to think of ourselves as living in a radically new global setting that could be properly identified as the Nuclear Age. But that time was superseded rather rapidly by the normalization of the threat posed by nuclear war and the treatment of nuclear weapons as weapons of last resort, yet part of the logic of war where the survival of "our side" is the unconditional priority, no matter what the costs in lives and devastation. Beyond this, it was possible for an American leader to threaten, without encountering serious objection, the nondefensive use of nuclear weapons. Dwight D. Eisenhower did this in 1952 to bring the Korean War to an end and faced no significant public protest. Today there is little objection when Israeli or American leaders talk rather openly about developing nuclear weapons with potential battlefield roles such as destroying underground targets. Such an outlook refutes the claim often made that the only reason to possess the weaponry is to deter attacks and conceivably to retaliate with these weapons if attacked with nuclear weapons.

Krieger: Regardless of what one calls the time in which we live, we have the technological capacity, made possible by nuclear weapons, to destroy the human species. Actually, this capacity did not arise immediately from the first atomic weapons. These weapons were frightening, but not nearly as frightening in their potential for destruction as the thermonuclear weapons that would be developed and tested in the 1950s. These weapons were thousands of times more powerful than the first atomic weapons. You're right that the threat posed by nuclear war has been largely "normalized." For most people, nuclear weapons have become a part of the background of their lives, and only occasional crises have reminded them of the threat. The general public has seemed comfortable with retreating into a kind of nuclear complacency. It is a complacency that is unwarranted, however, given persisting threats of nuclear devastation by accident, miscalculation, or the intentional use of nuclear weapons, as well as post-9/11 concerns about nuclear weapons falling into the hands of nonstate extremist organizations, including the al Qaeda network.

A Hypothetical Opening to the Nuclear Age

Falk: Except for periodic crises during the Cold War, perhaps most dramatically during the Cuban Missile Crisis of 1962, the public lost interest in nuclear weaponry, and governmental establishments went about their business with an extra dose of stealth, but always proceeding on the assumption that the weapons were here to stay, constituting vital elements of a flexible security posture for any leading state in the world. I have often thought that had the Nuclear Age started differently, say with a Nazi nuclear weapon used against a British city in the closing months of World War II, the status of the weapons might have been decisively different in two principal ways: The incredible devastation and suffering caused by such a German attack would likely have inhibited the use of such a weapon by the United States against Japan; and had the victory over Germany and Japan been achieved with only this German use of the weapon, then whoever on the German side ordered the weapon used would have been prosecuted for war crimes and almost certainly convicted. If the victorious liberal democracies had had "clean hands" with respect to these weapons in 1945, then it is quite reasonable to suppose that nuclear weaponry would have been criminalized, making even development and possession distinct war crimes of the greatest severity and undermining the prestige incentives associated with the weaponry. If the United States had not possessed and used the weapon, then the Soviet Union would not, in all probability, have devoted the resources to achieve the capability, and the whole course of history would have been, or at least might have been, decisively different.

Krieger: You describe a very interesting hypothetical opening to the Nuclear Age. Surely, the public perception of nuclear weapons in the United States would have been very different if the Nazis had been the first to develop and use them. Had they done so, in one possible scenario they might have won the war in Europe, which was the refugee scientists' original rationale for promoting the U.S. nuclear weapons program. In the scenario you describe, in which the Nazis develop and use the weapon and still lose the war, the weapons would become associated in the minds of Americans with the evil of the Nazis, and the threatened or actual use of them would be considered a war crime or a crime against humanity. Of course, this didn't happen, and we are stuck with the history that actually unfolded.

Falk: The actual historical sequence produced somewhat the opposite result. The United States, as the first developer and user of nuclear weapons, was also the leader in the crusade against fascism and Japanese militarism, as well as victorious in the war. Its use of the weaponry was justified at the time as saving American lives—and in certain formulations, even Japanese lives—the reasoning being that the alternative to the atomic attacks was an invasion that would produce a million or more casualties on each side. Given the overall political climate, including the emerging rivalry with the Soviet Union, the media and public opinion gave a sigh of relief when Japan surrendered in the aftermath of the attacks, and the evaluation of nuclear weaponry was preoccupied with what might happen in the future. Here initial sentiment fearful of a future nuclear war favored following a path leading to world government or at least to total nuclear disarmament. Such a sentiment never took control of public debate and was soon subordinated to the realization that, in relation to the Soviet Union, the possession and further development of nuclear weapons gave the West an edge in the rivalry, as well as offset the Soviet advantage in conventional weaponry, and that nuclear weapons should not be eliminated unless a means could be found to retain the strategic advantages that they were believed to confer, either by retaining control of the stockpile of fissionable material or through superior technological know-how that would tilt any postdisarmament nuclear rearmament race in the direction of the West. In effect, great power rivalry, the old game of international relations, became reascendant, and the main nuclear weapon states never looked back, or even contemplated in any serious way, except for momentary departures, getting rid of nuclear weaponry.

Public Complacency and Despair

Falk: The fact that no weapon has been used since Nagasaki reinforces both governmental and public complacency, giving rise to a form of false consciousness supposing that since nuclear war has not taken place in these sixty-seven years, it will never happen—that the weapons are safe and secure, and there is no great cause for concern. This prevailing mood of complacency also undermines support for disarmament initiatives, making it more difficult to circumvent the obstacles placed in the path of moves to rid the world of nuclear weapons by the domestic nuclear weapons establishment (consisting of weapons makers, weapons labs, think tanks, and the Pentagon in the United States and comparable institutional forces in the other nuclear weapon states). Furthermore, since World War II every attempt to do more than regulate the costs and uncertainties of the nuclear arms rivalry or limit some of its risks has ended in frustration.

Even the collapse of the Soviet Union and post-9/11 concerns about political extremists gaining control of nuclear weapons has not generated a debate about whether security might be enhanced for the United States and others by getting rid of the weaponry altogether.

Krieger: The issue of public complacency is a critical one. So long as the public is complacent and remains unengaged in the issue, changing the status quo is unlikely. Finding the key that opens the door to public concern over the nuclear threat and its profoundly negative implications for the human future seems to me essential if we are to assure that we have a future.

Falk: To some extent this complacency may be hiding an underlying despair, a turning away because it seems impossible to get rid of the weaponry. There was a great outpouring of hope and enthusiasm when President Barack Obama gave his speech in Prague on April 5, 2009, in which he committed the U.S. government to the quest for a world without nuclear weaponry and generally nurtured the hope of people around the world that he was dedicated to achieving a better human future and would lead the world in that direction.[1] Unfortunately, this moment passed quickly, and attention shifted to the passage of a typical arms control measure, New START, which cut the size of American and Russian nuclear arsenals but did nothing to signal any effort to seek the elimination of the weaponry. On the contrary, to mobilize support in the U.S. Congress, the White House pledged support for an additional $85 billion for further development of nuclear weaponry and to continue work on missile defense. Yes, it is a Nuclear Age in the narrow, somewhat technical sense that it has proved politically impossible to remove this sword of Damocles that has been hanging by a slender thread over the fate of humanity for these several decades.

Krieger: It is interesting to speculate about whether the general complacency among the public is masking an underlying despair. I tend to think that it isn't. The complacency may be a way to cover over the fear associated with nuclear devastation, but I think it is mostly a failure to fully recognize the seriousness of the danger. As time goes by, particularly with the end of the Cold War, it must seem to many people that the dangers have receded so far that they are virtually nonexistent. What is missing from the equation is leadership, and I think that is why President Obama's Prague speech made such a strong impact. We should remember, though, that the speech was delivered in Europe, and in general the Europeans have been much more eager than Americans to see nuclear weapons eliminated. I viewed President Obama's Prague speech as a moment of hope, but when I reviewed it carefully, I realized that he had a little something for everyone in the speech. He said that America seeks "the peace and security of a world without nuclear weapons," but he then added that he was not naïve and that the goal would not be reached quickly and perhaps not in his lifetime.[2] In other words, he signaled that there is no sense of urgency and that we will continue for the foreseeable future to live in the Nuclear Age. This is an era in which some countries continue to hold the world hostage to their concept of security, which is really state terrorism. These same countries express the strongest concerns about nonstate nuclear terrorism, a possibility that their own arsenals make more likely.

Falk: Big events often lead us to affix labels to historical eras. Thus, after 9/11 numerous conferences and book titles contained the phrase "age of terror," but was that an adequate label for the preoccupations, priorities, and pursuits of most people in the world? I think not. It may have been descriptive of the immediate shock occasioned by the attacks in the United States and the abrupt realization that the country was acutely vulnerable to this sort of nonstate violence despite having the most powerful military capabilities in history. But for most of the world's peoples, the issues of poverty, development, conflict, corruption, and oppression were far more salient than nuclear weaponry, or for that matter terrorism, and it is important for all of us living in affluent parts of the world not to be insensitive to the outlooks of others facing their own overwhelming challenges.

In my view, it is acceptable for us to talk about the Nuclear Age because that is the focus of our concerns, and arguably this dimension of our world has global and species implications that are greater than any other challenge at this time, although even here this will strike many as an overstatement. At present, of the distinctly *global* challenges climate change seems currently to command the greatest global attention and is alone supported by a scientific consensus suggesting that without drastic adjustments urgently undertaken, the future of humanity is deeply imperiled, even apocalyptically. Recent widely read books such as Clive Hamilton's *Requiem for a Species*, James Hanson's *Storms of My Grandchildren*, and Gwynne Dyer's *Climate Wars* depict a dark, foreboding future, given the anticipated failure to reduce global warming by restricting the emission of greenhouse gasses. The public imagination of the post-Hiroshima era that gave rise to such cultural works as Neville Shute's *On the Beach* (1957), the film *Hiroshima Mon Amour* (1959), or even Jonathan Schell's *Fate of the Earth* (1982) has vanished from serious political discourse because other concerns have emerged, not because the risks associated with nuclear weaponry have diminished.

The Need to Raise Our Voices

Falk: For those of us who retain the fear and revulsion associated with these weapons, it is necessary to raise our voices, even if they are heard as cries in the wilderness. I believe we have a responsibility to make our case as well as we can. Our way of making our case relies primarily on reason, evidence, ethics, law, and a Plan B that is both feasible and desirable, but it also appreciates the role played by appeals to emotions and values via poetry, film, and fiction. Perhaps, this counter-societal commitment underpinning these dialogues provides enough of a justification for the designation "Nuclear Age," that is, precisely to pose a challenge to complacency. At least this justification is convincing for me.

Krieger: It is convincing for me as well. There will always be contending ways to define an era. For me, Nuclear Age is a defining concept because it contains within it the seeds for stirring people from their complacency. To focus attention on terrorism, President George W. Bush used the term "global war on terror." If you want to use your country's resources and send young men and women to die in distant lands, this is perhaps a useful concept. I think it is actually a dishonest concept, but one that has been useful for perpetrating and perpetuating endless war. The concept of the Nuclear Age draws our attention to nuclear technologies and hopefully to their dangers.

You're right that climate change has attracted much more attention among the public and among national leaders than has the nuclear threat. But the attention it has drawn has not been all positive by any means. Exposing the threats posed by climate change has resulted in extensive pushback among conservative political elites and right-wing media. There is a sense that large elements of the U.S. population are not guided by either truth or reality. Profits and desires to maintain domination supersede the risks inherent in climate change. The same attitudes are reflected in debates on nuclear weapons. Those who make light of the dangers of climate change are often the same people who seek nuclear advantage and oppose nuclear disarmament. Regardless of their attempts to maintain some form of nuclear supremacy, though, this will not be possible in the long run. That nuclear weapons may turn out to be "military equalizers" is being recognized by longtime conservative policy makers such as Henry Kissinger, George Shultz, William Perry, and Sam Nunn. These four former U.S. policy makers, sometimes referred to as the Gang of Four, have jointly written a series of opinion pieces in the *Wall Street Journal*.[3] They understand that nuclear terrorism is capable of leveling the playing field, even when one team on the field is as powerful as the United States.

Falk: Such conservative militarists as Henry Kissinger and George Shultz endorse a sophisticated national interest view that proliferation and potential access to nuclear weaponry both deter the United States in the use of force abroad and make the country more vulnerable to attack. Such antinuclear positions have little, if anything, to do with moral revulsion or legal condemnation of the weaponry, although they may be tactically useful in mobilizing public and elite support for embracing disarmament. At the same time, denuclearization without demilitarization is likely to be resisted eventually by several other countries, especially the secondary nuclear weapons states, and those that believe their security depends on the

U.S. "nuclear umbrella" would likely consider themselves more vulnerable to military attack with conventional weaponry and, if so, would either do their best to oppose nuclear disarmament or initiate a nonnuclear regional arms race by escalating defense expenditures. No issue of this sort is raised by the kind of arms control arrangements currently on the table, including New START, which leaves the hierarchy of nuclear weapons arsenals undisturbed. At some point we need to consider whether a nuclear disarming process is both viable and desirable if it is not extended to nonnuclear military capabilities in its final stages.

Krieger: A couple of other cultural works related to nuclear weapons, although they, like those mentioned above, also go back to the early decades of the Nuclear Age, are *Dr. Strangelove or: How I Learned to Stop Worrying and Love the Bomb* (1964) and *Fail-Safe* (1964). Both concern a failure in the command and control of nuclear weapons ending in nuclear tragedy. The more powerful of the two films, in my opinion, is *Fail-Safe*, although Peter Sellers does a brilliant comedic job of revealing the dark side of nuclear policy making in *Dr. Strangelove*. Another interesting film is *Amazing Grace and Chuck* (1987), about a young boy finding an improbable but effective means of challenging U.S. reliance on nuclear weapons and seeking the global abolition of nuclear arsenals.

Lack of Cultural Attention

Falk: It is worth noting that the public absence of these concerns at present is reflected in a lack of cultural attention to nuclear dangers, although the risks of a governmental use of the weaponry, while somewhat different than during the Cold War era, are still present and may have increased. The 9/11 attacks sparked some concerns about potential nuclear terrorism carried out by nonstate political actors, the Indo-Pakistan conflict, Iran's nuclear program, and the tensions on the Korean Peninsula, all of which could produce conditions in which nuclear weapons were used with catastrophic human consequences. To the extent that there remains a concern about the use of nuclear weapons, it focuses almost exclusively on what might happen if a regional conflict were to get out of control or the weapons were to fall into extremist hands by way of proliferation, the black market, or theft.

Among existing nuclear weapon states, it is generally agreed, Pakistan now seems the most unstable and dangerous country on the face of the earth, although Israel's threats directed at Iran have sometimes included suggestions that nuclear weapons could be used in carrying out attacks on the Iranian nuclear infrastructure. I mention these developments to make the broader point that the Nuclear Age is not a static conception of the impact of nuclear weaponry on world order but rather a dynamic reflection of the changing global setting, and it currently emphasizes the nuclear danger posed by nonstate actors and regional conflict, as well as dangers due to disasters of the Fukushima sort at nuclear reactors.

Krieger: The general cultural understanding of nuclear weapons in the United States seems to have moved from serious concern at various points during the Cold War to complacency in its aftermath. I would characterize the level of this concern for nuclear dangers as being extremely low at this time. Nuclear dangers, except for the possibility of nuclear terrorism, would hardly make the list of serious concerns for most Americans. In terms of these concerns, or lack thereof, this focus on nuclear terrorism is akin to a sleight-of-hand trick. The obvious hand distracts with the threat of terrorism, while the other hand, which is largely concealed, is busy modernizing the U.S. nuclear arsenal to make it more effective.

Since the creation of nuclear weapons, not everyone has been threatened to the same degree. Ironically, the countries most threatened are those with nuclear weapons. In the Nuclear Age, nuclear weapon states target other states but cannot escape being targeted themselves. Some countries with the technological capacity to develop nuclear weapons have chosen not to do so because they believe they are more secure without them. Yet, the overriding reality of the Nuclear Age is that all states and all people are potential victims of nuclear annihilation so long as the weapons exist in significant quantities.

Human Security versus National Security

Falk: I would also make explicit what might seem obvious. Agreement to consider labeling our historical epoch the "Nuclear Age" by no means implies that other human concerns are not vitally important. Issues associated with poverty, disease, global warming, self-determination, conflict resolution, human rights, global justice, and regulating the world economy are all of the greatest relevance to *human security*, a comprehensive perspective on public policy that privileges people rather than governmental regimes, which are given priority whenever security is associated exclusively with *national security*.

In this regard, it may be well to agree at the outset that we are viewing the Nuclear Age through an optic crafted by the priorities of human security. Such an optic contrasts with statist understandings of security that are preoccupied with grand strategy and the interests of bureaucratic and private-sector elites. It is important not to lose sight of the degree to which governmental policies on defense budgets and weapons are constrained by the hidden but powerful influences of the military-industrial-media complex.

Krieger: Of course, I agree that the concept of the Nuclear Age does not imply that other concerns, such as those you mention, are not of vital importance. I would say that the principal characteristic of the Nuclear Age is the fact that our technological capacities seem to have outstripped our social competence. We have created technologies that are more powerful than our capacities for control. We have poured our resources into developing ever more powerful weapons, weapons that could destroy civilization, and we remain uncertain as to whether we can harness these technologies to our use. There is a real possibility that our harnesses will not be effective in controlling the technologies. This is reflected in concerns about nuclear proliferation, nuclear accidents, and nuclear terrorism, but we should also be concerned by the intentions of those who possess nuclear weapons.

Our preoccupation in the Nuclear Age with our powerful technologies has led us to use our resources unwisely. The United States and Russia have poured valuable scientific and financial resources into developing nuclear arms and neglected the great gap that exists between the rich and poor of the world. In a sense, nuclear weapons appear to be used as an insurance policy in seeking to assure that the rich, or at least the dominant classes in the United States, United Kingdom, and France, will maintain their inequitable position in the world. Certainly the resources used on these weapons could have made an impact on alleviating poverty, reducing inequities, controlling diseases, and protecting the environment. Instead, the diversion of resources to the weapons has increased inequities, while the testing of the weapons has spread radioactive poisons and caused widespread destruction of the environment. The preoccupation of the rich countries with nuclear arsenals has been at the expense of working to resolve many of the world's other great problems, as well as serious social problems within countries. Nuclear arsenals have been developed in the name of national security, but at the expense of human security.

The Military-Industrial Complex

Krieger: You mention the powerful influence of the military-industrial-media complex. We shouldn't forget the attachment to this complex of academia and also the U.S. Congress. It has been fifty years since President Eisenhower referred to the military-industrial complex in his farewell address to the nation on January 17, 1961. He warned against the influence of this complex, which seems to have only grown since his time. He said, "The conjunction of an immense military establishment and a large arms industry is new in the American experience. The total influence—economic, political, even spiritual—is felt in every city, every state house, every office of the Federal government. We recognize the imperative need for this development. Yet we must not fail to comprehend its grave implications. Our toil, resources and livelihood are all involved; so is the very structure of our society."[4]

Eisenhower continued, "In the councils of government, we must guard against the acquisition of unwarranted influence, whether sought or unsought, by the military-industrial complex. The potential for the disastrous rise of misplaced power exists and will persist. We must never let the weight of this combination endanger our liberties or democratic processes. We should take nothing for granted. Only an alert and knowledgeable citizenry can compel the proper meshing of the huge industrial and military machinery of defense with our peaceful methods and goals, so that security and liberty may prosper together."[5]

After warning about the dangers of the military-industrial complex, to which we have added many other major institutions of our society, Eisenhower went on to share his disappointment with the meager gains in disarmament. "Disarmament with mutual honor and confidence," he said, "is a continuing imperative. Together we must learn how to compose our differences, not with arms, but with intellect and decent purpose. Because this need is so sharp and apparent I confess that I lay down my official responsibilities in this field with a definite sense of disappointment."[6]

Falk: I think it is appropriate to invoke Eisenhower's cautionary words, especially as they were uttered fifty years ago. They serve as a reminder not only that his warnings went unheeded but that the tendencies he found worrisome in 1961 are far more daunting now, yet went unmentioned in Obama's Prague speech. The only recent favorable development is the increasing American anxiety about financial overstretch, the gaping trade deficit, and the huge national debt; fiscal conservatives are beginning to realize that their economic priorities can be realized only if major cuts are made in the Pentagon budget or in such indispensable and very popular entitlement programs as Social Security and Medicare, or both. At present, fiscal conservatism is still subordinated to the bipartisan militarist consensus, which refuses even to discuss whether it is viable to maintain the costly projection of American power worldwide via a network of hundreds of foreign military bases, navies in every ocean, and the militarization of space.

But I have another point to make about this celebration of Eisenhower's wisdom regarding his contradictory moves as president when he possessed authority in relation to nuclear aspects of national security. Eisenhower and his notorious secretary of state, John Foster Dulles, were self-proclaimed fiscal conservatives, one manifestation of which was their contention that the defense budget could be reduced by achieving "a bigger bang for the buck," which, when translated into policy, meant a greater willingness to threaten, and if necessary use, nuclear weaponry. This was also the time when the U.S. government endorsed the policy of "massive retaliation" as a nuclear weapons posture, in effect threatening an enemy with unrestrained and indiscriminate devastation, an omnicidal threat if account is taken, as it should be, of radioactive fallout. Additionally, during the Eisenhower presidency, greater discretion was given to battlefield commanders to initiate the use of nuclear weaponry. This devolution of command authority was viewed at the time as an important move in the direction of *normalizing* reliance on nuclear weapons.

My intention is not to tarnish the reputation of Eisenhower or to raise doubts about the validity of the remarks that you have drawn to my attention. It is to point out that even those in public office most sensitive to the dangers of American militarism are caught within the existing structures of national security policy, and their challenges, if made at all, tend to be rife with contradiction.

I have one further concern about Eisenhower's famous speech. Why did he wait to voice these anxieties until he was leaving the office of the presidency? Why make these statements in a farewell address? Why not take some action, confront some opposition, raise the issues of concern in public debate? In fairness, Eisenhower isn't the first leader to look back on a militarist career with a belated skepticism. The father of the nuclear submarine, and a staunch advocate of submarine warfare fought with nuclear missiles, was Admiral Hyman Rickover, who at his retirement dinner also warned of the menace associated with the very capabilities he had done so much to establish and champion, fighting each year in Congress for every last Polaris submarine. Robert McNamara never stopped shedding tears about the Vietnam War after he was no longer in the government, although at the peak of his influence he was proud that the war was called "McNamara's War." According to distinguished psychohistorian Robert Jay Lifton, this behavior exhibits "the retirement syndrome," in which guilt accumulated for actions taken during career years is abruptly acknowledged, in effect, as an act of unconscious atonement.

The more serious point here is that nothing will be done about the concerns voiced when the authority figure waits until he or she lacks any formal or effective power. There is an understanding that such doubts as expressed are not really intended to influence public policy but are within a domain of piety, important for the cleansing of impurities from the person, and perhaps the audience, but not politically significant, and thus with a lasting resonance only for those outside the realms of governance. How often do active political leaders, even those with liberal credentials, warn of the military-industrial complex or remind the public or the Congress of Eisenhower's warnings?

Krieger: It's true that the timing of Eisenhower's warning about the "unwarranted influence" of the military-industrial complex is suspect and that he seems to have done very little to reduce the influence of this powerful complex during his eight years in office. In fact, at least with regard to nuclear weapons, the number of weapons grew dramatically on his watch, from some 1,400 in 1953 to over 20,000 when he left office. Perhaps Lifton was correct that Eisenhower's warning in his farewell address was an attempt to reduce his guilt and a form of unconscious atonement. I would focus, however, not only on the psychology of his motivations but on the impact he hoped to achieve. Eisenhower could have left office with no reference to the dangers of the military-industrial complex. His reputation was secured by his military leadership during World War II as commander of the Allied forces in Europe. He was a major military hero of that conflict. Yet, he did warn against the "unwarranted influence" of the military-industrial complex, and he regretted the lack of progress toward disarmament in his time, which was relatively early in the Nuclear Age.

I don't know if we can determine what motivated Eisenhower's warning at the end of his term in office, but regardless of his motivations, he left the presidency with this warning to the American people. Were Eisenhower able to return and witness the changes that have occurred in the United States and the world in the past fifty years, I think he might have celebrated that there has not been another world war. But at the same time, I think he would be appalled by the increased power of the military-industrial complex and its influence on American society, by the size of the U.S. military budget, by our unwarranted and illegal wars, and by the number of nuclear weapons remaining in the world.

Eisenhower, the great military leader, ended his two terms as U.S. president, and his farewell address, with a prayer "that the scourges of poverty, disease and ignorance will be made to disappear from the earth, and that, in the goodness of time, all peoples will come to live together in a peace guaranteed by the binding force of mutual respect and love."[7] Perhaps, like other leaders at the end of their public service, he felt freed of what he saw as the constraints of office, and he could be more honest and visionary in his views. I would take him at his word and accept that he was seizing an opportunity to issue a serious warning to the American people. Certainly his concerns for the unwarranted influence of the military-industrial complex have proven true and been borne out as an impediment to eliminating the scourges Eisenhower named, which continue to weigh so heavily on human security.

Peace Remains an Imperative of the Nuclear Age

Krieger: In my view, peace remains an imperative of the Nuclear Age. Nuclear weapons make war an outmoded means of settling disputes, a risk

that can no longer be tolerated, but one made more likely by the influence of the military-industrial complex. Nuclear war remains an ongoing and sobering risk of the Nuclear Age.

Falk: We should also recognize that in the fifty years that have elapsed since Eisenhower issued this warning, the conditions that he noted have become far more entrenched and dangerous from the perspective of either peace or the rule of law. For one thing, the military-industrial complex has been reinforced by a compliant media that is increasingly dominated by right-wing corporate ownership and by a network of reactionary think tanks that exert a huge influence on the formation of public opinion as well as on Congress and the presidency. Gareth Porter has recently argued, persuasively I think, that a more accurate current description of the American governing process is to regard it as a "permanent war state."[8] Porter stresses convincingly that this condition of permanent war preceded 9/11 but was greatly intensified by the attacks and the explicit embrace of the "war on terror." The Pentagon's avowed engagement in "the long war" against transnational extremist networks is one expression of this world order posture, which has been funded by a larger expansion of military spending than occurred in the early-1950s period of the Cold War. In effect, as has been evident over the course of the past ten years, the United States regards itself as engaged in a borderless war against Islamic extremism, highlighted by drone attacks in states far from what government officials call the "hot battlefield" of Afghanistan and legally justified by claims of an inherent right of self-defense. These exceedingly controversial policies produce intense anti-American sentiments in such countries as Pakistan and Yemen. Drone attacks have been responsible for the deaths of innocent civilians and spread fear among people living in the target societies.

It is also notable that this militarist approach to security is not challenged in mainstream political debate despite polls showing that a majority of Americans favor cuts in the military budget and a greater use of discretionary government spending on domestic social issues. Currently, over 50 percent of discretionary spending by the federal government goes to the military. It is notable that despite this extraordinary investment in hard-power militarism, almost equaling what the entire world spends, the United States has never, throughout its history, seemed as insecure and vulnerable as at present. At some point in our discussions, we will have to face more seriously this question of the link between the reliance on nuclear weaponry and the broader embrace of militarism in a circumstance of permanent war.

Finally, we should recall that the makers of the Constitution were divided over whether political democracy could be sustained if the federal government were allowed to maintain a standing army. Ever since 1941, when World War II started for the United States with the Japanese attack on Pearl Harbor, there has been an incredible buildup and entrenchment of the military bureaucracy deep in the entrails of government. We need to ask ourselves with as much care as possible whether both democracy and peace are any longer possible given this set of developments.

Dimensions of the Nuclear Age

Falk: Returning to the theme of the Nuclear Age, we notice two distinct effects that connect with the role of nuclear weaponry. First, it is difficult, if the society and government have assumed a permanent war footing, to build much support for or interest in any form of disarmament, especially if it involves the most powerful weaponry that has ever existed. Second, because political leaders have recognized a mutual interest in avoiding accidental or unintended war, a shared interest that never existed before the advent of nuclear weaponry, there is a managerial impulse to cut the risks, dangers, and costs of the Nuclear Age by engaging in arms control. From my perspective this is also a source of confusion because, in the public mind, arms control masquerades as disarmament, or at least as progress toward disarmament, which is not how it is perceived in the policy-making community, which understands that management is one thing and getting rid of the weaponry is quite another, with the first being often desirable and the second being either utopian or undesirable.

Krieger: There is, of course, strong evidence that we are now living in a state of permanent war. We moved fairly quickly from the Cold War, which ended surprisingly abruptly, to the global war on terror, a war seemingly without end. It is a perfect stage for the military-industrial complex to retain and exercise its influence on our society and its political institutions.

And, of course, our allocation of resources to the military and the industry that supports it continues to grow. It is sobering that the United States now spends over half its discretionary income, the portion allocated by Congress each year, on the military. As you point out, we are spending annually roughly the amount that the rest of the world combined, including our allies, spends annually on its military forces. Most tragic about this is the loss of opportunities as we pour these resources into the endless pit of militarism. It is shocking to realize that many of the greatest problems confronting humanity—those set forth in the eight Millennium Development Goals, including poverty, lack of basic education, child and maternal mortality, and environmental degradation—could be dramatically reduced and eliminated for large numbers of people with just a small portion of what is spent on military forces.

Despite our enormous expenditures on our military forces, we are not secure. Nor could we be secure even if we spent all of our discretionary funds on the military. In the end, it is not our military that makes us secure but the basic necessities of life, such as clean water, nutritious food, and a healthy environment, on the one hand, and education, health care, shelter, and opportunities to work productively, on the other. The great irony of the Nuclear Age is that our continued reliance on nuclear weapons makes it more likely that these weapons will end up in the hands of terrorists who may be eager to use them against us. In the Nuclear Age, the powerful weapons that we have developed may come back to haunt us. They threaten to destroy U.S. citizens and cities rather than protect them—just as they threaten people everywhere.

You are right that there is an important difference between arms control and disarmament. Arms control has often been used to secure strategic advantage and to manage arms and military power, often at the expense of disarmament initiatives. To the public, arms control and disarmament have not been clearly differentiated, and the one may look like the other. In fact, though, arms control is not sufficient. It simply tries to turn weapons that can destroy civilization into a managerial problem, when, in fact, they are a problem that affects the future of the human species. To treat nuclear weapons as a managerial problem invites disaster. The public needs to understand more clearly that in the Nuclear Age, national security and human security have taken divergent paths. To bring these paths back into alignment will require replacing arms control with disarmament.

Falk: Perhaps we have said as much as we can usefully say about living in the Nuclear Age, including our admission that for others situated elsewhere on the planet, such a designation seems ill fitting.

I do think that part of our justification for choosing this focus is that we seem to be living through a period in which there is this high level of unjustified complacency and misdirection when it comes to nuclear weaponry. The complacency arises in large part because, despite dire warnings of apocalyptic results, no nuclear weapon has been used in warfare for the last sixty-seven years. I think this has led to a subconscious belief that deterrence has worked even during the tensions and crises of the Cold War, recalling the old adage "If it ain't broke, don't fix it." Some counterterrorist and counterproliferation concerns are evident, but these have to do with blunting the possible acquisition of the weaponry by potential enemies, not with weapons themselves as possessed by existing nuclear weapon states.

I believe that the two of us assess the dangers and costs of continued reliance on this weaponry differently. First of all, regional tensions in South and East Asia could easily generate a war in which nuclear weapons were used. Also, the effort to prevent unwanted governments from acquiring the weaponry has already produced an incredibly destructive and costly war in Iraq and threatens another one with wider risks in relation to Iran. I would also emphasize the cultural degradation that arises when governments base their own security on threats to annihilate enemies in the future. It suggests that the United States, in particular, has learned nothing from the unspeakable suffering it inflicted on the civilian populations of Hiroshima and Nagasaki. It further bears witness to a secular absolutism that is willing and ready to murder tens of millions of innocent people and poison the atmosphere for decades for the sake of its own rather dubious assumptions about how to make the country secure from attack.

Nuclear Weapons Abolition: The Most Urgent Struggle of Our Time

Falk: True, President Obama made a statement that seemed sensitive to these concerns, and he did this while he was president, but he hedged and did little to follow up, conveying the impression that, for him, we are not in the Nuclear Age. I suppose this is our underlying claim: that unless we treat the menace of nuclear weapons and nuclearism as a moral and political priority, we have no realistic hope of eliminating this weaponry from our planet. By calling our time the Nuclear Age, we intend to convey a sense that this challenge of abolition is symbolically and substantively the most urgent struggle of our time, at least for those of us living here in the United States.

Krieger: You've summed up our discussion of the Nuclear Age admirably. I'd just like to add a few additional thoughts. First, one of the most important aspects of the Nuclear Age is that it is the time of those of us alive on our planet now. We are living in the Nuclear Age, and whatever responsibilities go along with the technological threats of our time are our responsibilities. Second, those responsibilities have been blurred by the absence of a nuclear war for the past sixty-six years. But it would be an abdication of those responsibilities to conclude that nuclear weapons have made us safer and that we can live with them indefinitely. In fact, the weapons have undermined our collective security, both by the threat they pose and by the enormous cost in resources that has resulted in lost opportunities to improve human security. Third, the current level of complacency regarding the dangers of the Nuclear Age suggests that there is a large gap in knowledge regarding these dangers; thus, there is a need for far more public education and discussion of these issues. Fourth, President Obama seems more committed at this point to nuclear arms control than to nuclear disarmament. Although he held out hope of a farther-reaching vision and more astute policies, in fact his policies so far have been consistent with those of other U.S. presidents during the course of the Nuclear Age. While he has spoken of nuclear disarmament, he has seen this as a distant possibility beyond his own lifetime and has not taken steps for nuclear disarmament but rather for nuclear arms control.

Finally, the survivors of the atomic attacks on Hiroshima and Nagasaki are the true ambassadors of the Nuclear Age. Their message, as written at the Hiroshima Peace Memorial Cenotaph reads, "Never Again! We shall not repeat the evil." This is a much more relevant and moral perspective on the Nuclear Age than that which says, "The genie is out of the bottle," offered by those who would dismiss attempts to rid the world of nuclear weapons. There is no genie; there is no bottle. But there are human beings on our miraculous planet who are willing to take a stand for assuring a future for humanity and all life. Each of us who cares about the human future must act to ensure that no other cities suffer the same fate as Hiroshima and Nagasaki. We must stand together, across boundaries, to assure that we find our way out of the Nuclear Age by achieving a world without nuclear weapons.

CHAPTER 2

Nuclear Deterrence

Falk: There is no doubt that the core rationale for the retention of nuclear weapons remains tied to the concept of deterrence. During the Cold War this seemed plausible, given the confrontation between two hostile superpowers, but even then nuclear deterrence was far more dangerous for the future of humanity than risks associated with a disarmament process that aimed at the abolition of this weaponry. Of course, it was not only the issue of perceived risk. It was the linking of security to the politics, legality, and morality of making credible threats to annihilate indiscriminately and in a massive manner the cities and people of a foreign country and to fill the world's atmosphere with lethal fallout that would cause death and disease in completely neutral societies as well as in those of the parties to the conflict. The political debate during this Cold War period always had an apocalyptic tone: The pro-deterrence security establishment argued in favor of what was called "mutual assured destruction," or "better dead than red," while opponents pointed out that the acronym for this reliance on deterrence was appropriately "MAD" and reversed the slogan of nuclearists by signaling their preference for "better red than dead."

A Critique of Nuclear Deterrence

Krieger: Nuclear deterrence has put a positive spin on the possession of nuclear weapons. It has allowed policy makers to argue that the weapons are not intended to make but to prevent war. Based on nuclear deterrence theory, some analysts have argued that nuclear weapons are actually instruments of peace rather than massive annihilation. The concept of nuclear deterrence has given the public a false sense of security. It has been used to give the impression that nuclear weapons are protective devices to keep another country's nuclear weapons from being used against one's own country. In this sense, nuclear deterrence is a very dangerous concept. It is certainly not a foolproof defense against nuclear weapons use or nuclear war, but it is considered by much of the public to assure the security of one's country.

When thinking about nuclear deterrence, it is important to keep in mind that it is only a theory of human behavior. It is not proven, and there are many ways in which nuclear deterrence could fail. It is worth reflecting on how we came to live so relatively comfortably with the concept of mutual assured destruction. In addition to threatening one's enemy, nuclear deterrence creates a condition that is obviously threatening to one's country, to one's community and family, to all one may love and cherish in the world.

Falk: Your criticisms of nuclear deterrence as an unproven instrument that generates both a false sense of security against a nuclear attack and feelings of unconditional dependence on nuclear weapons are well founded. Explaining nuclear deterrence along these lines undoubtedly also helps to account for public complacency about the risks associated with the possession, development, and spread of the weaponry. At the same time, criticism of deterrence will never be convincing unless it also addresses the uncertainties that accompany the attempts to get rid of the weaponry through negotiated and verified disarmament. Opponents of nuclear deterrence need a credible alternative that seems safer, cheaper, and more in accord with the values embedded in Western and other world civilizations, including respect for international law, while at the same time upholding national security as generally understood.

A further issue cannot be dismissed. Many trusted security analysts, including independent ones, argue that even if there are risks associated with retaining nuclear weapons and the option to use or threaten to use them, their elimination would greatly increase the risks of major warfare. This perspective credits nuclear weapons with preventing the Cold War from turning into World War III because they induced both Washington and Moscow to be more prudent than rival governments had been in the past and led to the establishment of tools for crisis management to reduce the prospect of the outbreak of unintended warfare, either nuclear or conventional. We need to have responses to these concerns if we want our position and proposals to be taken seriously.

Krieger: Nuclear deterrence may be comforting to some, but only if its limitations are not clearly understood. Nuclear deterrence seems to offer protection from nuclear attack, and this may generate complacency about nuclear threat. On the other side of the equation, nuclear deterrence is based on the threat of massive retaliation potentially leading to the deaths of billions of people—a risk no sane person or society would take. Sanity is judged within the context of a society, however, and since our society takes this risk, perhaps we can conclude that the norm of our society is insanity.

The safer, cheaper alternative to nuclear deterrence is nuclear weapons abolition. It is unclear, though, whether this alternative is more in keeping with Western values. There is a strong tension between respect for international law and concern for national security. I would argue that international law and national security coincide when it comes to nuclear weapons and that national security would be strengthened by abolishing the weapons as required under international law. Of course, I recognize that my perspective on this, and yours, may differ substantially from that of those who promote nuclear deterrence as a means of assuring national security. I draw some encouragement from the fact that Albert Einstein, Bertrand Russell, and many of the original atomic scientists recognized that nuclear weapons undermined national and global security.

Has nuclear deterrence prevented World War III through the potential for massive annihilation of the human species? While many so-called realist politicians and academics have supported that position, I have grave doubts. Nuclear deterrence theory involves too many unknowns and uncertainties. It is illegal because it contains the threat of indiscriminate slaughter, which is prohibited under international humanitarian law. It is immoral for the same reason. The theory is also unproven and cannot be proven. Nuclear deterrence risks too much that we have built painstakingly over the span of human civilization. We know what the failure of nuclear deterrence would entail. That should be an adequate incentive for rational leaders to build a global system of security based on international law and institutions as an alternative to nuclear threat.

Falk: Deterrence as a general idea is understood to entail discouraging a potential enemy from launching an attack or doing something perceived to be a fundamental threat to the security of the state. The term "nuclear deterrence" gained currency early in the Nuclear Age both as an acknowledgment of the special, and supposedly constrained and essentially defensive, role assigned to the weaponry and to back up the claim that the presence of such a powerful deterrent has kept the peace among major states ever since the end of World War II. Nuclear deterrence was initially articulated in the Cold War setting in which the United States and the Soviet Union each developed large arsenals of nuclear weapons, yet wanted to avoid using the weaponry, which was widely assumed to be a particularly catastrophic means for a nation to commit collective suicide. Only the extreme hawks, the "Dr. Strangeloves," in our midst had the moral temerity and strategic hubris to argue in favor of limited or preemptive nuclear war as desirable policy options, but despite some close calls, these crazies, although unnervingly influential, never got to steer the ship of state. The mainstream defense community seemed content with keeping the weaponry as a hedge against supposed Soviet expansionist designs, although within the nuclear weapons establishment, Faustian bargains were continuously being struck, including "clean bombs" that would spare people and "first-strike weapons" that would disable the retaliatory power of a rival state.

Krieger: The common understanding of deterrence you mention suggests that there is much room for misunderstanding. You refer to deterrence as "discouraging a potential enemy from launching an attack or doing something perceived to be a fundamental threat to the security of the state." Since deterrence is a theory about human communications and threat, precision is important if the theory is to work as predicted. But actually, the imprecision regarding the threat of nuclear retaliation is quite stunning, considering that with nuclear deterrence the future of civilization hangs in the balance. It is not at all clear that nuclear-armed country A would know with precision what would constitute for country B "a fundamental threat to the security of the state," or that country B would know what this was for country A. It is this imprecision that makes nuclear deterrence so dangerous over time. Of course, aggressive nuclear policies may be far worse than policies of nuclear deterrence, but nuclear deterrence leaves much room for misinterpretation and miscalculation that could trigger nuclear war.

Falk: I agree with you about this and would mention an additional problem. Nuclear deterrence is usually associated with the idea that in the Nuclear Age a country must possess a retaliatory capability to discourage a surprise attack on it. This might be true for some states possessing nuclear weapons, but it is certainly not accurate if applied to the United States. The role of nuclear deterrence for the United States seems more ambitious and ambiguous. If nuclear deterrence were confined to retaliation, then there would be no reason not to make a formal pledge never to use the weapons first and to encourage nuclear weapon states to join in a No First Use declaration, a commitment that the United States has refused to make even in relation to nonnuclear countries.

Beyond Deterrence

Krieger: The United States does have a more ambitious and ambiguous approach to nuclear deterrence than would be required to deter only nuclear attacks. It seeks to manipulate the policies of other countries by this more encompassing approach to nuclear deterrence. In doing so, it creates expanded uncertainties for other states. Some policy makers view greater uncertainty as contributing to a more effective deterrent force, but I would not be so sanguine about increasing the uncertainties in the system. It could lead to unanticipated results, which can be deadly when you are standing at the edge of a nuclear precipice.

No First Use declarations, particularly if made legally binding, would help to narrow the parameters of nuclear deterrence to retaliation for a nuclear first strike only. I would see this as a valuable indicator that those countries adhering to No First Use policies are prepared to limit their reliance upon nuclear threat as a means of upholding their national security. China and India have both made No First Use pledges. The United States has qualified its pledge and refused to apply it to other nuclear weapon states or to states it deems not to be in compliance with the Non-Proliferation Treaty. During the George W. Bush administration, the United States was explicit that it would consider using nuclear weapons in the event of a chemical or biological attack or some other form of surprise attack against the United States, its friends, or its allies.

Falk: Nuclear deterrence is supposed to be helpful for other diplomatic purposes, including dissuading adversaries by creating uncertainty about whether certain forms of perceived hostile moves might lead to a response with nuclear weaponry. There is a history of "deterrent" threats mounted during the Cold War that had nothing to do with retaliation against an attack: ending the war in Korea (1953), protecting the Taiwan offshore islands of Quemoy and Matsu from a Chinese attack (1954–1955, 1958), resolving the Berlin Crisis (1961), avoiding the deployment of Soviet missiles in Cuba (1962). Other nuclear weapon states also claim that their sole reason for acquiring these weapons is to secure themselves against threats and attacks, while they act in a manner suggesting that this infernal weaponry has been assigned other tasks. In my view, Israel, for instance, seeks to retain a regional monopoly of nuclear weaponry in the Middle East not only because it fears an attack but so that it will have a free hand in threatening or waging conventional wars against its neighbors without fear of nonnuclear retaliation because it would have the sole regional option of responding with nuclear weapons.

There are all these uncertainties as to whether the public argument underpinning nuclear deterrence constitutes full disclosure of the broad spectrum of possible uses of the weaponry. We know this topic is surrounded by great secrecy and that the public in the most democratic of countries is denied information about the actual strategic doctrines controlling the use of the weaponry. In effect, there is no transparency as to the actual scope of nuclear deterrence in the United States or in the eight other nuclear weapon states.

Krieger: I doubt the information released to the public regarding nuclear deterrence does include full disclosure concerning the possible uses of nuclear weapons. It should be kept in mind, though, that nuclear deterrence cannot be effective if it is not communicated to potential adversaries. But even if it were fully informed, clearly the public could be easily manipulated by government leaders into believing that nuclear threat posturing would benefit the country.

The combination of nuclear deterrence, nationalism, and secrecy is a dangerous narcotic. It induces policy makers to believe that nuclear weapons make them invincible. It breeds not only nuclear arrogance but a reckless-ness that makes leaders of nuclear weapon states and the citizenries they serve highly vulnerable.

Falk: I am increasingly inclined to think of deterrence as a *rationaliza-tion*, that is, an excuse for retaining and developing nuclear weaponry that hides rather than discloses the real reasons, rather than as a *rationale*, that is, an explanation for the persistence of the weaponry. If deterrence were the major part of the story, then it would seem reasonable to expect the United States especially to have initiated disarmament negotiations either during the peace-oriented leadership of Mikhail Gorbachev in the last years of the Soviet Union or certainly in the immediate aftermath of the Soviet collapse in 1991. But there was no move in this direction. Quite to the contrary, there were reports at the time that Washington was encouraging Boris Yeltsin's Russia to keep its nuclear arsenal intact and not to embarrass the United States by suggesting a receptivity to nuclear disarmament. In this sense, while acknowledging the significance of deterrence in explaining the public reluctance to part with the weaponry, I believe there are additional reasons that the security establishment, in this country at least, seeks to retain and spends billions to modernize the weaponry.

Krieger: Your observation that deterrence is a rationalization rather than a rationale is compelling, but it begs the question of what the weapons are rationalizing. You mention the billions of dollars involved in modernizing nuclear weaponry. Not just billions but trillions of dollars have been spent on nuclear weapons over the course of the Nuclear Age. I wonder, though, if money alone drives the retention and modernization of nuclear weapons. I suspect there is much more to it, what I might call a "nuclear mind-set" rooted in fear and driven by power.

Falk: No question. I never meant to suggest that resistance to denucle-arization was only, or even mainly, a matter of the market dimensions of nuclearism. I have been arguing that nuclear weaponry needs to be un-derstood in relation to the grand strategy of important states, especially for a global state such as the United States. This is another way of talking about fear and power.

Opting for Nuclear Disarmament

Krieger: Clearly, the grand strategies of powerful states have influenced and been influenced by nuclear deterrence, both broadly and narrowly conceived. It is possible to imagine that the new "modes of thinking" that Einstein felt were essential to avert catastrophe in the Nuclear Age might include a grand strategy of global cooperation to abolish nuclear weapons, among other important goals.

When Presidents Mikhail Gorbachev and Ronald Reagan met in Reykjavík, Iceland, in 1986, they came close to an agreement to eliminate their nuclear arsenals, perhaps as close as leaders of any of the current nuclear weapon states have come to achieving that goal in the Nuclear Age. At least on the U.S. side, there was not much support among policy makers for Reagan's vision of a world free of nuclear weapons. Interestingly, the deal faltered due to Reagan's insistence on continuing to develop the U.S. missile defense program and Gorbachev's fear of this program.

In light of our focus on nuclear deterrence, I would point out that missile defenses are, in effect, an admission that nuclear deterrence is insufficient to prevent a nuclear attack. If nuclear deterrence were taken seriously as reliable protection against a nuclear attack, then missile defenses would not need to be considered. In the aftermath of the Cold War, there has been progress in reducing the size of nuclear arsenals, but it has been slow, and nuclear deterrence has not been abandoned, at least not as a rationalization for maintaining the U.S. nuclear arsenal.

Falk: I would disagree somewhat here with your reasoning. One could quite honestly believe that nuclear deterrence is a necessary first line of defense against an attack with nuclear weapons, but that it is not foolproof and, further, that no claim is being made that nuclear weapons can deter a nonstate political actor that is not vulnerable to retaliation. Missile defense is ambiguous with respect to intentions but can be justified as complementary to deterrence by its capacity to nullify a disabling first strike by an enemy state.

Krieger: If one claims that nuclear deterrence works, it seems to me that one cannot, at the same time, assert that it doesn't work. Missile defense is, in essence, an admission that nuclear deterrence may fail. Missile defenses are complementary to nuclear strategy in another, more insidious way: These "defenses" could be used to mop up the remaining nuclear weapons of an adversary after a first-strike attack against its nuclear forces. This is the Russian anxiety about U.S. deployment of missile defenses in Europe: concern about a U.S. first strike.

Falk: My main argument against missile defense is that it seems inconsistent with nuclear disarmament as it renders lesser nuclear weapon states completely vulnerable to attack during the disarming process, depriving them of their retaliatory threat. A secondary argument is that it is an expensive and destabilizing new weapons system that is likely to generate new forms of military competition and raise tensions among states. A tertiary argument holds that one purpose would be to allow the United States to conduct its foreign policy more aggressively, and recklessly, because even crossing the nuclear threshold would not result in major retaliatory damage to the homeland.

Krieger: I agree with your three arguments against missile defenses. I would only add the following points: First, the deployment of missile defenses by country A is an incentive for country B to improve the quality and increase the quantity of its nuclear arsenal. This has the potential to initiate new nuclear arms races. That was the reasoning behind the Anti-Ballistic Missile Treaty, which the United States and the Soviet Union signed in 1972 and George W. Bush unilaterally abrogated in 2002. Second, missile defenses are highly unlikely ever to have the technological capability to provide the protective shield that some policy makers believe possible. Since it is primarily the United States that is developing and deploying missile defense technology, this deployment would not only give the United States a false sense of security but increase its nuclear arrogance.

Why Does the United States Insist on Nuclear Deterrence?

Falk: I would like to make one further observation that you might find provocative but that follows from the failure of the United States to launch a nuclear disarmament initiative in the 1990s. There is a strange feature of deterrence in the current global setting: The U.S. government is both the most vocal advocate of nuclear deterrence and the country for which nuclear deterrence makes the least sense. Why? First, because it possesses such dominance in conventional weaponry that it would be capable of devastating any country that dared to threaten or attack it with nuclear weapons. That is, to the extent that the logic of deterrence underpins security, the United States doesn't really need nuclear weapons, and in relation to the biggest current threat—a repetition of 9/11—deterrence is acknowledged to be irrelevant partly because of the lack of a sufficient retaliatory target and the presumed suicidal intent of the attackers. Unlike the United States, many countries can offset their feared vulnerability to attack by possessing nuclear weapons as a deterrent. Many commentators believe that Iraq in 2003 would not have been attacked if it had then been perceived as actually possessing nuclear weapons or stockpiles of chemical or biological weapons. Second, in a disarming world, American military superiority would be arguably much more relevant to shaping the outcome of political conflicts than it is in today's world, where, to some extent, risks of escalation lead the United States to be somewhat, although insufficiently, self-deterring, that is, seeking to avoid situations that might spiral out of control to the extent of crossing the nuclear threshold.

Krieger: Inasmuch as nuclear deterrence is basically a communications theory with psychological underpinnings, it is hard to assess the reasons leaders choose to rely upon it. In the case of U.S. leaders, I think the reason is largely fear based. These policy makers may be uncertain as to how much power is enough to prevent an attack. In deterrence theory there is always a question of how much is enough. Leaders may fear that, without a "sufficient" quantity and quality of nuclear weapons, their conventional forces would be unable to prevent a nuclear attack by another country. When it came to nuclear deterrence policy, the United States and former Soviet Union generally seemed to err on the side of greater numbers of nuclear weapons equaling a stronger deterrent force. In fact, there is no precise way to define "sufficient." Throughout the Cold War each side sent messages to the other about its obscene power in the form of nuclear weapon and missile tests. It resembled a nuclear Kabuki dance.

I agree with you that nuclear deterrence may be far more effective in the hands of a small and relatively weak country and that Iraq might well not have been attacked by the United States in 2003 had it possessed a small nuclear arsenal. The few nuclear weapons that North Korea has developed provide it with some sense of security against a U.S. attack aimed at regime change. This situation sets up dangerous incentives for nuclear proliferation among smaller countries that fear the possibility of attack by more powerful countries. Understanding this should motivate more powerful states to move away from nuclear deterrence and to embrace nuclear weapons abolition before nuclear weapons continue to spread.

Dietrich Fischer, a longtime peace advocate and scholar, has likened nuclear deterrence to trying to prevent traffic accidents by putting babies on the bumpers of all cars on the road. The babies would make more visible the risks of an accident and would presumably cause drivers to be more careful. This would not be sufficient, however, to prevent fatalities, because no matter how carefully drivers drive their cars, accidents still happen. This is the situation with nuclear deterrence. It is a high-risk enterprise. The high risk may make policy makers more careful, but it doesn't eliminate accidents or miscalculations. Nuclear deterrence is not foolproof, either for small countries or for large ones like the United States.

The Relevance of Worldviews

Falk: True, nuclear deterrence is high risk in its essence and catastrophic in its effects if it fails to prevent the use of the weaponry. But alternative approaches to security also have risks, and their failure would impose heavy costs. In the end, the argument cannot be resolved through intellectual debate. Neither side will give way as there is no evidence that can convince those with an opposing worldview. In the background is the age-old debate about whether human nature is inherently aggressive or naturally peaceful. Those who believe the former, including those who hold a tragic view of history, will incline toward retaining the weaponry, while those who believe in the underlying and potential goodness of people and their governments will incline toward disarmament. Unfortunately, governmental bureaucracies are overwhelmingly inclined to adopt a negative view of human nature and to build a foreign policy around worst-case scenarios and claims of "realism." Henry Kissinger, perhaps the most influential diplomat of the last sixty years, built his reputation around this tragic view of human nature as aggressive and world history as intrinsically war prone. His favorite bit of folk wisdom was "If you want peace, prepare for war."

Besides the relevance of underlying belief systems, there exists the disciplinary role of groupthink in governmental circles, which in turn encompasses career interests and relations between officials making policy and private-sector beneficiaries working in affiliated industries, think tanks, and weapons labs. Better arguments will not sway those occupying such entrenched positions where old habits of thought and vested interests prevail.

Krieger: Worldviews always provide frameworks for understanding the world. You single out Henry Kissinger for his influence on policy with his realist perspective. Kissinger no doubt exerted a strong influence on U.S. foreign policy and encouraged an international politics of power. He was a nuclear strategist who relied upon all forms of power, but particularly on nuclear forces. Interestingly, Kissinger has come around in recent years to arguing that nuclear deterrence is no longer sufficient to protect the United States, primarily due to the threats of nuclear terrorism. I think that he has surprised many people by joining George Shultz, William Perry, and Sam Nunn in arguing for nuclear weapons abolition. Of course, their vision is long range, but it is still unexpected given the realist perspective. In fact, I think for men like Kissinger, nuclear weapons abolition is the new realism, at least in the long term. They have recognized that the power of nuclear weapons cannot be contained and can be turned against even the most powerful states, including the United States.

Falk: At bottom, effective opposition to nuclear deterrence must be rooted in morality, law, and a sense of the spiritual destiny and potential of the human species. Deterrence involves threats to inflict massive, possibly apocalyptic, indiscriminate death and destruction on innocent civilians and their societal infrastructure, violating the most basic norms of morality and international humanitarian law. Such a societal and governmental embrace of nuclear deterrence is deeply corrupting. At the same time, warfare has rested on a habitual tension between legally mandated restraints, including respect for civilian innocence, and a political imperative to do whatever is necessary to destroy the capabilities and the will of the enemy.

In this fundamental sense, even Hiroshima and Nagasaki, shocking as these attacks were, represented more continuity than discontinuity in the manner in which World War II was conducted by the winners as well as the losers. Designed to maximize civilian loss of life and break the population's will to continue the war, the firebombings of German and Japanese cities amounted to an unapologetic reliance on state terror as a battlefield tactic. The Germans and Japanese were equally ready to do whatever they could to inflict damage and terrorize civilians. The rockets fired at London and other British cities were completely indiscriminate. Japan used biological weaponry and was guilty of atrocities in its war to conquer and subdue China.

To break with nuclear deterrence is to break with the ethics of warfare as practiced up until this time. The wars waged by the United States in Iraq and Afghanistan, or by Israel against Lebanon in 2006 and the defenseless people of Gaza two years later, exhibit this same refusal to constrain war-making within limits set by law and morality. The only difference in relation to nuclear deterrence is the availability of an argument based on prudence—that it is imprudent to rely on such weaponry—but that puts the issue back in the domain of rational debate, which will reflect the balance of interests and forces rather than deference to what is humane or favored by the values of democratic society. To me this suggests that the only serious hope for dislodging nuclear deterrence rests with civil society and a social movement that refuses to risk survival on threats to engage in genocidal warfare.

Finally, it seems that such a movement could only get off the ground if there were either an actual use of the weaponry that destroyed the credibility of nuclear deterrence as a preserver of the peace or an existential fear that these weapons might be used against our society. Such fear did exist from time to time during the Cold War and gave rise to a robust antinuclear movement, especially in Europe, but it could not be sustained sufficiently to challenge the nuclear establishment. I think we should not entertain hopes any longer of a top-down approach of the sort depicted in Barack Obama's Prague speech; instead, we must work and pray for a bottom-up approach catalyzed by events and developments less traumatic than the use of the weaponry.

Krieger: Nuclear deterrence, with its threat of massive annihilation of innocent people, is clearly morally abhorrent. Virtually every major religious body has reached this conclusion. Yet, the moral position has not been sufficiently influential. It would seem that fear and power have trumped morality when it comes to nuclear weapons and the human future. I agree with you that nuclear deterrence is deeply corrupting. The Nuclear Age is an era of corruption, a time in which leaders have accepted, and even promoted, policies of nuclear deterrence, which could lead to the massive annihilation of innocent people and foreclose the future to new generations. Those with an opposing voice on this issue need to speak out and be heard. One great problem with the complacency of large numbers of people on this issue is the lack of significant public debate. This, in essence, means that the mute button has been pressed on the most important public policy issue of our time. Even Henry Kissinger and his colleagues' surprising statements calling for a step-by-step approach to nuclear weapons abolition have engendered very little public debate on the issue.

You say that breaking with nuclear deterrence will require breaking with the ethics of warfare as it has been practiced. I think that is right. The Nuclear Age, with its omnicidal potential, demands that we change our approach to security. In the Nuclear Age, a serious split has developed between national security and human security. National security, based on nuclear deterrence, portends the destruction of all. The weapons we task with securing our nation are the same weapons that hold the potential to destroy other nations and to trigger an attack that will destroy our own. When you think about it, this is an absurd approach to national security. It leaves citizens exposed to annihilation. This would seem to be apparent on its face, and yet the overwhelming response has been complacency.

Finding Security without Nuclear Deterrence

Falk: Again I would stress that the political critique of deterrence cannot stand on its own but must be associated with an alternative that is safer, cheaper, and not vulnerable to evasion by real or imagined enemies. So far critics have not been able to make this case in a manner that engages public support. At most, if fear is generated by a global crisis—as occurred several times during the Cold War, most intensely, during the Cuban Missile

Crisis of 1962—then managerial adjustments are made, accompanied by a surge of temporary support for antinuclear activism. The moral critique of deterrence is unconditional, and if morality guided policy and governmental approaches to security, it would have long ago led to the abandonment of a security function for nuclear weapons, especially if the threat to use them is taken into full account. It should be noted, in passing, that deterrence rests upon the credibility of the threat to use the weapons in retaliation or if provoked. Thus, the political leadership of nuclear weapon states projects the belief that the security of their societies is based on a continuous and unconditional willingness to devastate an adversary with genocidal fury and an absence of wider concerns or any acceptance of responsibility for the radioactive fallout and harm suffered by peoples not even involved in the conflict. This posture contradicts the most fundamental and widely shared ethical commitment of all civilized societies to avoid violence toward those who are innocent.

Krieger: Perhaps you are right that rational debate cannot win the day on this issue, but at the same time it would be foolish to cease to attempt rational arguments to oppose reliance upon a theory as faulty and dangerous as nuclear deterrence. It is said that generals always prepare for the next war in the way they prepared for the last one. That is no longer possible in an all-out war. A country cannot escalate to the use of nuclear weapons without the risk of triggering national suicide and possibly a global holocaust. In a global nuclear war, there would be no victors, only losers. The U.S. president who recognized this clearly was Ronald Reagan, who concluded, "A nuclear war cannot be won and must never be fought." Drawing upon this conclusion, Reagan continued, speaking of the United States and former Soviet Union, "The only value in our two nations possessing nuclear weapons is to make sure they will never be used. But then would it not be better to do away with them entirely?"[1] Reagan was able to follow the logic of the situation to the need to abolish the weapons. If Reagan, a staunch Cold Warrior, could understand this logic, it should be clear to everyone who thinks about it.

You suggest that there are only two ways in which the public could become engaged in dislodging nuclear deterrence: first, through the destruction of the concept's credibility by the use of a nuclear weapon; second, through development of an existential fear that the weapons might be used against us. Many other people share this perspective. It is one that admits to the ineffectiveness of logic, but it also presupposes a failure of human imagination to come to grips with the real threat that nuclear deterrence poses to the human future. Perhaps we humans are not wired to imagine our collective demise. Perhaps, like the generals, we are still preparing for the last war—or the last peace. I would suggest, though, that a peace built on nuclear threat is a highly unstable peace, one that will lead to nuclear proliferation, nuclear terrorism, and nuclear war.

Awakening Civil Society

Krieger: We share a commitment to awakening civil society to the dangers of the Nuclear Age. It is a daunting task, but an absolutely necessary one. I don't know which is the longer shot: encouraging greater leadership from the top, in line with the hope engendered by Obama's Prague speech, or seeking to awaken and engage a largely complacent public to exert its power to end the nuclear weapons threat to humanity. Both paths present significant challenges. I feel we cannot give up on either possibility, and we must continue to encourage more effective and urgent political leadership on nuclear weapons abolition, while continuing to educate and advocate in a way that moves the public from complacency to engagement and action.

Falk: I think implicit in your words is the sense that a political climate capable of initiating a process of deep military denuclearization presupposes an interaction between pressures from below and leadership from above. Only this combination will yield the results we both seek. I believe the abandonment by Obama of his Prague vision of a world without nuclear weapons has taken place because no popular movement exists to promote this goal. There was a resonant reaction, which registered widespread public approval of the speech, but without an accompanying politics capable of challenging the entrenched interests of the nuclear weapons establishment, the vision will soon dissipate and disappear from the mainstream political arena. This has already happened. Our role as citizens and activists is to build a political climate that creates the space for a receptive leadership in Washington and elsewhere to move forward. It is a recipe for frustration to believe that we currently possess the leverage to strengthen the will of the policy-making community in Washington. If Kissinger's Gang of Four was unable to shake confidence in nuclearism, it is foolhardy to believe that we have the relevant clout. We need to concentrate on sustaining rational debate and encouraging grassroots opposition, which, when historical events conspire, can take the shape of a vibrant antinuclear movement. Until that day comes, we will have to be content with the thankless work of articulating necessary truth in the wilderness, that is, unheeded and mostly unheard by the mainstream.

A Moral Perspective

Krieger: Albert Camus imagined Sisyphus not as tortured but as happy in his work as he pushed his rock up the mountain, only to have it roll down again so that the arduous task could be repeated the next day. In this sense, I see our task not as banishment to serve as a voice in the wilderness but as a sacred duty. No matter what the emperor may believe about nuclear deterrence, it is the equivalent in security terms to wearing no clothes. The emperor may believe that nuclear deterrence provides security, but this is not appreciably different from believing he is wearing a fine suit when he is naked. In this case, the emperor represents not only the political leadership but also the people. They, too, generally believe they are protected by nuclear deterrence. They, too, must adjust their vision and their thinking. In the end, it is a matter of education, logic, and focus as well as politics.

Falk: It is hard not to be drawn to Camus's interpretation of the Sisyphus myth, but I don't think it fits fully. We recognize the imperative of persisting despite failure, but we are fundamentally expecting at some point to succeed, and we are motivated by the risks that persist. We are not resigned to the futility of our commitment to a denuclearizing world.

Similarly, I am not entirely in agreement about the naked emperor. As I have tried to argue, there are better prudential alternatives to deterrence, which is morally and legally unacceptable. At the same time, given an acceptance of certain security goals, in some situations there are grounds for believing that deterrence might work to reduce vulnerability. North Korea or Iran could reason in this manner that it is less likely to be attacked if its enemies believe it possesses and would use nuclear weapons if attacked. I feel we have to be careful not to paint our argument in overly broad strokes, which make it easy to put forth exceptions or to dismiss our reasoning as antinuclear piety.

Krieger: You're right that neither of us is resigned to the endless task of pushing the rock up the mountain. At least we can see the summit, that is, the goal of a world without nuclear weapons. It certainly helps in our efforts to know where we are headed, even if the path to get there is both uncertain and arduous. We also agree that nuclear deterrence is morally and legally unacceptable, despite the fact that some countries, particularly weaker ones, may find it useful in fending off stronger ones. Still, even for relatively weak countries, whose leaders may believe they have few other options, nuclear deterrence is rife with uncertainty and extremely dangerous.

CHAPTER 3

Nuclear Proliferation

Krieger: Nuclear proliferation has two variants: horizontal and vertical. Horizontal proliferation refers to the spread of nuclear weapons to other states or to entities such as terrorist organizations. Vertical proliferation refers to increases in the quantity or improvements in the quality of nuclear weapons in existing arsenals. Nuclear arms races such as the one that occurred between the United States and the former Soviet Union or that which is now taking place between India and Pakistan are examples of vertical proliferation. Nuclear weapon states have clearly been most concerned with horizontal proliferation, as opposed to increases or improvements in their own existing nuclear arsenals. I think we will mostly be speaking here about horizontal proliferation—that is, the spread of nuclear weapons—but it is worth noting that for many decades the most prominent form of nuclear proliferation was vertical.

Since the end of the Cold War, the U.S. and Russian nuclear arsenals have been shrinking. The United Kingdom and France have made more modest reductions to their nuclear arsenals. China has maintained a policy of minimum deterrence. Nonetheless, all five of these original nuclear weapon states have taken steps to improve the quality of their nuclear arsenals. It is unclear what Israel has done with its secret nuclear program, although it seems to have expanded its options for the delivery of nuclear weapons. In 1998, both India and Pakistan conducted multiple nuclear weapons tests, sending a loud message that they were now members of the nuclear weapons club. North Korea joined this club with a nuclear test in 2006 and another in 2009. There is deep concern in the international community that nuclear weapons will proliferate further to other states and to nonstate extremist groups.

Horizontal and Vertical Proliferation

Krieger: When thinking about nuclear proliferation, most analysts, policy makers, and members of the public focus on horizontal proliferation, or the spread of nuclear weapons to other states. I think we can agree, though, that vertical proliferation cannot be overlooked. The states that currently possess nuclear weapons pose the greatest danger to themselves and to the world. Dealing with the arsenals of the current nuclear weapon states requires not antiproliferation agreements but rather nuclear disarmament, most importantly through a nuclear weapons convention for the phased, verifiable, irreversible, and transparent elimination of nuclear weapons.

Falk: I am not sure that it is useful or clarifying to consider the development of nuclear weapons by states that possess the weaponry as a form of proliferation. It seems preferable that such issues, including weapons competition between rival nuclear weapon states, be discussed as matters of quantitative increase and qualitative improvement of existing nuclear weapons capabilities and that the interaction between nuclear weapon states be termed as either "competitive nuclearism" or a "nuclear arms race." The antidote to vertical proliferation would be a stagnant nuclear arsenal, but that misses the point argued by most nuclear critics, including myself, for whom the goal is getting rid of the weaponry. Freezing further nuclear weapons acquisition and development would be a form of arms control, seeking to reduce the risks and costs of competitive nuclearism without challenging the legality, morality, and prudence of relying on the weaponry.

In contrast, horizontal proliferation, or simply proliferation, is widely understood as associated with a political actor, whether a state or nonstate entity, crossing the nuclear threshold by acquiring the weaponry. The intense preoccupation of the United States with discouraging most instances of proliferation has to do with the idea that the more fingers there are on nuclear triggers, the more likely it is that a trigger will be pulled in a conflict or as a result of an accident or miscalculation. In one sense, the antiproliferation regime is at odds with deterrence as a rationale for acquisition and possession. Indeed, antiproliferation forces place most emphasis on discouraging states with the strongest deterrent justifications for acquiring nuclear weapons. In the current global setting, both North Korea and Iran are confronting hostile neighbors, geopolitical threats, and sanctions, and both would seem to have a rather good deterrent argument for the deployment of nuclear weapons that are not vulnerable to destruction by way of a first strike by their adversaries. We need in the discussion of proliferation to consider its problematic conceptual relationship to the deterrent rationale. For the moment, if we grant that a serious disconnect exists between these two centerpieces of the overall approach taken by the nuclear weapon states, then we should be on the lookout for additional explanations of the antiproliferation consensus.

Preventing Proliferation Is Not Sufficient

Krieger: I do think it's useful to understand that nuclear weapons proliferation can take place vertically in a state that already possesses nuclear weapons. It underlines the hypocrisy of a nuclear weapon state increasing or improving its arsenal while calling upon or requiring non–nuclear weapon states to refrain from developing nuclear arsenals. The self-restraint of nuclear weapon states from vertical proliferation would not change the status quo that divides nuclear haves and have-nots and would hardly be a solution to the nuclear dilemma. It seems clear that the only suitable and stable goal is a world without nuclear weapons, which requires both nuclear disarmament and barriers against nuclear proliferation.

You are absolutely correct in arguing that an antiproliferation regime is at odds with nuclear deterrence as a rationale for acquiring and possessing nuclear weapons. The former supports a two-tiered world of nuclear haves and have-nots, whereas the latter, the deterrence justification, supports nuclear proliferation. This is an important point. It makes clear that preventing proliferation is not sufficient; the circle must be completed by the nuclear disarmament of those countries possessing nuclear weapons. It is a serious concern that the current nuclear weapon states continue to rely on nuclear weapons for security and use these weapons to explicitly or implicitly threaten others, which, in turn, supports the rationality of countries under duress, such as North Korea and Iran, seeking to develop nuclear arsenals. What may seem rational for individual countries, however, may prove irrational for the international system as a whole.

Falk: Antiproliferation policies must be understood in relation to impe-rial or hegemonic geopolitics, which seek to ensure that certain states are vulnerable to threats and even uses of force without possessing major retaliatory capabilities. This is not essentially a security rationale for deny-ing these states a nuclear weapons option, but it has to do with controlling challenges that their governments are perceived to pose to the prevailing order regionally or globally. The geopolitical overlay of the nonprolifera-tion regime is exposed, as well, by the refusal to keep Israel from acquiring nuclear weapons or failing to induce the Israeli government to renounce nuclear weaponry or even to join the nonproliferation regime. In my mind, the peace and security of the Middle East would be greatly enhanced by the establishment of a nuclear weapon–free zone in the region, which all coun-tries except Israel seem prepared to do, and because of Israel's reluctance, the United States has no interest in such a stabilizing initiative. Perhaps this element of the broader proliferation context is better understood as driven by strategic alliance relationships, arms sales, and the compulsions of domestic politics in the United States, especially the extreme pro-Israel bias of the U.S. Congress.

Losing the U.S. Monopoly

Krieger: When the United States created nuclear weapons in the Man-hattan Project, there were already fears that the knowledge to create the weapons would spread to the Soviet Union. The United States shared its nuclear weapons know-how with its World War II ally, the United King-dom, but tried to keep it secret from another ally, the USSR. President Harry S. Truman unrealistically thought that the know-how to make the bomb could be kept under U.S. control for decades. In fact, it took the Soviet Union, with some help from spies, only four years to conduct their first nuclear weapon test. The United Kingdom, France, and China took longer, but all had conducted nuclear tests by the end of 1964. Israel reportedly had its bomb a few years later.

By the early 1960s, the first three nuclear weapon states—the United States, Soviet Union, and United Kingdom—were worried about nuclear proliferation to many other states and began negotiating an international treaty to prevent it. By 1968 the Non-Proliferation Treaty (NPT) was opened for signatures, and by 1970 it had sufficient ratifications to enter into force.[1] The principal purpose of the treaty, from the perspective of its strongest enthusiasts—the United States, Soviet Union, and United Kingdom—was to prevent the proliferation of nuclear weapons to other states. The non–nuclear weapon states, however, wanted something in return for their agreement not to develop or otherwise acquire nuclear weapons. They wanted a world without nuclear weapons and thus insisted upon the inclusion of a provision in the treaty that called for nuclear disarmament of the five nuclear weapon states recognized by the treaty: the United States, Soviet Union, United Kingdom, France, and China. The non–nuclear weapon states thus forced a provision for the leveling of the playing field. They were prepared to remain free of nuclear weapons, but not in a world where some countries had a continuing military advantage of possessing nuclear arms. The non–nuclear weapon states also negotiated a right to assistance in implementing programs for the "peaceful" use of nuclear technology. This provision of the treaty, which refers to peaceful nuclear energy research, production, and use as an "inalienable right," would increase the prospects for nuclear weapons proliferation, the principal goal the treaty was created to prevent.

The Geopolitics of Nonproliferation versus the Treaty Regime

Falk: At the outset we need, as hinted at earlier, to distinguish between the legal regime on nonproliferation established by the treaty and the geopolitical regime governing the same subject matter that is administered largely, if not exclusively, by the United States. In the legal regime, as you point out, there is the appearance of a bargain that gives nonnuclear states two important benefits: a legal commitment by nuclear weapons states to seek nuclear disarmament in good faith and a legal assurance to non–nuclear weapon states of an unimpeded right to take full advantage of nuclear energy technology. And there is also an opt-out provision, allowing a party to the treaty to opt out by giving three months' notice and making the claim that the "supreme interests" of the country require its withdrawal. The International Court of Justice (ICJ) in its advisory opinion of 1996, *The Legality of the Threat or Use of Nuclear Weapons,*[2] unanimously confirmed the legal obligation of the nuclear weapon states to pursue nuclear disarmament in good faith, a legal obligation derived from Article VI of the Nuclear Non-Proliferation Treaty.

The geopolitical regime is much more one-sided in support of the interests of the nuclear weapon states in preventing proliferation without making any pretense of embarking on a path leading to nuclear disarmament. As the disputes with Iran and North Korea have illustrated, when a state viewed with hostility by the United States and its allies ventures near the nuclear threshold, the geopolitical override of the treaty takes the form of interfering with both the rights of nonnuclear states to enjoy peaceful uses of nuclear technology and to withdraw upon notice from the treaty. In fact, the geopolitical claims are put forward so strongly as to provide a political rationale for threatening military attack directed at a state that approaches, even without crossing, the nuclear threshold, a process and claim of "enforcement" not set forth in the treaty itself. There is, as previously indicated, another side to the geopolitical regime that is tolerant of proliferation viewed as benign or politically expedient, which has allowed Israel to become a nuclear weapon state by stealth and to keep its distinctive posture as being understood to possess a weapons arsenal of several hundred nuclear warheads without even being compelled to disclose to the international community the reality of its relationship to nuclear weaponry. Does this tolerance of Israeli exceptionalism not undermine the integrity of the nonproliferation approach and erode its moral and legal authority? This glaring instance of what might be called "complicit proliferation" underscores the extent to which double standards pervade the implementation of allegedly global norms.

Krieger: I think it is useful to distinguish between the legal regime and the geopolitical regime governing nuclear proliferation. The first is at least purportedly rooted in fairness and, despite its two-tier structure, seeks to level the playing field; the second is rooted in power and seeks to maintain the dominance of the most powerful states. In the current international system, power still trumps the law. This is extremely dangerous in a system in which power, at least in part, rests upon the threat to use nuclear weapons. It creates strong incentives toward nuclear proliferation.

The International Court of Justice (ICJ) concluded its advisory opinion titled *The Legality of the Threat or Use of Nuclear Weapons* with unanimous agreement on the nuclear disarmament obligation, stating, "There exists an obligation to pursue in good faith and bring to a conclusion negotiations leading to nuclear disarmament in all its aspects under strict and effective international control."[3] The failure of the nuclear weapon states to take this obligation seriously, to view it as a "not in my lifetime" obligation, as President Barack Obama has done, paves the way for nuclear proliferation. The nuclear double standards that currently exist are not likely to hold; they create pressure for either nuclear disarmament or nuclear proliferation.

Falk: This evaluation of the two regimes is persuasive only if you grant sincerity and autonomy to the legal regime. In my view, the apparent fairness of the treaty was almost immediately belied by practice, reinforced over the years, in which the nonproliferation commitment was viewed as "hard law," while the disarmament commitment was viewed as "soft law," or not law at all. "Soft law" refers here to a commitment so weak as to be essentially voluntary and, in this instance, it was overshadowed from the outset by the major effort of nuclear weapon states to strengthen their weapons systems and to stay ahead of their rivals or keep their deterrent viable. I think a fair reading of this pattern would suggest that the nuclear weapon states, especially the United States, opposed as a matter of policy, as distinct from gesture, any serious effort to start disarmament negotiations. As Richard J. Barnet noted in his 1960 book *Who Wants Disarmament?*, there were good reasons to doubt that even when the United States and the Soviet Union tabled disarmament proposals, they were doing anything more than engaging in an elaborate public relations battle that offered the world the false impression of a genuine commitment to world peace.[4]

Krieger: It seems clear that, at the time of signing the Non-Proliferation Treaty, the nuclear weapon states were not serious about the nuclear disarmament obligation in the treaty. These states wanted to prevent nuclear proliferation and signed onto the treaty with its nuclear disarmament clause but showed no seriousness of intent in pursuing this portion of the treaty. For nearly two decades after the signing of the treaty in 1968, U.S. and Soviet nuclear arsenals continued to increase. The nuclear weapon states treated their disarmament obligations with disdain. In 1968, there were just under 39,000 nuclear weapons in the world, nearly all of them in the arsenals of the United States and USSR. This number reached its apogee in 1986 with over 70,000 nuclear weapons in the world. From that point the number of nuclear weapons in the world has declined, but there are still approximately 20,000 today, and they are still predominantly in U.S. and Russian arsenals. The most powerful states in the world have not behaved as though bound by their nuclear disarmament obligations under the NPT.

A Material Breach of the Non-Proliferation Treaty

Falk: In my view, the failure of the nuclear weapon states to pursue nuclear disarmament over a period of more than forty years, despite the injunction to do so by the International Court of Justice, is a material breach of the NPT that would give any party the option of pronouncing the treaty void. Some confusion has been created by the misleading claim that an arms control measure such as New START is a step toward nuclear disarmament and thus a responsive move to the ICJ ruling. Selectivity, with respect to permitting some states to complete a nuclear fuel cycle (Germany, Japan) while denying others such an option (most notably Iran), and the blind eye turned toward Israel's acquisition and development of nuclear weapons are further grounds for calling the treaty regime into question from the perspective of international law. I feel that the passivity of the non–nuclear weapon states in response to this long pattern of nonimplementation by the nuclear weapon states has not served either them or the wider interests of humanity well. It is time to try something different that challenges the complacency and nuclearism of the United States and its cohorts in the nuclear weapons club.

Krieger: Some non–nuclear weapon states have tried to call attention to the failure of the nuclear weapon states to implement their disarmament obligations, but to little effect. Mexico and a few other states attempted this at the 1995 Non-Proliferation Treaty Review and Extension Conference, but the arm-twisting of the United States and its allies overwhelmed most parties to the treaty. The New Agenda Coalition countries, seven middle power countries that include Brazil, Egypt, Ireland, Mexico, New Zealand, Sweden, and South Africa, tried to challenge the nuclear weapon states and push forward a nuclear disarmament agenda, but they didn't gain any real traction. It would be wonderful to see a strong and concerted effort by non–nuclear weapon states to challenge the nuclear weapons club. I think the most effective thing that such states could do would be to start the process of negotiating a nuclear weapons convention and, if necessary, to do it without the nuclear weapon states.

Falk: I have strong doubts that the nonnuclear states could ever be persuaded to take such an initiative, and if they did, it would almost certainly be ignored as an irritating gimmick. A serious challenge from these states, especially if one or more nuclear weapon states could be persuaded to join, would be an ultimatum of intention to the effect that, if no serious negotiations of a nuclear disarmament convention are commenced within two years, then the nonnuclear parties to the NPT will jointly withdraw in accordance with Article X of the treaty.

Krieger: What you are suggesting would indeed be a serious challenge, but a risky one. If the nuclear weapon states did not rise to the challenge, the international system could be thrown into even greater chaos than currently exists. If the non–nuclear weapon states that are parties to the NPT pronounced it void and withdrew in their national interests, the basis for the ICJ's opinion about the obligation to pursue complete nuclear disarmament would be undermined. That obligation is based on the language of Article VI of the NPT, calling for the nuclear weapon states to pursue negotiations in good faith for nuclear disarmament.

Is Arms Control Enough?

Krieger: I can appreciate your frustration with the lack of significant progress toward nuclear disarmament. It is understandable, and I share it. Still, though, I would not say that there has been no progress toward nuclear disarmament. The numbers of nuclear weapons in the arsenals of the United States and Russia have come steadily down since the mid-1980s. They have not come down rapidly enough, but they have at least moved in the right direction. New START provides a new platform on which to consolidate and build further downward momentum. It does not represent serious nuclear disarmament aimed at zero, but it creates further possibilities.

Falk: Here we do disagree. I do not interpret New START or any of the arms control measures, even if inherently desirable, as moves in the direction of nuclear disarmament. At most, such initiatives are neutral, but I tend to view them as negative from a disarmament perspective. Their effect is to add to the illusion of stability and to weaken incentives to produce change. Arms control embodies a managerial outlook, and the treaty ratification process in the U.S. Senate shows that there is no intention to move toward a world without nuclear weapons; instead, the trend is toward a compact with nuclearists to appropriate billions for a new and qualitatively better future nuclear weapons arsenal. We must not fool ourselves or fall victim to wishful thinking.

It is one thing to argue that New START is so important, because it cuts risks and costs, that it is worth ignoring the adverse effects on seeking disarmament; or that further proliferation is so dangerous that it is sensible to ignore the failure of intention and performance to implement the disarmament provision. But it is bad faith to pretend that the treaty remains intact after forty years of overt noncompliance, which developed a brazen character in the 1990s when the collapse of the Soviet Union removed the deterrence lynchpin of opposition to nuclear disarmament.

Krieger: I suppose one could say that, at various times during the Nuclear Age, arms control treaties have done more to diminish public concerns than to disarm the weapons. One prominent example is the Partial Test Ban Treaty of 1963, which followed considerable public agitation about atmospheric testing of nuclear weapons. The treaty quieted the public but didn't stop the nuclear testing, which was switched to underground testing. There have been many such instances when agreements have created an illusion of progress that has calmed public concerns about the dangers of the weapons. New START may be a part of that pattern, or it may represent a meaningful stepping-stone to far more significant steps actually aimed at zero nuclear weapons, the only truly stable number. President Obama's words point toward the latter outcome, but his actions thus far point more toward the former. I can understand your skepticism.

Double Standards: A Recipe for Failure

Krieger: I find it particularly frustrating in the area of nuclear nonproliferation that double standards are so ingrained in the system. This relates both to the actual possession of nuclear weapons and to the technology for developing weapons-grade nuclear materials. It is impossible to sustain a nonproliferation regime that carves out exceptions for friends and harsh punishments for others. Such hypocrisy is a recipe for failure.

Falk: I have long harbored doubts as to whether the nonproliferation approach, by reference to its legal or geopolitical dimensions, is a contribution either to world peace and stability or to the goal of nuclear abolition. Attention has shifted from the threat posed by the weapons and their possessors to that generated by states with only the alleged ambition to acquire the weaponry. It is certainly the case that some governments are more reckless and irresponsible than others, but it is also true that the states that have engaged in aggressive war since the end of World War II have been overwhelmingly the nuclear weapon states, headed by the United States. If we really believe in the elimination of nuclear weaponry, then I think we have to move toward the renunciation of the nonproliferation legal regime and, even more so, its implementation by way of threats and engagement in aggressive war.

Iran has been threatened constantly with attack if it does not give sufficient assurances that it is not seeking to attain nuclear weaponry. The Israeli computer worm Stuxnet, developed jointly by the United States and Israel, has been deliberately employed to disrupt Iran's nuclear program, reportedly in serious ways. This poses several disturbing issues. Stuxnet provides a means to "enforce" nonproliferation goals in relation to Iran through a coercive interference with its civilian nuclear program—a dangerous precedent that sets the stage for future cyberwarfare.

I think we need to appreciate that the "enforcement" of nonproliferation, or counterproliferation as it is sometimes called, is a geopolitical undertaking quite far removed from international law, and in practice it involves the flagrant disregard of international law, as was the case when Iraq was attacked in March 2003. The same mix of antiproliferation policy and unlawful threats of force have for several years been present in American and Israeli diplomatic postures adopted toward Iran's nuclear program. In the absence of a UN Security Council mandate, there is a contradiction between the geopolitical implementation of the Nuclear Non-Proliferation Treaty and adherence to the UN Charter, especially with regard to its core commitment prohibiting recourse to aggressive force.

Renouncing the Non-Proliferation Treaty

Krieger: You're right that enforcement of nonproliferation has often involved threats and actions that violate international law, such as the Israeli bombing of the Iraqi Osirak nuclear reactor and the threats to bomb Iranian uranium-enrichment facilities. Such violations of international law have been "protected" by the United States and have reinforced the international double standards in this area. We need to return to the UN Charter prohibition on the use of force, but to get there we will need somehow to level the playing field and end the era of nuclear haves and have-nots.

I disagree with you if you are calling for the outright renunciation of the legal nonproliferation regime. I think the legal nonproliferation regime has serious flaws, particularly its promotion of nuclear energy as an "inalienable right." I also think that the selective application of its nonproliferation principles is unconscionable. But the legal nonproliferation regime remains needed until it can be superseded by a nuclear weapons convention for the total elimination of nuclear weapons. Preventing nuclear proliferation and breakout will need to be part of an effective nuclear disarmament regime. Creating such a regime would demonstrate a far more serious effort to eliminate the threat of nuclear weapons than the current situation, which entails an obligation to nuclear disarmament embedded relatively weakly within a selectively enforced nonproliferation regime.

The use of the Stuxnet computer worm to slow down the Iranian uranium-enrichment program raises many important security questions. On the one hand, if it has succeeded, it may eliminate the perceived necessity of an Israeli or U.S. attack on Iran as a "vigilante" means of enforcing nonproliferation. I would far prefer to see nuclear proliferation prevented by a computer worm than by a war. On the other hand, it demonstrates the double standards of a system that allows nuclear-armed nations to use technological means to prevent other states from developing the same weapons that they have.

The use of the Stuxnet worm is a harbinger of the type of security issues that will emerge in future cyberwarfare. I suspect that, in this area, relatively weak states will over time be able to develop or replicate technologies that will put the complex military systems of powerful states at risk. In other words, the use of Stuxnet may be opening a Pandora's box, setting loose new furies on the world. A computer worm capable of exploding nuclear weapons in flight would be a far more useful and potentially dangerous tool than Stuxnet. We really don't know what effects such cyberwarfare technology of the future may have on the world.

Falk: I am not convinced by this line of reasoning. For one thing, there has been no proof that the Iranian nuclear program aims to produce weapons, and without proof, such coercive interference with peaceful nuclear technology seems a serious violation of the NPT itself. For another, unilateral uses of force, even in this form, seem to undermine the effort of international law to make unlawful all nondefensive uses of force. To validate such conduct because it averts a more blatant form of attack seems to underwrite the role of Israel and the United States as regional sheriffs, while Israel is itself an outlier that deserves to have its own programs disrupted by Stuxnet techniques at least to the extent that Iran deserves to be so obstructed. To adapt my thoughts to your phrasing, this is "vigilante injustice"!

Nuclear Energy as a Path to Proliferation

Krieger: One of the great problems with the NPT is that it encourages the peaceful use of nuclear energy, which actually opens the door to nuclear weapons proliferation. It ends up making the treaty work against itself. Of course, Israel is not a party to the treaty; nor are India and Pakistan. This demonstrates a fundamental weakness in international law, that is, the exemption of nations that do not sign a treaty from the law. This would be unworkable in domestic law and is equally so in international law. Some powerful states have been using "vigilante injustice" to enforce the law selectively, but this is unsustainable and will not prevent further nuclear proliferation. It will, however, enrage its victims, and over time they will find a way to level the playing field.

Falk: It may be, as you say, a weakness of the NPT that it encourages access to nuclear power, but such access was integral to the bargain whereby the nonnuclear states were persuaded to agree to renounce their weapons option. If that access had not been allowed, then the treaty regime would never have attracted such wide participation, as countries like Japan were determined early on to meet a large proportion of their energy needs with nuclear power. Furthermore, the nuclear weapon states indicated no willingness to join in a general prohibition on peaceful uses.

Krieger: It is unfortunate that there appears to be such widespread support, even enthusiasm, among states for nuclear energy. There remains no solution regarding the long-term storage of nuclear wastes that will endanger the health of humans and other creatures for tens of thousands of years. Even more critically, from the perspective of our discussion, nuclear energy provides a path to nuclear proliferation for countries with nuclear reactors.

Antiproliferation Warfare

Falk: Iraq was attacked in 2003, causing the deaths of up to 1 million Iraqis and the displacement of as many as 5 million, because it was supposedly seeking nuclear weapons and possessed a stash of chemical and biological weaponry of mass destruction. This antiproliferation war would still have constituted aggressive war under the UN Charter even if Iraq had been found to possess weapons of mass destruction. The unlawfulness of the invasion and occupation of Iraq was reinforced by the failed effort of the United States to gain authorization from the UN Security Council for the attack and, despite this, proceeding with a massive use of nondefensive force. In this respect, there is an uncomfortable link between geopolitical antiproliferation policies and international criminality. The Obama administration has done nothing to back away from this approach to Iran, pointedly refusing to take the military option off the table and failing to criticize belligerent Israeli threats directed at Iran.

Krieger: It is unfortunate that one of the justifications for initiating the illegal U.S. invasion and occupation of Iraq was based on the false charge that Iraq had a nuclear weapons program. This must be viewed as a Nuremberg-type criminal conspiracy to commit aggressive warfare, which occurred at the highest levels of the U.S. government and unfortunately remains untried and unpunished. Let's consider a hypothetical situation. What if Iraq had truly had a nuclear weapons program and had been close to achieving a nuclear weapons capability? What would be the responsibility of the international community in such a situation? I assume you would say that the

United States had no right to initiate an attack on Iraq as it did, and I would agree, but what about the international community? What responsibilities would it have had? If the UN inspectors had found evidence of a secret Iraqi nuclear weapons program, would the United Nations have borne some responsibility for destroying it or pressuring Iraq to do so itself? Or would it have been appropriate simply to stand by while Iraq acquired nuclear weapons capability and became a new member of the nuclear weapons club? It may be difficult in actuality to be certain that a uranium-enrichment or plutonium-reprocessing program is aimed at developing nuclear weapons. This ambiguity perhaps makes the hypothetical more problematic.

Israel's Nuclear Weapons

Falk: I hate to keep harping on the tolerance of Israeli nuclear weapons acquired by stealth and the perceived justification for intervening to prevent Iraqi acquisition, but it exposes the untenable approach to proliferation that even you are partially endorsing. Why is Iraq more dangerous to world order than Israel? The United Nations and the international community lack the credibility to pick and choose among nuclear weapon states in terms of danger to future world order. By many criteria, the United States is the most dangerous of all nuclear weapon states, and yet it dominates the geopolitical regime without any real challenge. Returning to your hypothetical, both Israel and Iraq have engaged in expansionist wars. Iraq, more than Israel, would have risked annihilation if it were ever to deploy or threaten to use nuclear weaponry. Israel has been threatening Iran with military attack, including with nuclear warheads in some versions, receiving hardly any criticism and even tacit acquiescence from Congress and encouragement by conservative leaders like Dick Cheney.

Krieger: I abhor the double standards in the international system, particularly as they are applied to nuclear weapons. At the same time, though, I do not support the proliferation of nuclear weapons to any further states. I do not find Israel's developing of nuclear weapons a justification for Iran, Iraq, or any other state to do so. Rather than opening the door to further proliferation, I would prefer to see the countries of the world put pressure on Israel and the other nuclear weapon states to disarm their nuclear arsenals. The choices that confront us now are nuclear disarmament or nuclear proliferation. As long as some states continue to rely on their nuclear arsenals, the system will be unstable, and there will be pressure toward proliferation. Neither the legal nor the geopolitical regime will be able to hold back nuclear proliferation in the absence of significant steps toward nuclear disarmament.

Falk: But so long as there is no prospect of mounting pressure on Israel, why should a state such as Iran, facing threats of attack by stronger military powers and confronting efforts to destabilize its regime internally, not be entitled to exercise equivalent security options to those relied upon by its adversaries? You oppose double standards, but you seem to be ratifying their operational relevance given the realities of world politics, especially in the Middle East. This is comparable to our argument over the NPT itself. If double standards and nuclearism are not challenged, the result is a tacit accommodation to an unjust and unlawful structure. I think enough opportunity has been given to the nuclear weapon states to move away from double standards that it becomes almost mandatory to conclude that it will not happen and to make our assessments on that basis. For me, living with double standards for this weaponry is unacceptable. The relevant question is, What can be done to challenge such a regime in the name of nuclear disarmament, international law, and the equality of states before the law?

Krieger: I oppose double standards. My goal is to end double standards in the nuclear arena by achieving nuclear disarmament. I do not, however, favor any means whatsoever of ending double standards—for example, by promoting the spread of nuclear weapons to additional states. I think this would only compound the nuclear dangers in the world. I agree that it is necessary to challenge the current regime based on double standards, but I think we must do this by pressing for universal nuclear disarmament. I can understand your frustration with the current international system. I share it. But I do not believe that nuclear deterrence is reliable, and therefore I believe we must exercise caution when it comes to encouraging nuclear proliferation as a means of ending double standards.

Falk: I see our discussion leading—perhaps because it reflects my deep distrust of the nonproliferation rationale—to an insistence on the initiation of a disarming process in the near future. There is no credible excuse for delay. The proliferation regime is unfair and unstable and has been operated in a discriminatory manner. For this reason, I favor its repudiation, which seems to me the only way to make the United States and other nuclear weapon states assess carefully a nuclear disarmament option. Without pressure on this two-tier system, there is no reason to suppose that its disappearance will occur except, God forbid, in the aftermath of a major war fought with nuclear weaponry or through some kind of unexpected popular movement that makes nuclear disarmament and abolition of nuclear weaponry a central goal. After more than sixty years, it seems naïve to think that either rational argument or moral appeal will suddenly reverse the tide of nuclearism. If Kissinger's Gang of Four caused barely a ripple of interest in nuclear disarmament among the political leadership, I think the implications are obvious. And looking further back, if Ronald Reagan's determined effort in Iceland to negotiate total strategic nuclear disarmament with a receptive Mikhail Gorbachev could be so cavalierly cast aside by the American security establishment—incidentally, due to bipartisan skepticism at the time—is there any basis for thinking that nuclear disarmament will get a receptive hearing in the current climate of opinion? To be sure, Obama gave his visionary speech in Prague, and maybe that nudged the Nobel Peace Committee in Oslo and was appreciated and quoted by peaceniks around the world, but his failure to follow up is more expressive of the play of forces in the United States (and regrettably elsewhere as well) than was his affirmation of the goal of living in a world without nuclear weapons.

Krieger: We agree that the nuclear nonproliferation regime cannot continue to hold up and is showing increasing signs of weakness. It is already exceedingly dangerous that this regime is being stitched together by war, as in Iraq, and threats of war, as in Iran. In 1995, the parties to the Non-Proliferation Treaty, under considerable pressure from the United States and other nuclear weapon states, agreed to extend the treaty indefinitely. Some countries and many civil society organizations, including the Nuclear Age Peace Foundation, opposed this indefinite extension of the NPT, believing that it rewarded the nuclear weapon states that were parties to the treaty but had done virtually nothing to fulfill their nuclear disarmament obligations. I believe that the number of countries in the world frustrated by the failure of the nuclear weapon states to fulfill their nuclear disarmament obligations and level the playing field has grown substantially. It is time for these states to exert pressure on the nuclear weapon states to transition from a nuclear nonproliferation to a nuclear disarmament regime.

Mobilizing the Public

Falk: We need to get rid of these weapons, and with a sense of urgency, but no top-down approach is going to work. You are fond of citing Gandhi and Martin Luther King Jr. as visionaries who attained the impossible, but they did so only because each mobilized a movement that developed the political will and capacity to overcome the obstacles blocking the achievement of its objectives. Perhaps the role of Nelson Mandela is more suggestive as he seemed to participate in a top-down approach, but in my view, Mandela's totally unexpected release from jail and the historic surrender of the governing white elite only came about because the worldwide antiapartheid movement had succeeded in isolating South Africa culturally, in sports, and to some extent diplomatically and economically. Change of the magnitude we are demanding depends on a mobilized public with dedicated leadership, and that is missing in relation to issues of war and peace. If we are serious about advancing our goals, we must acknowledge this and struggle to understand what can be done.

Krieger: As you know, I have worked for three decades trying to mobilize public opinion on the issue of nuclear weapons abolition. I know how challenging it is. For the most part, the public, if asked in polls, does not favor nuclear weapons, but nor does it view nuclear disarmament as a high priority. Too many other problems in people's lives seem more immediately pressing. It would be a disaster, though, if it took the use of one or more nuclear weapons to awaken the public and political leaders to the importance of this issue. It would be a tragic failure of imagination.

India and Pakistan

Krieger: Before we move on from the subject of nuclear proliferation, we should consider the cases of India and Pakistan. Neither became a party to the NPT, and both decided to develop nuclear arsenals. India first tested a nuclear weapon in 1974, under the guise of testing for peaceful purposes. Indian leaders repeatedly said that they would prefer a world with no nuclear weapon states but would not remain a non–nuclear weapon state in a two-tier nuclear world. In 1998, a few years after the 1995 indefinite extension of the NPT, India conducted a series of nuclear weapon tests and left no doubt that it had joined the nuclear weapons club. Immediately following India's nuclear tests, Pakistan also tested, creating two hostile nuclear powers in South Asia, an area that must now be considered one of the most dangerous in the world. A. Q. Khan, the so-called father of Pakistan's nuclear program, became a national hero. He set up a secret commercial enterprise for selling nuclear plans, technology, and materials to other countries. Fortunately, his enterprise was uncovered and halted, and he was placed under house arrest in Pakistan. As punishments go, this was a slap on the wrist.

One of the most disturbing aspects of nuclear proliferation to India and Pakistan was how the George W. Bush administration twisted arms to allow for the sale of nuclear equipment to India. Bush managed to get both U.S. law and the rules of the Nuclear Suppliers Group changed so that India could import nuclear technology and materials for its nuclear power program. The United States–India deal required inspections of India's civilian nuclear power plants but not its military nuclear facilities. The result was to allow India, a self-proclaimed and proven nuclear proliferator, to create more weapons-grade nuclear materials in its military program and thus develop the capacity to build more nuclear weapons. This is yet another example of a clear double standard regarding nuclear proliferation in the international system. Pakistan will continue to press for similar treatment, and based on the U.S. precedent, it will be difficult to dissuade China, for example, from assisting Pakistan as the United States has assisted India.

It is also worth mentioning that some countries are already virtual nuclear powers. Japan is the best example. It has both the technology and the plutonium to become a major nuclear weapon state in a very short time, weeks or months. Japan has fifty to one hundred tons of reprocessed plutonium for its nuclear power industry. This plutonium could be quickly converted to weapons production if Japan desired to do so. The United States points to this possibility as demonstrating a need for extending its "nuclear umbrella" over Japan. The situation in Japan should make clear—as does the proliferation of nuclear weapons to Israel, India, Pakistan, and North Korea—that the spread of nuclear research reactors and nuclear power reactors opens the door to nuclear proliferation. Nuclear power plants are Trojan horses for nuclear proliferation. Any attempt to go to zero nuclear weapons in the world will have to deal with this reality.

Delegitimizing the Nonproliferation Regime

Falk: I appreciate and, of course, support your laudable efforts to promote the cause of nuclear disarmament, devoting your energy and intelligence to this great moral and political cause. At the same time, I feel it is no longer tenable to seek simultaneously these goals and continued support for the nonproliferation regime. This is not a matter of the best being an enemy of the good. It is an instance of the bad being allowed to insulate itself from pressures to embrace the good. In other words, the nonproliferation regime facilitates reliance on nuclear weaponry as a diplomatic tool. There is no alternative at this point, I believe, for those of us dedicated to a world without nuclear weaponry but to take these nuclear weapon states out of their comfort zone, and this we can only do by delegitimizing the nonproliferation regime.

As far as research reactors and nuclear power reactors are concerned, there is no doubt that their presence allows for movement across the weapons threshold. A disarmament regime would have to monitor not only phased elimination of the weaponry but the operation of these reactors. For me, this is a disarmament challenge more than a proliferation problem. As I have argued, given the refusal of the nuclear weapon states to take credible steps in the direction of nuclear disarmament, arms control and antiproliferation policies are neither legally nor morally justifiable and weaken whatever disarmament incentives exist.

Krieger: As you well know, pursuing the goal of nuclear disarmament requires perseverance. It is not subject to logic or fairness, and there are many obstacles to achieving the goal. Nonetheless, I am convinced that it is an essential goal if humanity is to have a future. The nuclear nonproliferation regime will remain illegitimate so long as nuclear double standards persist and nuclear disarmament is not achieved. We are challenged to find a way to end policies that are neither legally nor morally justifiable, but we must find means that do not place the future of humanity in even greater jeopardy. I think we agree that the way forward must be to achieve nuclear disarmament and that time is not on humanity's side. We must pursue an end to the nuclear weapons era with a sense of urgency.

Falk: I share this goal, but how much perseverance is sufficient to demonstrate that relying on persuasion will not do the trick? Patience is no longer a virtue; it has become a vice. The time has come to push for some other way of challenging the nuclear status quo. There is not the slightest indication that any of the nuclear weapon states are even in the process of preparing proposals for negotiating a phased nuclear disarmament treaty, much less willing to advocate such a course of action as a genuine political project that goes beyond the visionary affirmations of some distant future when conflict disappears or we have arrived at a point where "ultimate" goals are converted into attainable goals.

Krieger: The most common response to the continued threat of nuclear weapons is complacency, and I do see virtue in persevering in the struggle to awaken individuals and countries to the need to rid the world of nuclear weapons before it is too late. The alternative to nuclear disarmament now is future nuclear catastrophes.

Falk: Nothing presently suggests that the United States or other nuclear weapon states are at all interested in nuclear disarmament. Nor is there any sign of a popular movement taking shape to exert pressure that will encourage governments to move toward nuclear disarmament. Under these conditions, I believe relying on peace education and persuasion amounts to de facto acquiescence in the status quo—or worse, waiting for the bomb to awaken public outrage. In this sense, I believe that your allegations of complacency also apply to those of us who consider ourselves to be part of the antinuclear movement. We have been co-opted unless we can imagine a plausible strategy to make our advocacy of nuclear disarmament a political project rather than, as at present, a pipe dream. My proposal is a two-year ultimatum by as many nonnuclear states as possible threatening to withdraw from the NPT unless serious nuclear disarmament negotiations get underway.

Krieger: I appreciate your desire for immediate action and your concrete proposal, which deserves serious consideration. As you know, though, I'm reluctant to see the Nuclear Non-Proliferation Treaty scrapped in the absence of a nuclear weapons convention to replace it. Many questions come to mind: Which countries would be willing to put themselves on the line to lead such an ultimatum? Would enough countries be willing to participate to be of concern to the nuclear weapon states? Would the nuclear weapon states party to the NPT be responsive? Would the nuclear weapon states not party to the NPT be responsive? In the event of failure, where would the world be with a wrecked nonproliferation regime and without a nuclear disarmament treaty to replace it? I think these questions deserve more thought. I suggest we return to your proposal for more in-depth consideration in our final chapter on the path to zero.

Falk: You raise questions that deserve a response and are relevant to my proposed ultimatum, but my confidence in this way of proceeding remains, although whether the nonnuclear states would be willing to mount such a challenge is uncertain. I agree we need to move on, but not before we address at least briefly the anxieties associated with the post-9/11 fear that nuclear weapons might fall into the hands of extremist nonstate actors. I think this is a credible risk, especially in national settings where extremists may have influence in the governing process, as in Pakistan. The fact that such an alarming threat has not called into question the nonproliferation approach is deeply disturbing. It suggests that the nuclear weapon states have such an infernal hold on the non–nuclear weapon states, by way of co-option and intimidation, as to make them unwilling and unable to protect their own security by challenging the proliferation approach. The retention of such weaponry by the nuclear weapon states remains beyond serious questioning, which is why the disarmament option is treated as an "ultimate" rather than a "proximate" goal.

CHAPTER 4

Nuclear Arms Control
and Nuclear Disarmament

Falk: Early in the Cold War, the idea emerged that it was mutually beneficial for the superpower adversaries to cooperate to the extent necessary to minimize both the dangers of the nuclear arms race, especially risks associated with accidents or mistakes, and its costs. There was also a widely shared concern about a misreading of intentions in the midst of an international crisis that could lead to a nuclear World War III. The Cuban Missile Crisis of 1962 brought home this American-Soviet shared sense of urgency about managing the risk of nuclear confrontation. An additional contributor to this managerial approach was the common interest in avoiding expensive additions to the cost of national defense, especially if seen as destabilizing in relation to mutual assured destruction (MAD). In this vein there was a widespread belief among war planners, at least until the presidency of Ronald Reagan, that defensive weapons systems designed to destroy incoming missiles should not be developed because doing so would seem to weaken confidence that an attack could be deterred by the threat of retaliation. Even if there existed skepticism about the effectiveness of defensive systems, once a superpower adversary embarked on such a course, the pressure on the other side to do the same or to take countermeasures to neutralize the defensive option would prove irresistible. The Anti-Ballistic Missile (ABM) Treaty was negotiated against this background but eventually scrapped by the war-prone presidency of George W. Bush in the aftermath of the Cold War.

Managing Nuclear Threats

Krieger: Nuclear arms control has always been a means of attempting to manage nuclear threats, particularly threats between the United States and Soviet Union. Most arms control agreements have tried to manage the most immediate dangers of nuclear weapons without altering the power relationship between the nuclear weapon and non–nuclear weapon states. For the most part, arms control agreements have "given up" only what the nuclear weapon states perceived as unnecessary. A good example is the 1963 Partial Test Ban Treaty, in which the United States, United Kingdom, and Soviet Union gave up testing nuclear weapons in the atmosphere, oceans, and outer space. Since these countries were able to move their nuclear testing underground, they no longer needed to test in these other environments.

The ABM Treaty was negotiated by the Richard Nixon administration and signed in 1972. The United States and Soviet Union viewed it as putting a lid on the nuclear arms race by keeping each side vulnerable to a retaliatory attack by the other. Even with the ABM Treaty in place, though, both sides continued to increase their nuclear arsenals up to 1986. Presumably, without the ABM Treaty, their arms race would have been even more wasteful. The treaty was unilaterally abrogated by George W. Bush in 2002. Russia didn't like the idea of ending the treaty then and continues to voice serious concerns about what it views as a potentially dangerous nuclear imbalance created by U.S. plans to deploy missile defenses in Europe.

Falk: This psychology of arms control was very much in keeping with the reliance on nuclear weaponry for various forms of deterrence, as well as with the continuous development of ways to bolster the credibility of retaliatory capabilities with new protection of launch sites and greater accuracy of guidance mechanisms. It should be acknowledged that, all along, right-wing critics sharply attacked arms control as a form of appeasement. The neoconservative cabal set forth their views within the Pentagon in the notorious Plan B, which argued that all treaties with the Soviet Union involving security issues were undesirable, weakening the pressure exerted by the West. Since 2000, and until Barack Obama's presidency, Plan B advocates such as Donald Rumsfeld and Paul Wolfowitz were in control of national security policy, and arms control arrangements were no longer pursued. It was this neoconservative outlook of most Republicans in the Senate that made the fight for New START so intense. In effect, the Democratic Party and liberal America support arms control, and they are opposed almost exclusively from the Far Right, which has been gaining strength during the Obama presidency.

The McCloy-Zorin Accords

Falk: The McCloy-Zorin Accords of 1961 were the climax of the pro-disarmament posture relied upon by the United States and the Soviet Union early in the John F. Kennedy presidency.[1] These eight principles set forth a plausible framework of phased, monitored, and verified disarmament of all weaponry, not just nuclear weapons. McCloy-Zorin represented a response to General Assembly Resolution 1378 (XIV) (1959), and its preamble affirmed that "the continuing arms race is a heavy burden for humanity and is fraught with dangers for the cause of world peace." Negotiated by high-level officials representing the two governments, it was as close as these geopolitical actors have ever come to committing themselves to a general and complete disarmament process. It did produce outlines of proposals on the basis of the accords but seemed to lack any governmental will on either side to test the other side's seriousness. It accepted the rhetoric of a world without war that goes well beyond a world without nuclear weapons, but there is no indication that the political leadership in either country regarded prospects for nuclear disarmament as more than atmospherics associated with the propaganda dimensions of the Cold War.

Krieger: The McCloy-Zorin Accords sought to provide a framework for general and complete disarmament. The accords, which were signed on January 20, 1961, were titled "Joint Statement of Agreed Principles for Disarmament Negotiations." The third of the eight principles called for an end to "all military forces, bases, stockpiles, weapons and expenses." This principle stated, "To this end, the programme for general and complete disarmament shall contain the necessary provisions, with respect to the military establishment of every nation for: The disbanding of armed forces, the dismantling of military establishments, including bases, the cessation of the production of armaments as well as their liquidation or conversion to peaceful uses; the elimination of all stockpiles of nuclear, chemical, bacteriological, and other weapons of mass destruction, and the cessation of the production of such weapons; the elimination of all means of delivery of weapons of mass destruction; the abolition of organizations and institutions designed to organize the military efforts of States, the cessation of military training, and the closing of all military training institutions; and the discontinuance of military expenditures."[2]

The McCloy-Zorin Accords' eighth principle calls for states to "seek widest agreement at earliest date while continuing to seek more limited agreements which will facilitate and form part of the overall programme for secured general and complete disarmament in a peaceful world."[3] The "more limited agreements" mentioned may be viewed as arms control, but they are clearly placed within the context of a program for general and complete disarmament. I think we would have moved much closer to serious disarmament if the United States and the Soviet Union had actually attempted to follow the McCloy-Zorin Accords. The tragedy is that they did not and reverted instead to seeking to manage nuclear threats through arms control agreements.

Nuclear arms control agreements have diverted attention and effort from seeking nuclear disarmament. The fact that the neoconservatives on the Far Right oppose even modest arms control agreements, as they did with New START, has made arms control seem more valuable than it actually is. But the benefits of arms control are perceived as valuable primarily because of the foolhardy bullying tactics of the neoconservatives, who seek not fairness and balance in negotiated agreements but U.S. advantage. They play a dangerous game, especially considering that the stakes are the survival of both countries and civilization.

Toward Nuclear Disarmament

Falk: Since the end of World War II, there have been periodic discussions of nuclear disarmament and a variety of proposals to achieve the elimination of nuclear weaponry; revealingly, however, there have been none since the end of the Cold War, a time that seems most propitious for seeing whether nuclear weaponry could be prudently eliminated. Nuclear disarmament as a goal from the outset has been built on the fear and revulsion associated with weapons forever associated with the horrible human and physical damage caused by the atomic bombs dropped on Japanese cities at the end of World War II. The great majority of governments, as well as world public opinion, viewed any use or threat to use nuclear weaponry as a crime against humanity, an extension of international criminality originally recognized at Nuremberg. The UN General Assembly adopted Resolution 1653(XVI) in 1961 to this effect. The use of or threat to use nuclear weaponry represents an unprecedented assault on widely held views of morality and legality, as well as poses threats to human survival.

Nevertheless, disarmament as a calculated policy pursued by the first and only user of this weaponry was always beset by ambivalence. Powerful states do not give up their most destructive weapons unless compelled to do so in a peace treaty signed after losing a war. The historical background of the Cold War accorded great respect to "the lesson of Munich"; this was interpreted after 1945 as warning against appeasing an expansive Soviet Union, which it became fashionable to believe was contained only because of deterrence coupled with the credible readiness to use countervailing force if and when provoked by challenges to the vital national interests of the West. There was also institutional resistance based on the role of the nuclear weapons establishment, which was well entrenched in the government bureaucracy but also had deep roots in the business world, scientific establishment, and weapons labs.

Finally, there was the prevalent view that the Soviet Union as a closed society had the means and incentive to cheat if a disarmament process proceeded toward the elimination of the weaponry. It was argued that a few hidden weapons in a disarming world could wield extraordinary influence, including as blackmail against the West. Considering these obstacles, it should not be surprising that pressures at home from civil society and a propaganda rivalry with Moscow led the United States to put on the table of diplomacy some disarmament proposals. Missing from this process was any sense of commitment by either government to sell disarmament to its own public from the perspectives of national security and political culture. In both instances, this selling would have had to confront and refute "hard-power realism" and make the case for a safer, more secure and legitimate, and more morally self-confident country due to the willingness to eliminate this weaponry and renounce forever the intention to use it for any purpose whatsoever.

Krieger: Unfortunately, it seems that despite lofty statements and UN resolutions, the moral and legal arguments for nuclear disarmament have not been widely taken up by people everywhere. I wish that they would be, as it seems clear that only with widespread public involvement will there be enough pressure to cause governments to act on nuclear disarmament. Overall, the nuclear weapon states have framed the issue in such a way that nuclear weapons are perceived to provide rather than undermine security. It is a significant moral failure that citizens of the nuclear weapon states have not demanded serious action by their governments to achieve nuclear disarmament.

Potential cheating is an important issue, but one that can be resolved by assuring verifiability through onsite inspections, as well as by technical means. Most importantly, though, proceeding with nuclear disarmament in phases will provide the opportunity to build increasing confidence in verification procedures with each phase. I agree with you that the U.S. government has never taken the lead in a serious way, either internationally or with its own citizens, in promoting nuclear disarmament.

Lack of Good Faith

Falk: My position, prefigured earlier in our discussion, is that a good faith and dedicated commitment to nuclear disarmament has never existed on the part of the U.S. government; nor has disarmament been a high priority for the American public. This exhibition of gross moral callousness is itself a civilizational and world order disgrace. It is probably the case that the United States is not alone in these failures of political will and cultural sensitivity and that the Soviet Union itself was uncertain about whether, in the last analysis, it would be willing to entrust its future security to a world without nuclear weapons. This uncertainty, or calculated embrace of nuclearism, is now also characteristic of the deep politics of nuclear weaponry as descriptive of the other seven members of the nuclear weapons club. At present, then, I am arguing that nuclear disarmament is not a *political* project for the United States or for any of the other nuclear weapon states.

Krieger: The U.S. failure to lead on nuclear disarmament is a tragedy both for the United States itself and for the world. President Obama has tried to lead with regard to preventing further nuclear proliferation, particularly to nonstate extremists, and in arms control matters with Russia, but he has not yet acted upon his vision of nuclear disarmament.

Falk: I think you are far too kind. The failure of Obama to lead goes beyond the absence of a sense of urgency in my view but is something far more significant, the absence of seriousness, by which I mean some conception of the relationship between means and ends. I have seen no evidence of a commitment that goes further than embracing the rhetoric of desire, not even some attention devoted to figuring out how the desire for what doesn't now exist might yet be achieved in some altered future.

Another criticism that I would make of the approach taken by the Obama presidency, in common with prior administrations, is that it pretends to itself and the world that arms control agreements constitute legally and politically relevant steps that lead the country and the world closer to disarmament. I believe that such claims are false and misleading and that whenever a major arms control agreement is accepted, it weakens public interest in and support for the disarmament agenda. Managing the risks of nuclear war by measures designed to stabilize the global setting and overcoming these risks by the elimination of the weaponry are very different things. Of course, disarmament critics deliberately complicate the discussion by contending, with some reason, that getting rid of the weapons will not eliminate the risks and may in certain situations actually increase the risk of nuclear war due to the possibility of noncompliance or the marketing and use of nuclear knowledge to and by nonstate actors or so-called rogue states.

Distinct Goals and Rationales

Falk: I am pointing to both conceptual and policy issues that tend to get overlooked due to the ways in which the arms control–disarmament distinction is manipulated: Conceptually, I believe that arms control and disarmament have distinct goals and rationales; in the policy domain, I believe disarmament advocacy is generally viewed as antithetical to the embrace of an arms control approach, although the two are quite often presented as complementary or even mutually reinforcing by liberal constituencies, which tend to believe that disarmament will only come about at the end of a long negotiating history that generates a series of small (arms control) steps that over time build public and governmental confidence in going much further. In my view, if we are ever to achieve disarmament without the traumatizing push of a prior catastrophe, it will be necessary to regard arms control as a parallel rather than a complementary path to a more secure, just, and peaceful world. In my terminology, we will become serious about nuclear disarmament only when we expose the diversionary effects of these arms control agreements. The arms control enterprise draws energy and talent away from nuclear disarmament, advocacy of which the Washington establishment views as both tiresome and irrelevant.

Krieger: You refer to Obama's "rhetoric of desire." It is perhaps a way to understand the distance between his rhetoric and his action. He has been strong in his rhetoric, particularly in the Prague speech in 2009, but his actions have not matched his words. As time passes, the rhetoric fades, and the lack of action becomes far more defining of his position. Still, it seems that he cannot be held solely to account for failing to match action with desire. For the most part, the American people have not broken through their complacency sufficiently to grasp the desire in Obama's rhetoric. If enough American people were enthusiastic about, or even positively responsive to, the rhetoric of a world free of nuclear weapons, that would put far more pressure on and give support to the president to take tangible steps to match his rhetoric.

Falk: I understand your effort to balance criticism with encouragement in your assessment of the Obama approach, but I am less willing to accord such a wide margin of good will. If Obama were genuinely committed to nuclear disarmament, it would have been clear by now. To begin with, he would not have launched his efforts in Prague rather than in an American city associated with the defense industry. At least he would have followed Prague with a second speech in St. Louis or Houston, and he would surely have appointed a credible working group to come up with a disarmament plan by a time certain. Admittedly, after sixty-seven years of nuclearism, it would require impressive leadership to move America toward nuclear disarmament, and it would require support from the heartland.

The Need for Leadership

Krieger: Of course, I would have liked to see Obama do far more, but at least he has highlighted the dangers of nuclear weapons, among the many serious issues that he has had to deal with. You are right that after sixty-seven years of nuclearism, it is not easy for a president to turn the nuclear juggernaut around quickly. Even for necessary radical change, restraint is built into the political process. There is also the need to assure that other nuclear weapon states are prepared to go to zero too. Obama talked a lot about his concerns about nuclear dangers in U.S. cities during his campaign for the presidency; he also convened a UN Security Council summit on gaining control of loose nuclear materials and preventing nuclear terrorism. If his efforts have not been sufficient, they also have not been insignificant. But he certainly does not deserve all the blame in this area; there has been little constituency for nuclear disarmament to support him.

As we've experienced nuclear arms control and disarmament measures up to the present, they have been on different paths. But I can conceive of some integration, assuming that arms control is not being used cynically as an alternative to nuclear disarmament. For example, UN Secretary-General Ban Ki-moon has proposed a five-point plan for nuclear disarmament. In his first point, he urges "all [Non-Proliferation Treaty (NPT)] parties, in particular the nuclear-weapon states, to fulfill their obligation under the treaty to undertake negotiations on effective measures leading to nuclear disarmament. They could agree on a framework of separate, mutually reinforcing instruments. Or they could consider negotiating a nuclear-weapons convention, backed by a strong verification system, as has long been proposed at the UN. I have circulated to all UN members a draft of such a convention, which offers a good point of departure."[4] The draft convention that he mentions was actually developed by civil society organizations and submitted to the UN General Assembly jointly by the Republic of Costa Rica and Malaysia.[5]

Ban Ki-moon is suggesting either "a framework of separate, mutually reinforcing instruments" or a nuclear weapons convention, which would be an actual treaty for nuclear disarmament. In my view, the nuclear weapons convention would be preferable, but a framework agreement could also move toward nuclear disarmament so long as it is clear from the outset that the goal of the "mutually reinforcing instruments" is a world free of nuclear weapons within a reasonable time frame.

Missing today is the political will on the part of any of the nine nuclear weapon states to pursue nuclear disarmament. Until this political will is present, public concern for nuclear dangers, to the extent it exists in any substantial measure, will likely be dealt with through periodic negotiation of arms control measures, such as New START. It seems clear to me that this will not be sufficient to prevent either future nuclear proliferation or future nuclear catastrophes.

Falk: Prestige is certainly associated with nuclear weapons, but several governments also see their possession as a hedge against certain foreseen and unforeseen contingencies. India worries that Pakistan could soon be governed by anti-Indian extremists. Pakistan worries that India may want to demonstrate its superpower status by attacking Pakistan. Russia and China are worried about being pushed around by the United States. Israel and North Korea seem concerned that in the future they might not be able to defend their borders and interests without holding in reserve a nuclear threat. The United Kingdom and France do not want to be perceived as no longer capable of defending their homelands against any adversary, making nuclear weaponry appear to compensate for the absence of sufficient conventional weaponry. To be serious then, in my sense, requires a big leap of faith that security can be better found in this century by relying on diplomacy and soft power, incorporating human rights and democracy into notions of security at home and abroad.

Justifying the Need for Nuclear Arsenals

Krieger: As you point out, there are many ways by which states can and do justify the need for their nuclear arsenals. The leaders and so-called national security experts in these states believe that nuclear weapons serve their national interests, and in a world of nuclear haves and have-nots, their position may appear rational. As I'm sure we agree, though, it's not rational—it's dangerous. This has been understood up to a point, and arms control has sought to maintain a middle ground of controlling and managing nuclear dangers while maintaining the perceived "advantages" of possessing nuclear weapons. This is a strategy of short-term advantage, but it runs the serious risk of longer-term failure. The system of power politics in the nuclear weapon states seems to reward those leaders and security experts who put emphasis on power rather than justice, or who at least want justice to be backed up by the greatest power possible. You are suggesting that a change in mind-set with regard to security is needed. I think you are correct, but changing mind-sets with regard to power is a daunting task. I would say, though, that it is also a necessary task.

Falk: I would quibble with you slightly about whether the retention of nuclear weapons, as stabilized via arms control, confers "short-term advantages." I do not see any essential difference between the short term and the long term with respect to nuclear weapons. If they are immoral, unlawful, and imprudent in the long term, then surely the same holds true in the short term. If you mean "apparent" short-term advantages as calculated by reliance on amoral and alegal strategic doctrine, then I understand the point.

Krieger: I mean "perceived" advantages, which doesn't necessarily imply real advantages. Apparently, many policy experts believe that nuclear deterrence provides advantage to the deterring state. I would view this as a very narrow and dangerous perception of advantage.

Shifting the Mind-Set

Falk: To achieve a breakthrough, as in Zen consciousness, we need to aim above the target to have any chance of hitting it. More concretely, it will be necessary to disentangle the understanding of security from a deeply layered set of beliefs about the linkage between hard-power superiority and the security of the state or political community. In most societies that linkage has been partially broken and other approaches adopted. One of the triumphs of the period since 1945 has been the establishment of a culture of peace in Europe such that borders are porous and there is virtually no expectation of war between any of the members of the European Union. Even in the European setting, though, France and the United Kingdom retain nuclear weapons and do not seem motivated to get rid of them or to push the United States to take the lead. In effect, in Europe, the culture of peace has not yet gone deep enough to reach the nuclear weapons issue either within the government or among the citizenry. Indeed, there was more antinuclear sentiment during the Cold War era when existential fears often grew intense that Europe could become a nuclear weapons battleground, and war thinkers in the United States, such as Henry Kissinger and Herman Kahn, conjectured that a so-called limited nuclear war could be rationally fought for control of Europe, yet allow the continent to recover in a manner not radically dissimilar from its recovery from the ravages of World War II. Nuclear disarmament has only risen to the surface of public consciousness when enough persons in society are scared that nuclear war might actually happen. As long as that anxiety about nuclear war is absent or weak, we have no chance of awakening enough of the public to the dangers and indecency of relying on this weaponry.

Krieger: I'm pleased that you have brought Zen consciousness into our discussion. Trying to unravel the issues related to security has the quality of a Zen koan, a mind-bending riddle that helps one awaken to reality. The task we confront is how to break through the seemingly intractable walls that now surround and protect the concept of security in the minds of national security elites. The concept of hard-power superiority seems to be hardwired into the national security establishment. This has changed very little despite the failure of hard power to prevail in war after war. The United States has experienced the limits of hard power in Afghanistan and Iraq for roughly a decade. It finally ended the war in Iraq, but continues in Afghanistan with little success.

Another way to look at nuclear weapons is through the prism of dependency. With regard to Europe, I think that neither France nor the United Kingdom wants to be dependent upon the United States for its security. Nuclear weapons give both of these countries at least the illusion of independence. That is a powerful psychological concept. In this sense, nuclear weapons are serving other needs than security. These needs require deeper exploration. For some countries, the weapons serve needs for recognition, prestige, status, and power in addition to security. Other countries, such as members of NATO and Japan and Australia, seem content to be dependent upon the U.S. nuclear umbrella. One necessary shift in mind-set is the realization that this umbrella is flimsy and that being under the umbrella is more dangerous than being beyond it. Carrying this shift of mind-set one step further leads to a questioning of deterrence theory itself; it is as flimsy as an umbrella protecting against a nuclear attack.

There is no doubt that the fear of nuclear war has subsided among the general public. For many people, it doesn't exist. The Cold War ended, and the nuclear threat receded in the minds of most people. It's necessary now to rely not on fear as a motivator but on imagination. Perhaps, though, without fear the imagining of nuclear dangers cannot be adequately triggered. That is why public education is so important. If people do not use their imaginations to awaken to the nuclear threat that remains present, the consequences could be catastrophic for all countries, including the most powerful ones, and for the human species. Albert Einstein put great faith in the human imagination. I do as well. Perhaps the Zen riddle is this: What casts a dark shadow when dormant and a fiery cloud of death when brought to life?

Falk: Against such a background of interpretation, I am wary of becoming co-opted by the arms control community. I prefer to be a shrill outsider than a patient enabler. The dedicated arms control advocate will be unlikely to get even a bad seat at the diplomatic table or in the counsels of security planning and is lucky to be allowed in the room at all. The arms control advocate is pigeonholed by the media and Congress as someone on "the left," while the disarmament advocate is totally ignored in the corridors of power, except every so often when an important leader is either worried or troubled by the continued reliance on nuclear weaponry. Sometimes, it is a hardened realist such as the architect of "containment" during the Cold War, George Kennan, who fears that a nuclear genie at large destroys our better angels even if only kept in reserve. I want to emphasize the importance of changing our tactics in relation to the challenge of achieving nuclear disarmament.

Krieger: I don't blame you for being wary of the arms control community, which has tried to make nuclear weapons acceptable by their management. Perhaps in some cases it has reduced the danger of their use or proliferation. But I think it is also correct that the arms control community has been effective in diminishing public concern for nuclear dangers. It has taken incremental steps that appear to be in the right direction but have diverted attention from the weapons and dangers that remain.

I believe we have reached a fork in the road, one direction being continued nuclear arms control through incremental agreements, a path almost certain to lead to disaster sooner or later. The other path would lead to a serious commitment to nuclear disarmament, as was promised more than forty years ago in the Non-Proliferation Treaty. This is the path we need to take. I'm not sure that your shrillness will help move the world onto this path, but I have faith that your insightful mind, clear voice, and persistence will make a difference. Can you summarize the change in tactics you are proposing?

New Approaches to Nuclear Disarmament

Falk: This is a fair and difficult question. I advocate an approach based on the end of patience and trust: (1) unconditionally declare No First Use of nuclear weaponry, followed by negotiation of an accord to this effect with other nuclear weapon states; (2) call upon Obama to speak about nuclear disarmament to the American people; (3) call on the U.S. government to put forward plans for both a nuclear disarmament convention and a general and complete disarmament process in accord with the McCloy-Zorin Accords; (4) recommend to nonnuclear states the issuance of a joint ultimatum to the effect of a joint withdrawal from the NPT if there is a failure to produce a detailed nuclear disarmament proposal and initiate a negotiating process within two years; (5) propose the negotiation of a multilateral treaty to establish an upper limit on defense spending of 1 percent of gross national product, with the agreement coming into force as soon as ratified by more than five of the ten countries with the largest defense expenditures; (6) adopt the principle of closing foreign military bases, to be implemented by closing fifty or more American overseas military facilities each year until the number is reduced to under fifty, with those remaining being scrutinized from perspectives on global security and each justified on an annual basis to Congress and to the American public.

Now it's your turn to provide a different program of action. I realize that my six points may sound radical, but I believe that the liberal posture of pleading and grasping at straws has gotten nowhere for over six decades and that there is less interest in nuclear disarmament today than during the 1950s and 1960s.

Krieger: The tactics you suggest are broader than I was expecting. They go beyond the nuclear disarmament path and follow in the path of general and complete disarmament initially set forth in the McCloy-Zorin Accords. In terms of tactics, though, it may be better to keep a focus on nuclear disarmament before proceeding to general and complete disarmament, rather than having them move in parallel. I have some concern that attempting to have the two move in parallel could result in progress on nuclear disarmament becoming dependent upon progress in general and complete disarmament. At any rate, I agree with all of the tactics you propose, with the exception of the two-year ultimatum by the non–nuclear weapon state parties to the NPT. I think this is too restrictive a time frame, and I would give the nuclear weapon states until 2015 to put forth a serious nuclear disarmament proposal.

Falk: On the coupling of nuclear disarmament and general and complete disarmament, I am agnostic, and so I believe it is useful to keep both paths to a safer, more peaceful world in our minds and hearts. There are good arguments for the position you take, which reduces to nuclear disarmament first, but there are also serious objections based on the danger of unleashing a new cycle of conventional warfare if the fear of nuclear war were abruptly removed from the international scene. There may also be greater appeal to the vision of a warless world than the image of a world without nuclear weapons. At this point, we are so far from embarking on either path that I would maintain my stress on nuclear disarmament and general and complete disarmament as benevolent alternatives with the choice of which is preferable left to the future. In the interim, of course, those who are committed to one or the other approach, as you are, can pursue the path they believe is more promising. I find myself more ambivalent on this issue.

One more item of response: Why is two years too short a period? If the commitment were forthcoming, the additional time needed to bring to the table a credible proposal would be happily extended by the international community. If we do not act as if we take seriously the urgency of the problem, how can we expect to be taken seriously? Besides, nuclear weapon states would have ample advance warning beyond the two years as support for the ultimatum was being generated and building throughout the world. And keep in mind that my tactic is partly designed to challenge the current mood of complacency, maybe not "shock and awe," but at least "shock and act."

Krieger: If there were a sudden wave of true enthusiasm for general and complete disarmament, I could also ride that wave, but absent that, I would keep my focus on nuclear disarmament. My reason for allowing more than two years for the nuclear weapon states to bring a proposal to the table for nuclear disarmament is twofold: First, the path forward is complicated, and it is important that the details be worked out carefully; second, it is an ultimatum with consequences that could prove highly detrimental. Even keeping in mind your desire to challenge the current prevailing mood of complacency, I think that the next Non-Proliferation Treaty Review Conference in 2015 provides a natural point at which to act upon such an ultimatum. It would also take a while to find countries willing to raise and act on such a challenge to the nuclear weapon states. I don't know of any that would actually be prepared to do so now.

Let me return to your earlier question about my approach to a program of action for nuclear disarmament. The briefing booklet I prepared for the 2010 Non-Proliferation Treaty Review Conference, *Nuclear Non-Proliferation and Disarmament: Shifting the Mindset,*[6] enumerates the following five priority goals proposed by the Nuclear Age Peace Foundation:

1. Each signatory nuclear weapon state should provide an accurate public accounting of its nuclear arsenal, conduct a public environmental and human assessment of its potential use, and devise and make public a roadmap for going to zero nuclear weapons.
2. All signatory nuclear weapon states should reduce the role of nuclear weapons in their security policies by taking all nuclear forces off high-alert status, pledging No First Use of nuclear weapons against other nuclear weapon states, and No Use against non–nuclear weapon states.
3. All enriched uranium and reprocessed plutonium—military and civilian—and their production facilities (including all uranium-enrichment and plutonium-separation technology) should be placed under strict and effective international safeguards.
4. All signatory states should review Article IV of the NPT, promoting the "inalienable right" to nuclear energy for peaceful purposes, in light of the nuclear proliferation problems posed by nuclear electricity generation.

5. All signatory states should comply with Article VI of the NPT, reinforced and clarified by the 1996 World Court Advisory Opinion, by commencing negotiations in good faith on a nuclear weapons convention for the phased, verifiable, irreversible, and transparent elimination of nuclear weapons and completing these negotiations by 2015.

Adopting a program of action based on these goals would provide a strong impetus to achieve nuclear disarmament. Actually there are more than five goals here. Some of the above points contain more than one action. For example, the first point refers to an accurate public accounting of nuclear arsenals, a human and environmental assessment of nuclear weapons use, and a public roadmap for going to zero. A public accounting of nuclear arsenals would be an important step in achieving transparency and form a basis for verifying the size of nuclear arsenals and arsenal reductions. I think that a human and environmental assessment of nuclear weapons use in a potential nuclear war could be a powerful way to awaken a dormant public on this issue. And a public roadmap for going to zero nuclear weapons would demonstrate that the nuclear weapon states had actually developed a plan and recognized that there was a way to get to zero. Each of these steps would be significant in advancing toward the overarching goal of nuclear disarmament.

The second point above refers to reducing the role of nuclear weapons in the security policies of the nuclear weapon states. It combines the need to de-alert nuclear arsenals with the need to commit to No First Use against other nuclear weapon states and No Use against non–nuclear weapon states. These would be practical steps in moving toward nuclear disarmament. The third and fourth points are pragmatic in calling for international control of nuclear materials and a reconsideration of the proliferation problems inherent in nuclear power generation. The fifth point would give the nuclear weapon states until the next NPT Review Conference in 2015 to negotiate a nuclear weapons convention, a new treaty for complete nuclear disarmament.

Generating the Political Will for Change

Krieger: I believe that the United States should be the country to lead the world to nuclear disarmament, but the political will in the United States at present is dismally lacking. Perhaps I am wrong about the United States being the country to lead and we should be looking for other countries to do so, as you have with your proposal for an ultimatum by the non–nuclear weapon state parties to the NPT. In seeking to find the needed political will, proponents of nuclear disarmament will need the power of Zen consciousness to which you referred: the power to stay balanced, focused, persevering, and unwavering yet flexible in the face of resistance to change and massive indifference to the overriding global threat posed by nuclear weapons.

Falk: I think we need to allow many flowers to bloom, encouraging leadership in the struggle to awaken public consciousness in multiple sites of concern, including in settings where policies on "sustainable development" are being set or where "dialogues of civilization" are taking place. The 2011 uprisings in autocratic countries throughout the Middle East suggest two relevant lessons for those of us working toward a less nuclearist and less militarist world: (1) the impossible happens; (2) positive political change erupts in a manner that the best experts fail to anticipate.

In this spirit, I agree with you that the United States is the most logical leader for a move toward genuine nuclear disarmament, but logic and experience are unlikely to move in the same direction. I mean by this that we should keep our imaginations as open as possible to that which may not seem plausible but may turn out to open up these unanticipated opportunities. I maintain hope for the future not by any faith in the rational becoming the real but in the sense that all human progress seems to have resulted from the commitments sustained by those who care even in circumstances where the outlook for success is bleak. It is a matter of bearing witness in a period of waiting and hoping, a vigil prompted by our repudiation of nuclearism in all its aspects.

Krieger: I agree with the two conclusions that you draw from the recent nonviolent revolutions in the Middle East: The impossible is possible, and its happening is nearly always unanticipated by the experts. For these reasons I continue to choose hope and still believe that a world without nuclear weapons is possible. It has always been a relatively small group of committed people who have challenged the status quo and brought about meaningful social change. This is true of abolishing slavery, achieving and expanding human and civil rights, and, most recently, ousting dictatorships through nonviolent revolution in the Middle East. I think, though, that it is perhaps more than bearing witness that is essential; it is being a voice of conscience and thereby awakening and engaging others in the struggle for a more decent world.

CHAPTER 5

Nuclear Weapons and Militarism

Krieger: Militarism is, unfortunately, widespread in our world. Many countries are continuing to invest heavily in military forces and weapons. Currently, more than $1.5 trillion is spent annually on the world's militaries, with the United States spending roughly half of the total amount. Military expenditures by countries generally appear to be significantly greater than those used to provide human security in areas such as poverty reduction, health care, and environmental protection or programs for individual and community benefit, such as education, sustainable energy, and mass transportation.

We live in a militarized world, and among all the countries of the globe, the United States leads the way. In addition, it continues to celebrate its military, even as it finds military solutions to be nearly totally ineffective. Reliance on military force is not a path to peace and security. It is far more likely to lead to war, with tragic and foreseeable economic, social, and human costs.

The United States is thus far the only country to have used nuclear weapons in war, and it did so twice, in 1945, against an enemy who was already essentially defeated and had no means of retaliation. A deepening taboo seems to be building against the use of nuclear weapons, but we cannot rely on this disinclination in looking ahead. The dormancy of nuclear weapons use could end at any time through accident, miscalculation, or design.

It is surprising that more countries have not sought to add nuclear weapons to their military arsenals. Perhaps this is explainable in terms of costs as well as the relative success of the Non-Proliferation Treaty. Related to both of these reasons, the United States has promoted the concept of extended deterrence to its allies, by which it means that it extends its "nuclear umbrella" over an allied country. The NATO countries, plus Japan, South Korea, and Australia, have allowed themselves to be placed under this umbrella. They expect that the United States will use nuclear retaliation against a country that attacks them with nuclear weapons. It has always been questionable, though, whether the United States would actually do so and thereby put its own territory at risk. The United States has in part dealt with this uncertainty in Europe by placing tactical nuclear weapons in five European countries (Belgium, Germany, Italy, the Netherlands, and Turkey) and authorizing use of these weapons, in the event of war, by the host country.

The countries that seem to have the most incentive to acquire and possess nuclear weapons are those most vulnerable to attack by a more powerful country. In this sense, I consider nuclear weapons to be a far more effective military instrument in the arsenals of relatively weak countries than in those of powerful countries. The United States, for example, has powerful enough conventional forces that it does not need nuclear weapons to bolster its military might or its retaliatory capacity. North Korea, on the other hand, can use its relatively small arsenal of a handful of nuclear weapons to deter a U.S. or South Korean attempt to launch a military takeover of its territory. Iraq under Saddam Hussein would have been able to prevent the U.S. attack against it, as well as regime overthrow and occupation of its territory, if it had actually had nuclear weapons, as the United States claimed but knew to be untrue. The Qaddafi regime in Libya was similarly overthrown in 2011 with NATO assistance after having given up its nuclear program eight years earlier.

Possession of nuclear weapons alters military dynamics. They are really weapons not of war but of mass annihilation. I am struck by how many leading military figures of World War II claimed to oppose the use of nuclear weapons. They did not like the idea of killing civilians—men, women, and children. The use of these weapons insulted their sense of honor and decency, rightfully I think. I view nuclear weapons as long-distance killing machines that destroy indiscriminately. Their most understandable use is that of giving a relatively weak country an equalizing threat against a powerful country. But even this is not truly justifiable. The far better approach to the protection of weak countries is to enforce the UN prohibitions against aggressive war and to hold leaders to account, as they were by the Nuremberg Tribunal.

U.S. Leadership in Militarism

Falk: I think you develop the case against militarism, and its most virulent embodiment in nuclearism, very effectively. I would underscore the disproportionate degree to which the United States leads the pack on whatever dimension of militarism is examined. This is true for all categories of weaponry, extending to land, sea, and air theaters of potential conflict. This militarist posture is also reflected in its network of several hundred foreign bases that establish an American military presence in every region of the planet. No other country currently projects its power beyond its own region. We need to understand this extraordinary reliance on military power that defies American pre–World War II traditions of noninvolvement in overseas conflict and an eagerness to demobilize in times of international peace.

Part of the explanation certainly lies in the Cold War, which involved a constant readiness for maximal warfare and involved the core doctrines of preventing Soviet expansion, protecting allies, and intervening in Third World countries to oppose leftist or Marxist governments and movements. This long period of international militarism entrenched pro-military bureaucrats deep in the recesses of the unelected portions of the government and created a variety of private-sector allies in defense industries, think tanks, and the media. This permanent warfare state then became reenergized by the 9/11 attacks and the preset neoconservative foreign policy agenda that prevailed during the eight years of the George W. Bush administration and has largely persisted during the presidency of Barack Obama, although with reduced stridency. As you suggest, this militarist orientation, endorsed with overwhelming bipartisan support, is outside the domain of "responsible" debate, thereby exempting the military budget from the kind of scrutiny that would seem mandatory given the failures of military approaches to conflict resolution in recent years and considering the urgency attached across the political spectrum to deficit reduction and economic recovery.

I fear that this rigid adherence to a militarism that does not even deliver security in traditional terms (Americans have never felt less secure) has now become embedded in the dominant sectors of American political culture. It has become, most tragically, "who we are." If this interpretation is correct, it helps us to understand the persisting overreliance on military approaches to foreign policy and disposition to solve conflicts by a reliance on force. It also explains somewhat the inability to learn from failures arising from militarism.

Krieger: Militarism appears to have become part of the ideology of the American political class. It is pervasive, and it is bipartisan. When a member of Congress stands against some aspect of militarism, be it a weapons system or a war, he or she often stands alone or nearly so. The political class seems to close ranks behind war, war preparations, and military solutions to conflicts. It tends to isolate those who seek cooperative and peaceful alternatives. Representative Dennis Kucinich comes to Congress from a working-class district in Ohio. He has been an outspoken critic of U.S. wars, but mostly he has stood alone or with a small number of other representatives, while the vast majority of congressional representatives act as cheerleaders for militarism and U.S. wars.

When you say that militarism has become "who we are," we need to examine who the "we" is. I don't find ordinary U.S. citizens to be so militaristic in their views, but they are led, and often misled, by the political elites. Obama appeared to offer a different kind of leadership when he expressed opposition to the war in Iraq during his presidential campaign. His position appealed to large numbers of Americans who believed that Bush had lied to the people about the reasons for going to war. However, as president, Obama has maintained a militaristic stance by transferring U.S. troops from Iraq to Afghanistan. He has also increased the portion of the U.S. budget going to the military and the "defense" industries to its highest level ever, higher even than under Bush. Lyndon Johnson also campaigned on a peace platform and, when elected, dramatically escalated the war in Vietnam. The culture of war and the ideology of militarism is that of the political elites. U.S. citizens allow this to happen through conformity and complacency. To change direction will require more critical thinking and engagement by ordinary citizens. This is possible. I see it, in fact, as a hopeful possibility.

Falk: In my view, these features of the militarist reality also underpin the seemingly unshakable foundations of nuclearism. First of all, nuclear weaponry is a heightening of modern warfare, but it shares many characteristics, including the ability to inflict devastation at a distance or impersonally, with missiles, strategic aircraft, and drones. True, these lack the apocalyptic qualities of nuclear weapons, which are once more tragically present in our political imagination due to the catastrophic damage to the Fukushima Daiichi complex of nuclear reactors, but the willingness to kill defenseless civilians in massive numbers was a prenuclear trait present in the sort of city-busting strategic bombing characteristic of the repeated air raids against German and Japanese cities during World War II. I think we need to go to the roots of this militarist syndrome that fundamentally contradict the major premises of international law and morality, as well as religious values, if we seek to gain support for the repudiation of weaponry of mass destruction. Without such a broad-based analysis, I fear that we will be continually disappointed by our failure to make any real progress in our political and ethical engagement with the vision of a world without nuclear weaponry.

Beyond Nuclearism

Falk: I do not think this means that we have to tie nuclear disarmament to general and complete disarmament or to a pacifist ethic, but I do feel that the possibility of drastic conventional arms limitations may need to be coupled with a credible approach to nuclear disarmament. I do think that some degree of demilitarization must accompany any form of substantial denuclearization. This is obvious in relation to other forms of weapons of mass destruction, but it seems to me to be a more general point. I believe, further, that it is a mistake not to discuss alternative approaches, including even the vision of a world without war as a possibly necessary, and certainly desirable, complement to a world without nuclear weapons.

Krieger: In the post–World War II period, nuclearism has become central to militarism. The nuclear era began with wartime atomic attacks on the general population of two Japanese cities. These attacks were clear violations of international law. The atomic weapons dropped over the cities did not discriminate between combatants and civilians, the latter of which comprised the large majority of the dead and injured. As long-distance killing machines, nuclear weapons became the prototype for other less encompassing means of long-distance killing in warfare or threats to kill in peacetime. The political elites who have closed ranks around militarism and nuclearism must enjoy living on the edge, since reliance on nuclear weapons places them, and the citizens they are supposed to protect, on a precipice. An accident, a miscalculation, or an irrational leader could push them and their societies over the brink and into the nuclear abyss.

I have always felt that the relationship between militarism and nuclearism is complex. Even if we could wave a magic wand and instantly end nuclearism, militarism would still remain in place. Ending militarism would certainly require dealing with nuclearism. I don't think a culture of peace could exist in a world in which some countries still threaten others with nuclear annihilation. Coming to grips with nuclearism will require dealing with imbalances in military forces, weaponry, and expenditures. So, I agree with you that in the process of abolishing nuclear weapons and ending nuclearism, it will be necessary also to take steps toward demilitarization.

It makes no sense to continue to rely on nuclear weapons when this could result in the destruction of civilization. But nuclear disarmament must be accomplished in a way that does not simply make the world safe for conventionally armed bullies and conventional warfare. The civilizational need for nuclear abolition could provide the impetus to reassess the militarization of the planet. If the most militarized countries, though, fail to grasp the need for denuclearizing the planet, we will miss the opportunity to make progress toward a more peaceful, less militarized world. Again, I think the United States should be leading the way but is held back from doing so by the pervasive support for militarism among its elites.

Falk: It seems misleading to imply that the atomic attacks were perceived or should be considered a departure from the behavior of the United States and its allies in World War II. In the last stages of both the European and Asian theaters of the war, strategic bombing on a large scale deliberately sought maximum destruction of civilian populations concentrated in cities. The bombing was both massive and wildly indiscriminate and had as its acknowledged purpose the demoralization of the enemy society via this form of state terror.

I agree that the atomic attacks involved added features, especially the radiation and long period of medical risk, which made these weapons and attacks particularly horrifying, including in their implications for the future. Yet, it is important to recognize that those who conducted warfare on both sides had much earlier concluded that winning the war as quickly and cheaply as possible was paramount. Such an outlook meant abandoning the legal restraints embodied in the law of war whenever these stood in the way of military necessity. I make this point to underscore my conviction that we must not create too large a gap between the military behavior surrounding the role of nuclear weaponry and the military practices relied on in the prenuclear era of warfare. I believe this is important. Getting rid of nuclear weaponry but continuing to endorse the idea of unconditional warfare poses two dangers: First, in times of crisis, an attempt to repossess nuclear weaponry would be more likely; second, without a credible commitment to abide by the limits set by the law of war, there would be immense pressure to bolster conventional weaponry as an offset to the phased elimination of nuclear weapons, with technological possibilities likely to enable the development, free from scrutiny, of destructive weaponry of near nuclear capability. In some ways this reality might indeed be more dangerous, as it would not bear the stigma attached to nuclear weapons, which seems to have had an inhibiting effect in situations where their use was contemplated after 1945.

The Need for a Moral Revolution

Falk: My main argument here is that the disposition to eliminate nuclear weapons requires "a moral revolution" if it is to avoid generating a series of disastrous side effects. Nothing else will suffice. In effect, we have to work simultaneously to build a culture of respect for international law and the authority of the United Nations and to discourage the retention of nuclear weaponry. If the realist abolitionists—that is, Henry Kissinger's Gang of Four—rest their main case on the erosion of American military dominance in the likely event of further proliferation of the weaponry, then we should rest our case on the stabilizing and practical benefits of linking nuclear disarmament to a strengthening of the global rule of law and the authority of the United Nations. On their side is geopolitical pragmatism; on ours is a normative commitment reinforced by an interpretation of historical trends relating to conflict resolution. One practical benefit of adhering to international law is the recognition that military intervention, even with overwhelming capabilities, is rarely successful at acceptable costs given contemporary realities, and it should not be undertaken from a cost-benefit perspective. Helpfully, the core prohibition of international law against nondefensive uses of force in foreign policy encodes this guideline in Articles 2(4) and 51 of the UN Charter. If the U.S. government, for instance, had adhered to this guideline in pursuing its interests, it would have avoided its worst failures in foreign policy over the course of the last seventy-five years (the wars in Vietnam, Iraq, and Afghanistan).

Krieger: I recognize that the atomic attacks at the end of World War II were, in effect, a continuation of policies seeking the large-scale destruction of civilian populations. But they also added some new dimensions to our capacity for destruction. They added the long-term threat of radioactivity, genetic mutations, and the scaling up of our human capacity for mass annihilation. Ridding the world of nuclear weapons is not a panacea. It is a step back from the precipice of total annihilation, of omnicide. You suggest that we must simultaneously rid the world of nuclear weapons and the possibility of unconditional warfare. I'm highly sympathetic with this desire, which calls for restraining warfare to the boundaries of international humanitarian law. Unfortunately, this hasn't yet been achieved. Warfare remains an organized effort to slaughter the "enemy," and it has proven very difficult to restrain the means of doing so. If nuclear weapons possession teaches us anything, it is that restraints in warfare are essential for the continuation of the human and most other species.

Again, I am sympathetic with your idea of a moral revolution. Gandhi and Martin Luther King Jr. led such revolutions. They demonstrated the power of moral behavior to achieve important changes in the world. They were powerful advocates of nonviolence, of speaking truth to power. When King spoke out against the Vietnam War, many of his associates tried to dissuade him from continuing to do so. He responded, in an essay titled "Conscience and the Vietnam War," by explaining the reasons for bringing Vietnam into the field of his moral vision. He stated, "I was increasingly compelled to see the war not only as a moral outrage but also as an enemy of the poor, and to attack it as such."[1] I would extend his vision, and I'm sure he would do so himself, were he alive today. The moral outrage is not just the Vietnam War; it is war itself. War may be especially the enemy of the poor, but it is also the enemy of all humanity. It diminishes us. When we dehumanize "the other," we dehumanize ourselves. Speaking of the Vietnam War, King said, "Somehow this madness must cease."[2] The same must now be said for nuclear weapons and for war generally: It is madness, and it must cease.

King ended his essay with a prophecy: "If we do not act, we shall surely be dragged down the long, dark, and shameful corridors of time reserved for those who possess power without compassion, might without morality, and strength without sight."[3] The question is, How are we to act? The starting point is to speak out against the militarism and nuclearism that plague our countries and our world. I keep coming back to the concepts of awakening and engaging. The first requires a concerted commitment to education for peace; the second requires advocacy for peace. And both, taken together, are the Herculean tasks of our time. The acceptance of this challenge, the demand from below for adherence to the UN Charter and the laws of war, would move us in the right direction, while those who lay claim to U.S. exceptionalism move us in the wrong direction. The Gang of Four base their arguments for nuclear weapons abolition on claims that it would improve U.S. security relative to the rest of the world. While they are right about this, they do not rest their arguments on a moral foundation and thus raise doubts about U.S. intentions in the rest of the world. The moral revolution that is needed must be based first and foremost on an acceptance of our common humanity across all borders. This would lead to an effort to create nonkilling societies and a nonkilling world, as Glenn Paige advocates.[4]

Falk: Of course, our views are quite convergent on these matters, and I agree with almost all of what you are saying. My point is that waiting for the moral revolution is a constructive form of passivity and is quite consistent with preparing the way. Gandhi and King did not act in a political vacuum but stood on the shoulders of others who had resisted the abuses of colonialism and racism. We must do our best to prepare the way for a moral revolution that will center on the repudiation of war as an instrument of policy, even if it does not go all the way to Glenn Paige's vision of nonkilling societies. We have seen in the course of the Arab Awakening, with its ups and downs, that revolutions come in all shapes, sometimes without evident preparation or exemplary leadership. With regard to nuclearism and war, we must open our imaginations to the unexpected, to pathways toward the future built on the foundations of what I have called in the past a "necessary utopianism." We will never make progress toward our goals if we operate within the confining horizons of feasibility, which will at best get us more and more arms control, if all goes well, but will not move the world an inch closer to nuclear disarmament or a nonkilling world.

My other observation in response to what you say is that we must be careful about the linkages between the pursuit of nuclear disarmament, militarism, and the likelihood of major warfare. I think there are respectable differences of opinion, deriving from contrasting views of human nature (as fundamentally either conflictual and aggressive or harmonious and peaceful) that lead different persons to assess risks differently. It would be very unfortunate if antinuclear "realists" were able to combine nuclear disarmament proposals with a dramatic ramping up of various sorts of conventional ultramodern weaponry. Precisely because anxieties would undoubtedly accompany the removal of nuclear weaponry, an unstable and dangerous arms race in conventional weapons could unintentionally result in a war-prone political climate.

Is Nuclear Disarmament Dangerous?

Krieger: I'm not sure waiting for a moral revolution is, as you call it, "a constructive form of passivity." In fact, I'm not sure any form of passivity is constructive. I think, though, that by this you mean passivity not in the sense of doing nothing but rather in the sense of doing what is possible in the present, even if limited, and keeping alive the possibility of moral revolution in the future. I believe that, once we understand the level of threat inherent in nuclear weaponry, we are obligated to try to confront this threat. I see that obligation, in fact, as the great challenge of our time. To meet this challenge will require perseverance and maintenance of what you have called "necessary utopianism," even in the face of seemingly overwhelming obstacles. I have considered this situation in the light of choosing hope, and I had a dialogue with the Japanese Buddhist philosopher and peace advocate Daisaku Ikeda on this subject.[5] We concluded that hope gives rise to action and leads to change, whereas a failure to choose hope leads to despair, complacency, and inaction. Choosing hope, even in the face of tremendously difficult obstacles, is essential. It is a manifestation of "necessary optimism" and keeps one engaged, despite the apparent odds against success. No great movement for social change has ever had an easy path to success. All have faced significant struggles. I expect the path to achieving a world without nuclear weapons to be difficult, but it is also essential. We must continue this struggle.

It would be a very unfortunate outcome if, in the end, nuclearism were replaced with new and virulent forms of militarism on steroids. We must be vigilant to ensure that this is not the result of efforts to end the nuclear weapons era. In fact, I don't think this outcome will be possible. It is unlikely that we will arrive at a nuclear weapon–free world if some countries attempt to attain military superiority with conventional weapons. The negotiations for a treaty banning nuclear weapons will undoubtedly have to take into account imbalances in conventional weaponry. If they fail to do so, states will not have sufficient confidence to go forward with the treaty. The moral revolution that is necessary must take into account that, if we wish to assure the future of civilization by eliminating nuclear weapons, it will be necessary to reign in conventional weaponry and warfare as well.

Falk: A short clarification is in order here. My concern is that if antinuclear realists manage the disarmament discourse, it will make other governments nervous about their intentions. The call for nuclear disarmament would be accompanied by arguments about the increased possibility of using non-nuclear armaments to achieve the various goals of grand strategy, including some probable increases in military spending to offset the drawing down of the nuclear arsenal. In such an atmosphere, other governments would likely become nervous about American intentions, assuming that these bureaucratic establishments were still mainly led by those adhering to a war ethic expressed by way of a realist frame of reference, and take steps of their own to uphold their security that might include increased arms purchases. It is impossible to anticipate exactly what would happen in the somewhat unlikely event that nuclear disarmament were accompanied by undiminished militarism in the disarming countries. I am merely pointing out that it would be important in the context of negotiating nuclear disarmament not to agitate nonnuclear countries with loose talk about a greater ability to make use of military superiority if no longer fearful of generating a nuclear confrontation. Under these circumstances, where nuclear weapons were being removed from the scene, it might lead ambitious realists to believe that expansionist and interventionist foreign policies pose smaller risks than previously, and this could induce other defensively minded governments to seek countervailing power sufficient to overcome such perceptions.

This is all very speculative, but it relates to widely shared objections to separating nuclear disarmament altogether from the quest for general and complete disarmament, or at the very least the design of postnuclear military capabilities in agreed defensive configurations. All offensive weapons systems and doctrines would be made unlawful to the extent possible. I believe such a scenario should be kept in mind but not regarded as probable. This added dimension of concern might seem to burden and complicate the call for nuclear disarmament unduly, but to the extent that existing elites would have to agree to any disarming process, this set of concerns seem plausible and should be articulated and discussed. Much depends on the climate within which the movement for nuclear disarmament evolves, especially within the United States. The relevance of the concern is likely to depend on the extent to which such a movement enlists support from within the established order, even if the disarmament impetus comes mainly, as is almost certain to be the case, from a future mobilization of civil society.

Who's Afraid of Nuclear Realists?

Falk: When you said earlier that it makes no sense to rely on nuclear weapons because a nuclear war would mean the end of civilization, you do not take account of the contrary view equally reliant on an opposing appeal to reason and probable effects. Such an opposed view argues that, in a world where nuclear weapons exist and are possessed, retaining rather than eliminating them is more prudent and also more likely to avoid nuclear war. This may seem strange to peace-minded persons, but this view rests on the idea that, as the arsenals are lowered, the temptation increases for unscrupulous political actors to cheat either by retaining a secret cache of weapons withheld from inspectors or by engaging in a covert program of nuclear rearmament. This outlook follows the common realist claim that nuclear disarmament would actually raise the risk of nuclear weapons being used either for diplomatic blackmail or to mount a surprise attack. We cannot win such an argument by reliance on rationality and common sense or through assertions about the character of human nature. As we know, such considerations can in good faith always be interpreted in contradictory ways, and we have no means to assess the comparative merits of opposing positions. This inconclusiveness on the level of rationality gives entrenched interests a great advantage in public debate, especially given the leverage exerted by pro-militarist forces in the mainstream media.

Against this background, I rest my entire case against nuclearism and militarism on morality and law. It is unacceptable to kill or threaten to kill innocent people on the basis of a weaponry and a strategic doctrine that is indiscriminate in targeting and would almost certainly result in inflicting mass destruction. As E. P. Thompson pointed out in a memorable essay written decades ago, a society that prepares for and implicitly approves of such reliance on instruments of mass terror is itself deeply corrupt and complicit, adopting a form of security that is indistinguishable from a readiness to commit massive genocide, or what he less anthropocentrically and more aptly described as "exterminism."[6] After all, it is not just the fabric of human society that is rent by nuclearism; nature itself is put profoundly at risk of enduring, long-term, if not irreversible damage, including the death of millions of animals. If we are to survive as a species, we need not only to tame the gods of war and militarism but to take seriously our inevitable role, so long neglected, as the ultimate custodians of Mother Nature, rather than as, during modernity, being ecologically disruptive and predatory in our relations with nature. Only those premodern brothers and sisters who are being faithful to their traditional ways of life are fulfilling this mandate that is partly sacred and partly the embodiment of a guide book for planetary survival.

Krieger: I have never accepted the argument that nuclear weapons have maintained the peace. I think it is a poor argument, one that seeks to justify the nuclear threat and one that cannot be proven. It is subject to proof, however, that the possession of nuclear weapons makes possible massive and indiscriminate annihilation and, at worst, the death of all. Nonetheless, you are right that rationality has little chance of prevailing in the culture of militarism that engulfs us.

"Exterminism" is a deeply disturbing concept. Both militarism and nuclearism corrupt the human spirit. They are not alone in having caused such corruption, but they have made us poor stewards of the earth and its abundant forms of life. It is true that we hold much of nature in the balance, as we hold our own existence in the balance. By the cleverness of our destructive inventions, we have traveled as far as possible to the edge of the precipice. Exterminism, as an existential threat, would in an ideal world be a strong incentive to action.

We need a moral awakening, even a moral rebirth, if we are to fulfill our responsibilities as trustees of the earth for nature and future generations. Modern civilizations have been dominated by an acute form of hubris that embraces dangerous technologies while putting us and our fellow inhabitants of earth at risk of annihilation. Social structures shaped to encourage complacency rather than public engagement have allowed this hubris to dominate our societies. The combination of hubris and complacency have undermined our stewardship of the planet and left us vulnerable to our instruments of mass annihilation. Both hubris and complacency, which have resulted in militarism and nuclearism, must be confronted and brought to an end. I only wish there were a clearer way forward.

Falk: You are correct that debate can never resolve the argument about whether nuclear weapons prevented World War III during the Cold War. It represents a clash of worldviews that generate very different assessments of risk. A hyperrealist, such as John Mearsheimer, is as convinced of the war-inhibiting impact of nuclear weapons as you are of their diabolical implications. Reason cannot bridge this chasm, which embodies those contrasting views of human nature and world politics that I have mentioned previously.

Breaking Down Walls of Complacency

Krieger: There may be geopolitical reasons to conclude that this would be an ideal time to push forward a nuclear abolition agenda, but the public, at least in the United States and most of the developed world, remains complacent. Our goal must be to continue to point to the need for a negotiated agreement to end the nuclear weapons era, as required by both morality and international law. The task is made far more difficult by the length of time since the weapons were used and by the receding tangibility of their threat to humanity. The public, like the president, seems to have more pressing priorities. In a world that remains extremely dangerous, how can we break through the existing walls of complacency to make the abolition of nuclear weapons and the taming of militarism a global priority? How can we generate sufficient commitment to this goal to succeed?

Falk: Since Prague, I feel that Obama has retreated to a standard arms control position, which in effect is an abandonment of the disarmament track. If Obama is not willing to challenge what you are calling the complacency of the public under current extremely favorable global conditions and given the deficit and threats of nuclear terrorism presently so alive in the public mind, it is unlikely that circumstances will ever be seen by politicians in Washington as conducive to establishing a genuine disarmament process.

To wait for complacency to disappear would mean waiting either for Godot to arrive or for a catastrophe to jolt the public into a mood of acute anxiety. Neither option seems helpful from our perspective. I believe we must express our disappointment with Obama's failure to plan for nuclear disarmament in very direct and critical language so as to keep faith with our own seriousness of purpose, claimed urgency, and belief that now is the time. As an aside, I believe the Japanese ordeal arising out of the unfolding disaster at the Fukushima Daiichi reactor complex has encouraged renewed public concern about nuclear issues and provides an opportunity for raising public consciousness on both questions of nuclear energy and nuclear weapons. My main point here is that, at this time, we should ourselves be taking clearer and more decisive advantage of an opportunity to raise awareness and mobilize support, but we must be clear.

Krieger: I agree with you that the Obama nuclear weapons agenda looks far more like traditional arms control than a plan for comprehensive disarmament. Actually, in many respects, it looks like a nuclear arms restoration project, given all the funds he is proposing for the modernization of the U.S. nuclear weapons infrastructure, the weapons themselves, and their delivery systems. He is showing far less leadership on nuclear disarmament than he seemed to promise at Prague and certainly far less than is needed.

I don't think public complacency regarding nuclear weapons will disappear miraculously; rather, I believe that the leadership for change must come from below, from organizations like the Nuclear Age Peace Foundation and others committed to this goal. Of course, we cannot wait for nuclear weapons to be used again to awaken the public and break through the complacency that currently exists. But even if we shout at the top of our lungs, there do not seem to be enough people listening and prepared to engage. Somehow we need to find more effective strategies.

CHAPTER 6

Nuclear Weapons and Nuclear Energy

Falk: Ever since the advent of the Nuclear Age, there has been controversy about the promise and relevance of nuclear energy. On one level, the nuclear weapons governments, especially the United States, initially touted the benefits of nuclear energy ("power too cheap to meter") both as a way of removing the taint from nuclearism and as a bribe to nonnuclear states: If you give up the weapons option, we will share the nuclear energy technology, and this will be a great contribution to energy economy and independence, as well as development, for the whole world. As we know, nuclear energy has never lived up to this promise and has caused anxieties that in some respects resemble those generated by the weaponry. Both Three Mile Island and especially Chernobyl frightened world public opinion, conveying the sense that nuclear reactors somewhat resemble nuclear bombs, being capable of spreading radioactivity and generating fear far from the sites of accidents. The March 11, 2011, events in Fukushima, Japan, have rekindled these fears and perhaps raised them to new levels.

This Japanese disaster at Fukushima took place at a time when there was a new surge of support for nuclear energy as a necessary component of any successful transition to a postpetroleum economy. Nuclear energy proponents argue that alternate forms of energy, especially solar and wind, would only contribute, at most, 30 percent to energy needs, and without nuclear energy, the world would have to rely on coal, which, as the argument goes, is much more detrimental to human well-being. In the foreground, then, suddenly increased anxiety about nuclear accidents is casting a shadow on the viability of nuclear energy and the construction of additional reactors. This is balanced against the economic and social pressure to rely on nuclear energy as a path to a more prosperous future, minimizing the risks and claiming that, despite Fukushima, nuclear energy is far safer than coal, and, in any event, the reactors of the future will be constructed to be less susceptible to catastrophic accidents.

The Weapons Dimension of Nuclear Energy

Falk: In the background, rarely discussed recently, is the weapons dimension of nuclear energy. The whole anxiety about Iran's nuclear program is illustrative. Despite reassurances from the leadership of Iran and an international inspections system, there is the widespread perception in the West that Iran's supposedly peaceful nuclear energy program is a smokescreen shielding a robust effort to obtain sufficiently enriched uranium to enable the production of nuclear bombs and warheads. In effect, a sophisticated nuclear energy program provides a country with a threshold capability to produce weaponry in a short period or by covert means. Japan and Germany, for example, are non–nuclear weapon countries but reportedly could produce a few nuclear weapons in a matter of months because they possess the entire nuclear fuel cycle.

Here we run up against the Faustian bargain embedded in the Non-Proliferation Treaty (NPT) of 1968. The non–nuclear weapon states forego their option to develop weaponry in exchange for a promise of full access to nuclear energy technology devoted to peaceful purposes. But it is precisely this access that inevitably provides these states with a weapons option, if vital national security interests or geopolitical ambitions point them in such a direction. As part of the bargain, the nuclear weapon states commit to good faith negotiations to achieve nuclear disarmament but have never followed through. In effect, this element of major noncompliance erodes the legal inhibition of the treaty, while, to a degree, providing non–nuclear weapon states with a latent capability to develop the weaponry erodes the inducement to give it up. The treaty even provides a loophole by allowing states to withdraw with notice in deference to their "supreme interests."

I suppose the central issue, often overlooked, is that there is an interface between nuclear weaponry and nuclear energy, in terms of both avoiding disastrous Fukushima-like events and facilitating acquisition of the weaponry. There are two predominant issues: how to avoid latent proliferation under the guise of developing nuclear energy capabilities, and how to induce nuclear weapon states to level the playing field by fulfilling their long-deferred legal obligation to seek, in good faith, nuclear disarmament. As argued in the last chapter, the global setting has never been more propitious for a serious endeavor to achieve nuclear disarmament than it is at present. The question we need to address is whether the quest for nuclear disarmament is properly separated from issues bearing on the viability and desirability of nuclear energy or whether nuclear disarmament cannot go forward unless the pursuit of nuclear energy is also renounced.

Krieger: Nuclear energy is a significant problem. From my perspective, it has always been oversold by its promoters, beginning with the claims that it would produce energy "too cheap to meter." This clearly hasn't turned out to be the case. In fact, it seems fairly certain that, without major societal subsidies, nuclear power would make no sense economically. As the accident at Fukushima and the one at Chernobyl twenty-five years earlier have shown, the costs of dealing with nuclear power accidents are enormous. Utility companies would not bear the risks involved without subsidies in the form of liability limits. Also, the plants produce long-lived radioactive wastes that will be a long-term burden on society. In fact, these wastes will be a burden for many times longer than civilization has existed. These radioactive wastes are a terrible legacy to bequeath to future generations.

The nuclear fuel cycle that accompanies nuclear energy generation has always engendered proliferation concerns. The chapter titled "Nuclear Power and Nuclear Disarmament" in the *Global Fissile Material Report 2009* states, "A civilian nuclear power program provides a state a foundation to produce fissile materials for nuclear weapons. It allows a country to train scientists and engineers, to build research facilities, to construct and operate nuclear reactors, and possibly also to learn techniques of reprocessing and enrichment that could later be turned to producing weapons materials. Even small civilian nuclear energy programs have large stocks and flows of nuclear-weapon-usable materials."[1]

Some types of nuclear power plants use enriched uranium in their operations. Enrichment entails increasing the percentage of uranium 235 (U-235), which comprises less than 1 percent in the uranium ore found in nature. Often this uranium is enriched only to low levels (2 or 3 percent U-235), but the same process can increase the percentage to the 80 to 90 percent level for bomb production. There has been such concern about Iran having a nuclear weapons program, despite its protests to the contrary, because it is using the centrifuge uranium-enrichment process. A uranium-enrichment capability, without a foolproof inspection program, may be considered a potential nuclear weapons program. There are currently some 1,475 metric tons of highly enriched uranium in the world, enough for some 60,000 nuclear weapons.[2]

The other part of the nuclear fuel cycle that raises weapons concerns is the reprocessing of plutonium, an element aptly named for the Greek god of the underworld. Plutonium is a by-product of the fissioning of uranium. It didn't exist on earth in any significant quantity before the World War II Manhattan Project to create nuclear weapons. Plutonium 239 (Pu-239) is an extremely dangerous radioactive material. Even a microgram of it, if inhaled, will almost certainly cause lung cancer. More immediately relevant to our dialogue, Pu-239 can be used to make nuclear weapons. Nuclear power plants create Pu-239. If this plutonium is reprocessed—that is, if more highly radioactive elements are separated out—it can be used in nuclear weapons programs. There are approximately 485 metric tons of weapons-grade plutonium in the world. Since the amount of plutonium required to make a nuclear weapon is about one-third the amount of enriched uranium, there is enough plutonium in current stocks to make some 60,000 nuclear weapons.[3]

The enrichment of uranium and the reprocessing of plutonium create very serious weapons proliferation problems. It is highly ironic that the Non-Proliferation Treaty describes peaceful uses of nuclear energy, which would include power generation, as an "inalienable right." This means that in a very real way, the treaty works against one of its principal objectives, that is, preventing nuclear weapons proliferation. I have always thought that the NPT lacked appropriate caution in its characterization and encouragement of nuclear energy programs.

My understanding is that the uranium stocks in the world as a source of fuel for nuclear power plants is limited and may be available only for the next few decades. To operate beyond that time horizon, nuclear power plants would have to use recycled plutonium for fuel, which would result in making nuclear weapon–capable material available in international commerce. Widespread commerce in plutonium would make it extremely difficult to control and thus make nuclear weapons abolition far more difficult, if not impossible.

Virtual Nuclear Weapon States

Krieger: You have raised the issue of virtual nuclear weapon states—those having the materials and technology to become nuclear weapon states in a very short period. There are a number of such states, and Japan and Germany are prime examples. These states are now positioned where other states would be after eliminating their nuclear arsenals. After completing nuclear disarmament, the former nuclear weapon states would also have the materials and the technology to rebuild their nuclear arsenals. This shows, I think, how much the goals of nuclear disarmament and nuclear power generation are at cross purposes. Where nuclear power programs exist, there will always be the possibility of nuclear weapons proliferation unless safeguards are foolproof, and I don't think we humans are capable of creating foolproof systems. This is one of the most prominent lessons of the accident at the Fukushima Daiichi Nuclear Power Station.

The authors of the chapter "Nuclear Power and Nuclear Disarmament" in the *Global Fissile Material Report 2009* share the concerns we are discussing about the potential for nuclear weapons proliferation from civilian nuclear power programs. They argue, "Even with stringent and equitable new rules to govern nuclear power, its continued operation and certainly any global expansion will impose serious proliferation risks in the transition to nuclear disarmament. A phase-out of civilian nuclear energy would provide the most effective and enduring constraint on proliferation risks in a nuclear-weapon-free world."[4] Unfortunately, even in the aftermath of Fukushima, it does not seem likely that a phaseout of civilian nuclear power will be forthcoming. President Obama, for example, has already reiterated his support for building more nuclear power plants in the United States, and the greatest growth of nuclear power is likely to occur in the rapidly developing giants, China and India, both of which have plans for large-scale nuclear power development (although China seems to be having second thoughts in the aftermath of Fukushima).

Nuclear Energy after Fukushima

Falk: Let me continue your last line of thought. Even more than was the case with Hiroshima, there is a tendency to look at the catastrophic accident at Fukushima and then reaffirm the viability, even the necessity, of going forward with plans for the expansion of nuclear energy capabilities. Of course, reassurances are offered: Greater caution will be taken in the future as far as the sites chosen for nuclear reactors; more stringent safety standards will be imposed on the nuclear industry; nuclear technology is being developed that is less prone to accidents.

Behind these contentions are a series of energy arguments: However bad the final accounting of the Fukushima disaster turns out to be, it will be far lower than the health consequences of relying on the only energy source available in sufficient quantities, namely, soft coal. The case for nuclear energy rests on two claims treated as compelling: that the demand for energy, no matter how wastefully high, must be met and that assessing harm should be calculated by statistical comparison of deaths and illnesses without taking into account the apocalyptic worst-case scenarios associated with a total reactor meltdown and massive releases of radioactivity. This kind of prudential risk assessment applied to nuclear energy, one frequently made for various scenarios involving reliance on nuclear weapons, somehow overlooks the psychic damage done by what amounts to an embrace of massive state terror as a calculated security risk. Recall that Henry Kissinger made his original impact on public policy by writing a book arguing that limited nuclear war in Europe would not be a catastrophe for the United States, or even for Europe, and could be a potentially necessary form of anti-Soviet containment. My point here is that instrumental rationality is not capable of comprehending the permanent damage to the human condition that could result either from any use, including threatened uses, of nuclear weapons or from future catastrophic events affecting nuclear energy facilities.

Krieger: I have been surprised to witness the strong defense of nuclear energy from some quarters following Fukushima. I attribute this defense to the corporate profits involved in building and operating nuclear power plants by an industry that has bided its time and persistently downplayed the dangers to the public. In the past decade or so, nuclear industry, largely rejected after the Three Mile Island and Chernobyl reactor accidents, has revived itself by claiming to be compatible with reducing global warming. In actuality, if one takes into account the nuclear fuel cycle in its entirety and the carbon dioxide emissions from building nuclear power plants, the plants are not nearly as beneficial as the nuclear industry claims.

Nuclear Industry Has Not Gone Away

Krieger: I want to make the point that the nuclear power industry has been very tenacious and has not gone away. I think the corporations that promote the industry have considerable concerns for profit but little concern for the risks posed to humanity and the human future. The nuclear plant operators are willing to downplay for short-term gain the catastrophic risks involved in the use of nuclear reactors to boil water. They are willing to generate wastes that will adversely affect the health and well-being of untold generations to follow us on the planet. They are unwilling, however, to build and operate the plants without government subsidies that limit their liability in the event of a catastrophic accident.

Corporations are not humans. They have no vision, no compassion, and virtually no accountability. They measure success by the bottom line only, and they seek to pass on the risks of their enterprise to the societies in which they operate. The tragedy is not that the nuclear industry focuses narrow-mindedly on profits and ignores risks. This is to be expected. The tragedy is that governments embrace and support this industry, demonstrating that they also do not place the interests of their people and the future at the forefront of their planning and decision making.

Falk: Corporate pursuit of profits is part of the story without doubt, but it is reinforced by the societal conviction that energy supply must keep pace with energy demands, however fatuous and environmentally harmful. Consumerism and militarism amount to absolutes for American culture, and elsewhere in the world they are strong and at times invested with an almost religious intensity. As long as these pressures exist, it will be almost impossible to effectively oppose continued reliance upon, and the likely expansion of, the nuclear power industry, regardless of reactors' uneconomical character, posing of catastrophic risks, and vulnerability to attack.

Another concern here elaborates on your appropriate stress on human fallibility: the preoccupation with what took place in the past. In other words, the main lesson drawn from Chernobyl was that Soviet inefficiencies were responsible for the accident, which could not happen in an advanced industrial country operating within a capitalist framework. Fukushima is significant because it illustrates that a private corporate actor, in this instance the Tokyo Electric Power Company, had a long pre-Fukushima record of cover-up and mismanagement, and yet the supposedly efficient and health-conscious Japanese government turned a blind eye toward the evidence. Some adjustments will likely be made relating to the retirement of old reactors, but even these may be relaxed over time if major profits are at stake and corporate managers have their fingers on triggers of policy influence. Only after Fukushima did Chancellor Angela Merkel in Germany temporarily close down seven reactors with designs similar to those in trouble in Japan, establish a moratorium on extending operating permission to overage reactors, and announce a phaseout of nuclear energy in Germany by 2022.

Terrorism, Sabotage, and Acts of War

Falk: The human capacity to anticipate the future is exceedingly limited, which should engender humility and caution in activities involving nuclear capabilities, be they related to weaponry or energy. Things could go terribly wrong. Looking forward, we do not know whether the next catastrophic event in either nuclear domain might result from nuclear terrorism or sabotage by a disaffected worker. The vulnerabilities exist, and so do, in all probability, schemes to circumvent efforts at protection, prevention, and mitigation. Does the human species really want to place its bets on the capacities of human institutions and procedures to prevent such accidents or deliberate acts from happening anywhere on the planet at anytime? Surely only a collective mentality that represses such uncertainties would accept such a burden. In Greek classical tradition this prideful refusal to acknowledge unlikely but possible dangers was regarded as the tragic flaw in human character called "hubris"; in more modern explanations of insensitivity to risk, with a greater emphasis on psychology, the stress would more likely be placed on what is often referred to as denial.

Krieger: Each time there is a major accident or near accident at a nuclear power plant, the nuclear industry tries to assert that it is distinguishable from potential future accidents. I believe that we humans must either be very gullible or very complacent to accept such explanations and promises. As you rightly point out, the accident at Fukushima demonstrates that such catastrophes can occur in even technologically advanced societies. It is not accidents alone, however, but also hostile acts of volition that should concern us. Terrorism and sabotage are two possibilities. Another is an act of war. There can be no certainty that, in the future, terrorism, sabotage, or acts of war will not result in the types of radiation releases that have occurred by accident and incompetence at Chernobyl and Fukushima. Since nuclear power plants are often built near metropolitan areas, cities throughout the world are vulnerable to terrorists, saboteurs, or acts of war turning nuclear reactors and their spent fuel pools into so-called dirty bombs. The plants will not explode, like nuclear weapons, but will rather release their deadly radiation so as to cause cancers, leukemia, genetic damage, and general dread among the people downwind.

I think hubris is much on display on the part of the nuclear industry and its government supporters, but I don't think it is necessarily rooted in denial. I would suggest that denial is a means of coping with fear. Ordinary citizens, though, are generally too poorly or wrongly informed about nuclear power dangers to be fearful. Rather, they are led to believe that nuclear energy is a modern miracle. However, when the nuclear industry and government attempt to place a power plant in their backyard, people tend to grasp the danger without denial and to face it squarely. When the plant is in someone else's backyard, perhaps there is denial, but more likely there is simply a lack of concern.

Falk: Maybe it is not so important, but I understand the relevance of denial in a somewhat different way. I regard it as a psychological mechanism of resisting a realistic appraisal of risk. Robert Jay Lifton relied heavily on his view of the phenomenon of denial to explain how Nazi doctors could commit crimes against humanity during their daytime jobs and behave benignly, even tenderly, at home with their families in the evening. We suppress that part of our awareness that interferes drastically with our preferred self-image or comfort zone. Denial is relevant in my formulation in allowing promoters of nuclear power to insist in good faith that it is relatively safe and necessary to meet energy needs while leaving out of the picture the vulnerabilities to terrorism, sabotage, and war that you correctly point out. If those vulnerabilities were taken into account in terms of appropriate security arrangements, the costs of nuclear power would soar to levels that would make it commercially nonviable or lead to its outright rejection. In this regard, we are dealing not just with the profit motive but also with the basic belief embedded in contemporary capitalism that the health of society is dependent on a continuous flow of technological innovations underpinned by a consumerist mentality. The idea of energy austerity based on needs and a more accurate calculation of risks and costs is generally avoided because its results would be devastating, given the hierarchy of cultural norms prevailing in modern society. Traditional societies and, to some extent, the green movement are of interest because of their rejection of these dysfunctional cultural norms, due either to their worldview or to a more rational interpretation of sustainability and the earth's carrying capacity.

Nuclear Power and Proliferation Risks

Falk: You also make some illuminating remarks about the proliferation implications of nuclear energy. I am more ambivalent than you about this concern. I am reluctant to create a new global setting in which the ex–nuclear states, because of their nuclear energy capabilities, have a nuclear rearmament option that other political communities do not possess. This would entail a new kind of dualism in world order that closely tracked the present disparity between nuclear weapon states and their nonnuclear counterparts. It would be essential in a nuclear disarmament process to do all that is technically possible to disable nuclear rearmament options. Of course, as elsewhere, there are some complexities here. If the disarming states did not retain an edge in relation to rearmament, there would be less incentive to get rid of the weaponry and more resistance from national security establishments. The rearmament option has been declared in the past as helpful, even by such a strong abolitionist as Jonathan Schell, in meeting concerns that there would be a temptation to cheat if the disarming process went very far.

Questions that linger include the following: Supposing that many countries opt for nuclear energy, does that make complete nuclear disarmament a virtually impossible political goal, or might it be possible by means of a combination of technical fixes and international inspection to verify compliance with disarmament obligations? How serious is the proliferation danger? If the proliferation risks arising from nuclear reactors could be minimized, should the objections of those of us advocating nuclear disarmament and demilitarization be dropped? In a central sense, this question asks whether under some, but not all, circumstances, nuclear disarmament is separable from the debate on the future of nuclear energy. And finally, supposing that nuclear power development continues as before Fukushima, does it modify our thinking about nuclear disarmament and, more generally, military uses of nuclear weapons? If so, in what ways?

Krieger: You raise important questions, and I will do my best to respond to them. If many more countries opt for nuclear energy, it may, indeed, make nuclear disarmament an impossible political goal. It will certainly raise very serious concerns about possible nuclear weapons proliferation and breakout that will not make nuclear weapons abolition easier. Of course, some representatives of governments and the nuclear power industry will claim that technological fixes and international inspections will be suffi-cient to allow for nuclear disarmament. I would say that trying to achieve a world free of nuclear weapons in which there is widespread use of nuclear energy can be analogized to a professional boxer trying to fight with one hand tied behind his back. While perhaps not impossible, success is un-likely. Certainly inspections would have to be very thorough and frequent. Worries about secret programs and diversion of fissile materials would be constant, and such concerns would not be nearly as prominent in a world without widespread use of nuclear energy.

I view the proliferation risks arising from nuclear energy production as serious. In a world without nuclear energy and a nuclear fuel cycle, such risks would be greatly limited. The phases of the fuel cycle that pose the greatest threat of proliferation are uranium enrichment and plutonium reprocessing. Countries with such programs must be considered as proliferation risks. A good example is Iran with its uranium-enrichment program, which has generated such serious concerns that there has been talk about Israel or the United States taking out Iran's enrichment facilities militarily. Israel did in fact bomb and destroy nuclear reactors in Iraq in 1981 and Syria in 2007.

You ask about the situation if the proliferation risks arising from nuclear reactors could be minimized. This raises a big if. It also raises the ques-tion of what level of minimization would be required. All systems of risk minimization would be human systems and therefore not foolproof. Prior to the Fukushima accident, we were assured that those risks were minimal, but even with the attempt at risk management, things went wrong. The basic assumptions were wrong, making the calculations of risk also wrong. The natural disasters that occurred turned out to be more extreme than expected; the earthquake was more powerful, the tsunami more massive. When natural disasters were combined with human error, the accident that the nuclear power plant owners claimed was impossible happened. Similarly, even with assurances that the risks of nuclear weapons proliferation are minimal, they could turn out to be far greater than anticipated.

Unfortunately, the likelihood seems to be that nuclear power development will continue, even in light of the unfolding tragedy at Fukushima. Those of us committed to achieving a world without nuclear weapons should be extremely concerned with this possibility. A great challenge of the Nuclear Age is to eliminate the nuclear weapons threat to humanity—a major responsibility that we owe to ourselves and to future generations. Any impediments to achieving this goal should be opposed. For that reason, I view nuclear energy unfavorably. I believe the principal challenge of our time is to end the nuclear weapons era. If one accepts this premise, then nuclear energy must be seen as an impediment, phased out, and replaced with renewable and sustainable forms of energy.

Let me pose a question to you: Can you imagine achieving a world free of nuclear weapons with thousands of nuclear power plants scattered across the globe? It seems to me that this would require of imperfect humans an unattainable level of perfection in applying safeguards.

Falk: Your question is both fair and fundamental. I would share the view that it seems more difficult to handle proliferation risks if an increasing number of nuclear reactors are situated throughout the world, resulting in a growing number of facilities capable of uranium enrichment and plutonium reprocessing. I also agree that the pressures to satisfy energy demands by expanding nuclear energy capabilities are being posed in such a way as to encourage their acceptance even in the aftermath of Fukushima. Already mainstream media have widely branded Germany as "irresponsible" because it prudently shut down its seven nuclear reactors built according to the same GE design as those at the Daiichi complex at Fukushima and placed a moratorium on extending the life of other reactors. It does seem irresponsible to reject nuclear power if energy projections are taken as an absolute, risks can supposedly be minimized, and alternative energy sources are presented as worse or insufficient. This latter view is contested by a variety of environmentalists who contend that solar and wind, in conjunction with more efficient energy use, can satisfy projected energy demands at acceptable costs, especially if combined with a turn against excess consumption.

Krieger: It is shocking actually that Germany would be branded as irresponsible for exercising caution with regard to its civilian nuclear program in the aftermath of Fukushima. I think this demonstrates the global effectiveness of a powerful industry and its lobbying force. To fail to exercise caution after observing the damage caused by the Fukushima accident strikes me as the height of irresponsibility. A principal purpose of government is to regulate dangerous technologies, those that could cause widespread and serious harm. When industries overstate their capability to prevent catastrophic damage and governments fail to regulate appropriately, the people ultimately suffer, as the people in the vicinity of Fukushima Daiichi are suffering now. And, of course, other people further from the disaster will also suffer the consequences of the radiation release.

Cultural Hubris and Energy Demands

Falk: I will repeat what I tried to say earlier because I believe it to be fundamental: In addition to the crass materialism of the profit motive, at issue here is the cultural hubris associated with unchecked growth that depends on fulfilling energy demands under conditions of an increasing scarcity that reflects the degree to which human activity threatens to exceed the carrying capacity of the earth. I believe this unwillingness to live within limits is the deep structural flaw of capitalism and modern secular civilization, both of which rest their hopes for a brighter future on essentially unrestrained and limitless economic growth.

At issue is who calculates the risks on the basis of what range of information and contingent events, giving what interests and values priority. This is inevitably an interpretative undertaking performed in ways that exhibit self-interest directly and indirectly, although claiming objectivity. The debate on nuclear power, or nuclear weapons for that matter, is worrisome in that the participants given access to the biggest platforms to disseminate their views are those linked to pro-nuclear industrial representatives and government bureaucrats who reflect cultural norms about consumerism and technology. The issues are put forward and resolved in what seems superficially like a reasonable manner befitting a democratic society, but in actuality antinuclear positions are rarely, if ever, given access to influential media to express their viewpoint. They must depend on either alternative media or the Internet to get their perspective heard at all.

Krieger: I agree with you that there exists a cultural hubris that seeks growth at nearly any cost and is concerned with immediate gratification, including profit seeking, rather than with employing restraints that would preserve the planet and demonstrate concern for future generations. Unfortunately, this desire for unbridled growth is spreading across the globe like a cancer. The push for growth began with the industrialized Western countries, but it can now be seen nearly everywhere on the planet. In the case of nuclear power, the demand for new reactors to fuel growth has been coming largely from China and India. Lifestyles of abundance, communicated via film throughout the world, are being emulated in developing countries with tragic results for our common future. Desire for growth has blinded Western culture and much of the world to the need for caution in pushing against the earth's limits. It also seems to have blinded us to the extraordinary dangers of creating radioactive materials that we cannot control and have no adequate plans to store effectively for tens of thousands of years.

Who calculates the risks of a dangerous technology and how the risks are calculated are key considerations. It is worth keeping in mind that the nuclear industry calculated the risk of catastrophic accident as sufficiently high that it required liability limits before it would build and operate nuclear power plants. These liability limits, which have been in place in the United States for decades, should be regarded as warning signals to the public and to countries choosing to emulate the West by investing in nuclear energy. They, as much as the accidents in Chernobyl and Fukushima, are flashing lights admonishing caution.

Financial self-interest is on the side of those who promote nuclear energy, not those who purchase it for electricity. The self-interest of opponents of nuclear energy lies in preventing radiation poisoning for themselves and for others. Concerned NGOs have acted for the public interest rather than seeking personal gain.

Falk: I think concerned NGOs such as the Nuclear Age Peace Foundation do their best by way of education and public information, but I doubt that such methods can surmount the walls of disinformation erected by an array of well-paid lobbyists and self-interested advocates. Often direct action of a provocative character is the only way to challenge rampant nuclearism or other forms of societal abuse, whether in energy or weaponry or on civil rights issues. It was mainly the crusade of Nobel scientist Linus Pauling that finally created a global climate of awareness about the health dangers of radioactive fallout, which stopped the atmospheric testing of nuclear weapons and led to the Partial Test Ban Treaty. I would have thought that Chernobyl and Fukushima would at the very least allow for the sort of debate that encourages all voices to be heard, but this is not the case.

Krieger: You point to direct action being effective in the past, particularly the action of Linus Pauling on the Partial Test Ban Treaty. Direct action was a powerful way to bring the dangers of nuclear fallout from atmospheric nuclear testing into the public imagination. Governments responded not by giving up nuclear testing but by moving it underground. In other words, governments were able to disarm public concern by ceasing atmospheric testing while still continuing to test and presumably improve their nuclear weaponry underground and out of public view.

Pauling, a great scientist, brought both scientific information and other respected scientists into the public arena. He was in the minority among scientists in being willing to challenge the status quo and express his concerns publicly. Many scientists today are paid experts of the nuclear industry, and those in government regulatory positions often have links to nuclear industry. Their self-interest must make them suspect in any debate on nuclear risks.

The Manipulative Power of Spin

Falk: The issues you have raised here about the vulnerabilities of nuclear facilities to deliberate acts intended to cause a disaster are never brought seriously into discussions of the viability of nuclear power. All attention focuses on an event that raises immediate concerns and on providing reassuring demonstrations that such instances are highly unlikely ever to happen again.

For instance, the Fukushima events are discussed as the freak outcome of a massive earthquake beneath the sea that generated a devastating tsunami of unprecedented magnitude, a combination of factors so unusual as to be disregarded in evaluating future safety. In contrast, former Soviet president Mikhail Gorbachev, in a publication released just after Fukushima, writes that Chernobyl should be regarded as "a shocking reminder of the reality of the nuclear threat."[5] He has written that the nuclear industry only survives through secrecy and deceit, having hidden 150 significant radiation leaks at various nuclear power reactors around the world.

Krieger: It is not just that spin masters have effectively manipulated the public discussion, to the extent there is one, about these catastrophic events and possibilities. The nuclear industry has also effectively co-opted scientists, or at least sufficient numbers of them, to raise confusion in the public discourse. Large numbers of people still see nuclear energy as a modern miracle rather than as a ridiculously complex way to boil water and a serious danger to the planet and its inhabitants.

Following an accident like Fukushima, the public reassurances from the nuclear industry and its experts that such an accident could never happen again are a form of public tranquilizer. The meager public challenge to these assurances reflects the same public complacency with regard to the risks of nuclear weapons. I would say that most societies do not do well in analyzing, evaluating, and communicating catastrophic risks to the public. We badly need truly independent agencies charged with these functions. Without such independent assessment, the public is left largely to the spinning of industry "experts." Such technology assessment agencies must have the function only of assessing risks and dangers. Currently, regulatory agencies such as the International Atomic Energy Agency have dual functions involving regulation and also promotion of nuclear industry. This is unacceptable. Simultaneous regulation and promotion of a technology entails a built-in conflict of interest.

I believe Gorbachev is correct in saying that the nuclear industry survives through secrecy and deceit. Many other industries manage to survive and profit in this way, but few, if any, have the capacity to cause such massive damage to the health and well-being of large populations as the nuclear industry.

Misplaced Confidence in Technological Solutions

Falk: The problem is not just that certain interest groups stand to gain from a continuing reliance on nuclear energy. There is also a widely shared societal confidence that technology will find a solution for any problems created by technology. Further, there is a belief that it is inconsistent with the experience and values of our modern society and mentality to impose limits on economic growth or technological innovation. An accompanying belief holds that if really serious health problems do emerge from nuclear energy in the future, adjustments can be made when enough evidence has accumulated. The tobacco industry employed such tactics of self-interest obfuscation to postpone successfully for decades the public recognition of the health hazards of smoking. Climate-change skeptics are following the same pattern, funded by the oil and gas industry, which has a strong interest in avoiding restrictions on carbon emissions. In addition, as environmental specialist Patricia Hynes has pointed out, the U.S. government assumes liability for damages to life and property above $12.6 billion arising from a nuclear accident and is proposing to extend $36 billion in loan guarantees in 2012 for new nuclear plants. Hynes states that "without these entitlements the nuclear industry would collapse."[6] Adding that Wall Street concurs with this assessment, she mentions a major financial advisory service that warned investors that the nuclear industry was a "bet-the-farm" risk.

Krieger: The idea that technology will find solutions for problems created by technology is a dangerous conceit. I would describe it as technological arrogance. It is, of course, a useful frame of mind for an industry that wants to proceed in the face of serious dangers, such as having no reasonable solution to storing its waste products for the long term. The tobacco industry was able to conceal the health hazards of its product for decades. Medical doctors used to do advertisements for tobacco companies in which they wore white coats, hung stethoscopes around their necks, and talked about which brand of cigarettes they smoked. Only when it became apparent that the societal health costs of smoking tobacco were enormous were serious warnings placed on tobacco packages and advertisements by tobacco companies banned from television. Unfortunately for the public, the cancers, leukemia, and genetic defects caused by radiation from nuclear power plant accidents do not come with markers indicating their source. The environmentalist you quote, Patricia Hynes, is absolutely right about the nuclear industry. It would collapse without government subsidies, especially liability limits. We can conclude from this that, at least in the United States, the government is keeping nuclear energy afloat. This is as clear an abdication of responsibility to the people as would be a government subsidy to limit the liability of the tobacco industry for health hazards related to its products.

Falk: Without much hesitation, I would say it is prudent and morally imperative to oppose reliance on nuclear energy as persuasively as possible, while recognizing that, unfortunately, the ongoing struggle to achieve nuclear disarmament is taking place in a global setting likely to be characterized by an increasing reliance on nuclear energy. The fact that no nuclear weapon has been used in the sixty-seven years since Nagasaki has psychologically convinced the public that, by and large, nuclear technology, military and nonmilitary, is essentially safe and that antinuclear fears are exaggerated and alarmist and should be ignored.

Nuclear Technology and Catastrophic Risk

Falk: There is, finally, in my view a larger issue at stake with profound consequences for the future of humanity. It concerns the hazards posed by catastrophic risks of collective harm resulting from accidents or deliberate action. The Fukushima incident illustrates one type of risk, while the arsenals of nuclear weapons pose another. The severity and nature of the risk is a matter of controversy that scientific inquiry cannot resolve. Further, there are many disagreements about whether it is worth taking various costly steps to minimize the danger posed. A similar challenge is associated with the risks of climate change arising from anthropogenic contributions to the buildup of greenhouse gasses in the atmosphere. Human society has always lived with radical uncertainty arising from vulnerability to events that cause severe harm, but until recently these events were limited in scope and mainly a consequence of the vagaries of nature. Human agency with regard to catastrophic, even apocalyptic events has emerged as a game changer. For this reason some observers have talked about living in the first "anthropocentric age," characterized by the extent to which human activities, whether in the nuclear domain or with respect to global warming, severely threaten human habitation on the planet and the life prospects of future generations.

Krieger: There is a tendency for the public to treat nuclear weapons as out of sight, out of mind. It is difficult to generate opposition to what is out of mind, and the end of the Cold War has certainly put nuclear weapons largely out of the public mind. Major accidents at nuclear energy facilities, such as at Fukushima Daiichi, provide an opportunity to point out the high risks of not only nuclear energy but nuclear weapons as well. Nuclear energy disasters raise public consciousness about nuclear dangers, civilian and military. It is not easy to bring public attention to what is intangible, such as nuclear weapons and deterrence risks. It is far easier to bring public attention to what is tangible, such as the Fukushima disaster. If the full extent of the costs of this disaster were set before the public, perhaps a rare moment of breakthrough in public awareness would be created. Of course, such public discourse must emphasize that the catastrophic effects of nuclear weapons, used intentionally or by accident, are likely to be far greater than those of a nuclear power plant accident.

There is no doubt that human activities are changing our relationship to nature. Our technologies are having greater and greater effect, resulting in greater risks of catastrophe. I characterize the Nuclear Age, the years since the creation of nuclear weapons, as the time during which humans have created technologies capable of destroying our species and much of nature. Given the potential for omnicide in the Nuclear Age, we must raise our level of risk management and be far more prudent in our use of dangerous technologies. This is true with nuclear technologies and with respect to technologies that are causing climate change. Some of these technologies, and I would include both nuclear weapons and nuclear energy production among them, are too dangerous to be maintained by attempting to regulate and manage them; they must be eliminated altogether. This is one of the great challenges of our time: to eliminate technologies that put the future of humanity at risk of annihilation or create an enduring legacy of poisonous materials that cannot be adequately contained and prevented from causing harm to countless future generations.

A Question of Values

Falk: Personally, I would rather accept the vulnerabilities and limitations associated with foregoing both technologies because I find their role in human affairs unacceptable. Nuclear weaponry is genocidal in its tendency, if not omnicidal and ecocidal, while nuclear power is a hubristic toss of the dice that could at some future time release lethal radiation in massive doses severely harmful to health and societal serenity. I believe as a matter of spiritual commitment that these technological options are unconditionally unacceptable for ethical, cultural, and environmental reasons, and such considerations should prevail over alleged "practical" benefits, themselves hyped to sell these technologies to the public. Let me put my position this way: I would be proud to live in a society that rests its security on nonnuclear means of defense and energy sufficiency (even if it entails some consumer restrictions such as fuel rationing) and feel ashamed and afraid to live in a society that relies on nuclear weaponry and nuclear energy to sustain its security and prosperity.

Krieger: The choice between maintaining or eliminating technologies with apocalyptic risk is an easy one for me and clearly for you as well. The dangers of the Nuclear Age require humanity to move beyond its childish ways and to think anew. We cannot consider only immediate gratification, as seems to be behind the attachment to nuclear energy. Nor can we continue to find loopholes in the law to evade the fact that the use of or threat to use nuclear weapons, as weapons of indiscriminate mass destruction, is already outlawed under international humanitarian law.

You raise the issue of values, and I think you are right to do so. The values that undergird support for nuclear energy seem to me to be greed and power. To rely upon this form of energy requires a suspension of concern for the future in order to have at our disposal more energy today. Much, if not all, of the power currently supplied by nuclear energy could be replaced by requiring greater energy efficiency and developing renewable forms of energy. If there are to be societal subsidies for energy, they should be in the areas of conservation and renewable energy development.

The same values that undergird nuclear energy also support nuclear weapons: greed and power. Nuclear weapons pose the ultimate threat to humanity. They are omnicidal. They threaten not only the death of the other but the death of the self and the destruction of one's society as well. Perhaps this is the ultimate power: the willingness not only to murder indiscriminately but to die in the process. I doubt this is a power that ordinary citizens in the nuclear weapon states would support, if they fully understood the consequences of doing so.

The values most at play in opposing both nuclear energy and nuclear weapons are commitment to life and compassion for others. I believe, as you do, that there is a spiritual component to these values. A change in orientation toward our world is essential if humanity is to survive the Nuclear Age. If the disaster at Fukushima, as tragic as its consequences have been, awakens humanity to the need to eliminate nuclear weapons from the planet, it will have been a great gift. If the Fukushima disaster proves to be a catalyst for awakening humanity to the need for a spiritual shift toward valuing life and living with compassion, it will be a great turning point for a maturing humanity toward controlling dangerous technologies, treating each other with respect and decency, and extending compassion to future generations.

Falk: I want to register some disagreement with the tone and substance of your last comment. It seems to me unlikely, to the point of inconceivable, that the public reaction to the Fukushima disaster—even assuming that worst-case scenarios prove accurate, which seems increasingly to be the case—will lead to any greater mainstream support for the elimination of nuclear weaponry. So far, I have seen almost no acknowledgement of the linkage in the public debate, which is characterized rather by a mindless insistence that the planned reliance on nuclear power should proceed un-abated. I do think there may arise opportunities to raise sufficient doubts about nuclear power to forestall this nuclearist momentum, especially in light of the encouraging German decision to phase out its reliance on nuclear energy altogether.

In my view, serious questioning of nuclear weapons will not take place until there is either a revolt by the nonnuclear states against the NPT regime or there occurs the ghastly, feared event of a government or nonstate actor using a nuclear weapon. Until that time, the most we can expect is a series of more or less constructive arms control gestures and a continued refusal by the U.S. government to follow up on Barack Obama's Prague speech with a detailed set of disarmament proposals or the establishment of an intergovernmental group of nuclear weapon states to prepare draft proposals and a negotiating process. Until one of these eventualities occurs, I am very skeptical about any push for genuine nuclear disarmament. Take note that even the unanimous view of the International Court of Justice that the nuclear weapon states had a legal obligation under Article VI of the NPT to pursue nuclear disarmament in good faith had no effect whatsoever on the policy process. Neither the nuclear nor the nonnuclear states regarded this authoritative interpretation of legal duties as sufficiently important to press the issue. In view of this, how can we expect post-Fukushima public discussion to challenge such entrenched reliance on nuclear weaponry? I am not against raising the issue, as we both have done, but I believe that we should admit the difficulty of overcoming the deep emotional and political attachments to the weaponry.

Krieger: Neither of us knows what will trigger a strong movement to eliminate nuclear weapons. No one predicted the fall of the Berlin Wall, the breakup of the Soviet Union, or the end of apartheid in South Africa. I can say this: Major radiation releases from nuclear power plants, whether caused by accident or hostile action, are wake-up calls—first, to the dangers of nuclear energy itself and second, by extension, to the even more extreme dangers of nuclear weapons. Whether the alarm sounds strongly enough will depend on how the dots are connected.

Robert Jay Lifton did a good job of connecting the "peaceful" and warlike uses of nuclear technology in an April 15, 2011, *New York Times* article titled "Fukushima and Hiroshima."[7] His linkage moved from the dangers of nuclear weapons to those of nuclear power. Lifton wrote, "We do better to overcome our denial and dissociation and to instead acknowledge that radiation effects are one and the same no matter what their source, that the combination of nature and human fallibility makes no technology completely safe, and that the technology most dangerous to us can hardly be relied upon to provide something 'clean' or pure, or to otherwise redeem us." I am convinced, though, that a link also runs in the other direction, from nuclear energy to nuclear weapons. There is tangibility to a serious nuclear accident, such as Fukushima, that could awaken the public to the dangers of both nuclear energy and nuclear weapons. You may be correct that the likelihood of this happening is low, but this does not mean that the link is not there or that we should not do our best to connect the dots.

Falk: Of course, I hope that your qualified optimism turns out to be correct, and we as activists and educators must do our best to make this happen. Yet, we must also recognize that the examples you gave were both activist movements against oppressive political regimes. Even the ghastly representation of apocalyptic suffering in the wastelands of Hiroshima and Nagasaki did not generate a popular movement of sufficient intensity to challenge the militarists and realists who continue to run the show. Here with nuclear power, there are several additional obstacles to overcome: the causal and controversial difficulty of connecting the dots (calculations of the deaths caused by Chernobyl vary from 4,000 to over 1 million), the private-sector pressures to invest profitably, and the reluctance of modern societies to reject an energy source at this historical stage (China has by far the largest program underway to construct additional reactors, with more than 150 planned). Of course, some factors might make nuclear power easier to prohibit than nuclear weapons: It does not engage national security interests to nearly the same degree as the weaponry, and to the extent that it does, it may work against nuclear power because of proliferation risks. If the true costs of nuclear energy are calculated, including liability insurance, the technology becomes a commercial black hole.

In concluding, we should remind ourselves and the public of the connections between the weaponry and so-called peaceful uses, and we need to remain ready to encourage a blend of moral, political, and economic arguments against any further proliferation of nuclear power capabilities.

CHAPTER 7

Nuclear Weapons and International Law

Krieger: In the aftermath of World War II, people throughout the world understood the terrible consequences of the use of nuclear weapons, instruments of mass annihilation whose force had been tragically demonstrated first at Hiroshima and then at Nagasaki. When Allied leaders agreed in the Nuremberg Charter to hold Axis leaders to account for crimes against peace, war crimes, and crimes against humanity, there was no consideration of nuclear weapons. These weapons, after all, had been used not by the Axis powers but by the United States, an Allied power. The Allies were not placing themselves or the weaponry they had developed and used on trial. Ironically, Hiroshima was bombed on August 6, 1945, the Nuremberg Charter was signed on August 8, 1945, and Nagasaki was bombed on August 9, 1945. In other words, Allied war crimes took place immediately before and after the Allies agreed to hold Axis leaders accountable for their crimes.

Even before Hiroshima was bombed, there were prohibitions in international humanitarian law, the law of warfare, against using weapons that did not discriminate between soldiers and civilians, that caused unnecessary suffering, or that constituted a disproportionate response to a prior attack. These prohibitions did not stop either the Allied or the Axis militaries from carpet bombing cities in Europe and Japan; nor did they prevent the use of the atomic bombs by the United States at the first opportunity in Japan.

Falk: There was, as you suggest, no willingness by the victorious powers in World War II to accept any accountability for their departures from the law of war, the most extreme instance of which was, of course, the atomic bombings at a time when Japan seemed ready, according to many reports, to accept defeat. More than this, led by the United States, there has been a consistent reluctance to allow questioning of the legal status of nuclear weaponry. The United States vigorously opposed referral of the issue to the International Court of Justice (ICJ) by the UN General Assembly.

But beyond resisting efforts to have these weapons considered formally unlawful and their threat or use declared a crime against humanity, as the UN General Assembly asserted in Resolution 1653(XVI) back in 1961, the U.S. government has been very touchy about acknowledging the suffering endured by the people in Hiroshima and Nagasaki. In a much publicized incident, for instance, politically powerful forces brought so much pressure to bear that an exhibit depicting the suffering of the civilian population in Japan, put together by the respected Smithsonian Institution in Washington, DC, to commemorate the fiftieth anniversary of these events, was cancelled. And shockingly, no U.S. president has seen fit to visit either Japanese city that experienced atomic devastation, although many American leaders have made it a point to visit Nazi death camps. Of course, the latter is entirely appropriate in memory of the Holocaust, but to avert our eyes from the devastation of Hiroshima and Nagasaki is to be guilty of a particularly serious form of denial, one that tends to withdraw stigma from the bombings and the weaponry.

Let me make the point differently. It is hard to imagine even the most cynical realist political leader setting forth a justification for genocide, while it is perfectly respectable in the media or in think tanks to propose strategic roles for nuclear weapons, including their use against cities.

The Nuremberg Promise

Falk: We should not forget what Justice Robert Jackson, the American chief prosecutor at Nuremberg, said in his extraordinary statement to the tribunal on that historic occasion in 1945: "And let me make clear that while this law is first applied against German aggressors, the law includes, and if it is to serve any useful purpose it must condemn, aggression by any other nation, including those which sit here now in judgment. We are able to do away with domestic tyranny and violence and aggression by those in power against the rights of their own people only when we make all men [*sic*] answerable to the law. This trial represents mankind's desperate effort to apply the discipline of law to statesmen who have used their powers of state to attack the foundations of world peace."[1] There is no doubt that this noble Nuremberg Promise has been broken many times by World War II's victors and that we have grown accustomed to living in a world of double standards: accountability for the weak and geopolitically vulnerable; impunity for the strong and geopolitically protected.

Krieger: Justice Jackson had wisdom and foresight. He could see clearly the need to make universal the application of the Nuremberg principles, holding to account all leaders who commit serious crimes under international law. The failure of the Allied powers to live up to the Nuremberg Promise in the aftermath of World War II is one of the great tragedies and certainly one of the lost opportunities of our time. The Nuremberg Promise was to end impunity for serious crimes under international law for all. So far, the promise hasn't been realized. Instead, powerful states and their leaders have sought to override the Nuremberg principles and build double standards of law and justice into the international system. A prime example of the application of double standards is found in the Non-Proliferation Treaty (NPT).

When the United States, United Kingdom, and Soviet Union sought to create the NPT in 1968, they agreed in Article VI to a provision calling for nuclear disarmament but phrased it ambiguously: "Each of the parties to the Treaty undertakes to pursue negotiations in good faith on effective measures relating to cessation of the nuclear arms race at an early date and to nuclear disarmament, and on a treaty on general and complete disarmament under strict and effective international control."[2] Since the NPT's entry into force in 1970, there has been little, if any, attempt at "good faith" negotiations on nuclear disarmament.

The World Court Pronounces on the Legality of Nuclear Weapons

Krieger: Not until twenty-six years later, in 1996, did the International Court of Justice address this issue by providing an advisory opinion, requested by the UN General Assembly, titled *The Legality of the Threat or Use of Nuclear Weapons*. After hearings and deliberations, the ICJ issued a multipart opinion and voted separately on each part. It found unanimously that there was in neither customary nor conventional international law any specific authorization of the use of or threat to use nuclear weapons.[3] It also found, by a vote of eleven to three, that there was no comprehensive and universal prohibition of such threat or use.[4] Three judges believed there was a comprehensive and universal prohibition. The ICJ went on to state unanimously that any threat or use that did not comply with the UN Charter would be unlawful.[5]

The ICJ agreed unanimously that any use of or threat to use nuclear weapons needed to be compatible with international humanitarian law. It stated, "A threat or use of nuclear weapons should also be compatible with the requirements of the international law applicable in armed conflict, particularly those of the principles and rules of international humanitarian law, as well as with specific obligations under treaties and other undertakings which expressly deal with nuclear weapons."[6]

The ICJ then split seven to seven, with the president's vote deciding the central conclusion of the advisory opinion:

> It follows from the above-mentioned requirements that the threat or use of nuclear weapons would generally be contrary to the rules of international law applicable in armed conflict, and in particular the principles and rules of humanitarian law;
>
> However, in view of the current state of international law, and of the elements of fact at its disposal, the Court cannot conclude definitively whether the threat or use of nuclear weapons would be lawful or unlawful in an extreme circumstance of self-defense, in which the very survival of a State would be at stake.[7]

In this latter section of the opinion, the ICJ introduced some doubts. It used the fudge word "generally" before the words "be contrary to the rules of international law." It went on to explain this by stating that the current state of international law didn't allow a conclusion as to whether "an extreme circumstance of self-defense, in which the very survival of a State would be at stake," would be lawful or unlawful. It is important to note that the ICJ did not say that the use of or threat to use nuclear weapons would be lawful in such a circumstance, only that the law was unclear. Three of the judges who voted against this position thought the law was in fact clear and that it was possible to conclude that any use of or threat to use nuclear weapons would be a violation of international law. The three were Judge Christopher G. Weeramantry of Sri Lanka, vice president of the ICJ; Judge Mohammed Shahabuddeen of Guyana; and Judge Abdul Koroma of Sierra Leone. The three judges wrote important dissenting opinions. Judge Weeramantry wrote, "My considered opinion is that the use or threat of use of nuclear weapons is illegal *in any circumstances whatsoever.*"[8] He also strongly challenged the word "generally" in the opinion, which modified "unlawful."

The ICJ concluded its opinion by stating, "There exists an obligation to pursue in good faith and bring to a conclusion negotiations leading to nuclear disarmament in all its aspects under strict and effective international control."[9] This was the ICJ's interpretation of Article VI of the NPT. It affirmed, in essence, an obligation not only to negotiate nuclear disarmament in good faith but also to conclude those negotiations and achieve nuclear disarmament in all its aspects.

Since the ICJ released its advisory opinion in 1996, there has been scant change on the part of the nuclear weapon states. The United States and Russia have negotiated to reduce the size of their nuclear arsenals, but they have not taken seriously the obligation set forth by the ICJ to pursue disarmament negotiations. Between the two countries, there still remain some 20,000 nuclear weapons. Both states have unfortunately demonstrated a gross indifference to international law, which I fear will have serious consequences for humanity.

Falk: You have provided an excellent summary of what the ICJ decided. I would add just a few observations. If read fairly, the majority opinion, although leaving some room for exceptional claims in the event that a state's survival is credibly at stake, goes a long way toward viewing nuclear weapons as unlawful. This view is inconsistent with the unwillingness of the United States and other nuclear weapon states to configure their weaponry and doctrine for defensive uses in survival situations. At minimum, this should lead all nuclear weapon states to make an unconditional declaration renouncing the option to use such weapons first. It would also preclude the development of so-called tactical nuclear weapons with battlefield missions.

A second observation is that, although the conclusions of the ICJ took the form of an advisory opinion, the legal assessments were the most authoritative attainable within the world legal system. These assessments of the relationship of the weaponry to the law were made by distinguished jurists from the world's major legal systems and would seem to deserve appropriate respect from all governments that purport to uphold adherence to the rule of law. The decision was also endorsed in a UN General Assembly resolution by a large majority of the membership of the United Nations.

A third observation relates to the failure of the United States and other nuclear weapon states to alter their approach to nuclear weaponry in response to this historic legal appraisal. In this regard, the imperatives of geopolitics, which continue to treat this weaponry as essential for national security, have taken precedence over respect for international law. Even the more modest unanimous finding among the fourteen participating judges regarding the obligation to pursue nuclear disarmament in good faith, as declared in NPT Article VI, has produced no appropriate initiative in the subsequent sixteen years. True, calls for nuclear disarmament and visions of a world without nuclear weapons are set forth from time to time, but there has been no concrete willingness to establish a mechanism at the national and global levels to frame a disarmament process that could guide intergovernmental negotiations.

Failure to Act on the ICJ's Opinion

Falk: This is not only a shocking disregard of the ICJ's clear finding but also a material breach of the Non-Proliferation Treaty that casts legal doubt on its continuing validity. It may be time for the General Assembly to put this question to the ICJ: What legal consequences arise from the persistent failure of the nuclear weapon states to fulfill their obligations under Article VI of the NPT? In my view, the nonnuclear states have also been irresponsible in not insisting on mutuality of respect in the nonproliferation setting. It may be up to civil society actors to bring wider attention to this pattern of disrespect for vital norms of international law bearing on the status of nuclear weaponry and the irresponsibility of governments in failing to seek compliance.

Krieger: I agree with you that the ICJ's advisory opinion goes a long way toward making the use of or threat to use nuclear weapons unlawful, particularly by concluding that any such act that violates international humanitarian law is illegal. It is almost impossible to imagine a scenario in which the use of or threat to use nuclear weapons would not violate the laws of war, even when "the very survival of a state" was at stake. It is not enough, though, to declare the use of or threat to use the weapons illegal. It is also necessary to declare their possession illegal and to eliminate them altogether if we are to ensure we prevent either threat or use. Possession alone can be construed as an implicit threat to use, and reliance on nuclear deterrence makes the threat explicit.

As we have discussed before, a declaration of No First Use of nuclear weapons would be a step in the right direction, but it is only a step and not sufficient. So long as the weapons are held in the arsenals of states, a pledge of No First Use can be quickly overridden. Such a pledge must be followed by negotiations for a nuclear weapons convention for the total elimination of all nuclear weapons.

The ICJ's advisory opinion is all the more remarkable when one considers that the Court's composition included judges from the five initial nuclear weapon states, those that are defined as nuclear weapon states in the NPT: the United States, Russia, the United Kingdom, France, and China. Without these five countries represented, the ICJ would quite likely have gone even further and ruled, as Judge Weeramantry expressed in his dissent, that the weapons were illegal "in any circumstances whatsoever." ICJ president Mohammed Bedjaoui of Algeria wrote in his separate opinion that nuclear weapons were "the ultimate evil." He found the existence of nuclear weapons to be *a challenge to the very existence of humanitarian law,* not to mention their long-term effects of damage to the human environment, in respect to which the right to life can be exercised."[10]

Judge Bedjaoui pointed out the irony of the ICJ's conclusion regarding its inability to find the threat or use of nuclear weapons illegal when "the very survival of a state" is at stake. He wrote, "The fact remains that the use of nuclear weapons by a State in circumstances in which its survival is at stake risks in its turn endangering the survival of all mankind, precisely because of the inextricable link between terror and escalation in the use of such weapons. It would thus be quite foolhardy unhesitatingly to set the survival of a State above all other considerations, in particular above the survival of mankind itself."[11] For this reason, the law as it stands is not sufficient, and it is necessary for states to fulfill the advisory opinion's final unanimous directive "to pursue in good faith and bring to a conclusion negotiations leading to nuclear disarmament in all its aspects." I think those who have looked carefully at the behavior of the NPT nuclear weapon states would share widespread agreement that they have not engaged in "good faith" negotiations on nuclear disarmament and thus have not fulfilled their obligations under international law, specifically under Article VI of the NPT.

I'm not sure how it would help move nuclear disarmament forward to ask the ICJ for another advisory opinion, inasmuch as the nuclear weapon states have been largely unresponsive to the existing advisory opinion. The status of international law seems insufficient to bring the most powerful states into line with its dictates. The politics of power in the international system evidently takes precedence over the power of the law. In some respects, since the ICJ issued its advisory opinion, the nuclear weapon states have used international law cynically to justify their nuclear arsenals on the basis of their potential need in the event of "the very survival of a state" being at stake. In other words, powerful states have treated the ICJ's opinion as an excuse for relying on nuclear weapons for geopolitical purposes. Of course, in doing so, these states continue to put at risk, as Judge Bedjaoui pointed out, "the survival of mankind itself."

Civil Society and the Enforcement of International Law

Krieger: I believe it is incumbent on civil society to point out the dangers of nuclear weapon states failing to fulfill their obligations under international law with regard to nuclear disarmament. It is also incumbent upon civil society to push governments to take greater action: to push nuclear weapon states to engage in the good faith negotiations for nuclear disarmament required of them and also to push the non–nuclear weapon states to put serious pressure on the nuclear weapon states to fulfill these obligations. With no enforcement mechanism available to hold the nuclear weapon states to account, the law loses its power. Perhaps only civil society, if seriously engaged, would have the capacity to restore this power to the law by pressing its demands to end the risk that nuclear weapons pose to the human future.

Falk: I agree with your observation that significant progress toward nuclear disarmament will depend on the mobilization of civil society around this issue to a greater extent than has occurred in the past. How to make this imperative a viable political project is the great unanswered question hanging over all efforts to proceed in an atmosphere that is definitely not receptive at present to a serious movement either in the United States or elsewhere. In the past, movements only formed during those periods of the Cold War when there was widespread public anxiety about the possible use of nuclear weapons.

I hope that the new doubts raised about the expansion of and reliance on nuclear energy will foster a wider debate that links these concerns with those that we have focused on involving the weaponry, past, present, and future.

In these regards, I think you undervalue the continuing role of international law and the ICJ in challenging the legality and legitimacy of nuclear weaponry. In my view, we need to understand this role as a process not an event. Recall that the ICJ was asked four times to pronounce on the legality and legitimacy of the racist apartheid regime that prevailed in South Africa and was extended to Southwest Africa (now Namibia) in their role as administering mandatory power. The experience in the ICJ was not entirely favorable, and the case involving Southwest Africa perversely endorsed apartheid as a legal and legitimate means for South Africa to carry out its responsibilities. The composition of the ICJ at the time had some peculiarities that made it much more conservative on human rights issues than the general international climate. The decision outraged many governments and world public opinion, which accelerated rather than undermined the global antiapartheid campaign, leading the General Assembly to terminate South Africa's role as a mandatory power. International law was symbolically important even when perversely invoked to validate reactionary policies.

With respect to nuclear weaponry, another General Assembly resolution seeking to clarify the legal obligations of states to implement the earlier advisory opinion would have important educative and consciousness-raising implications. It would reinforce the impression that the nuclear weapon states have twisted the outcome of the 1996 advisory opinion to serve their essentially nuclearist purposes and paid little attention to their obligations under the NPT regime. It would not be expected to transform the behavior of these governments, especially the United States, but it could reinforce the idea that they are openly defiant toward international law on this issue of ultimate significance for the future of humanity.

Finally, I believe we in civil society should make maximum use of international law and global legal institutions to wage a legitimacy war against the possession and normalization of nuclear weaponry. Without such an orientation, I see little hope that educational efforts on their own can produce the sort of political outcomes we favor. As I have suggested at various stages in our conversations, the greatest challenge antinuclear activists face is converting their fervent concerns into a viable political project. At present, we are still operating as a prepolitical movement, that is, without a plan that we have any reason to believe will be implemented by leaders, will enlist widespread-enough support on the part of citizens, or will be given priority in the policy agenda of global civil society. There exist widespread dormant antinuclear fears and sentiments but insufficient will to achieve political relevance. I think, in this dialogue, we need further commentary on whether the struggle for nuclear disarmament can be waged, as I have suggested in passing, as a legitimacy war and the precise role we can assign to international law.

International Law versus Deterrence Theory

Krieger: I appreciate your point about looking at international law, as it pertains to nuclear weapons, as a process rather than an event. The process must involve the establishment of norms so strong that their violation would engage the public and cause a mass uprising. The problem as it exists now is that the public does not widely know about or understand the applicable international law related to the use of or threat to use nuclear weapons. This law also, and importantly, fails to go to the heart of the matter, which is possession of the weapons. So long as possession is deemed legal, at least for the five NPT nuclear weapon states and the four nuclear weapon states outside the treaty, the threat of use will be implicit, and the possibility of actual use will remain close at hand.

The possession of nuclear weapons is intertwined with nuclear deterrence theory, which posits that the threat of nuclear retaliation by country x will prevent the use of nuclear weapons and other proscribed behavior against country x. Many people believe that nuclear deterrence has prevented nuclear war and thus is beneficial. If leaders of a country believe that nuclear weapons are a shield against attack, they will be reluctant to give up the weapons regardless of their understanding of international law or the state of the law as expressed by the ICJ. In the "legitimacy war" to which you refer, nuclear deterrence is a major obstacle to delegitimizing the possession of nuclear weapons. Thus, we must call into question the legitimacy of nuclear deterrence. As we have discussed, nuclear deterrence theory has many flaws, including that it is subject to communication failures, requires rational leaders, and is not effective against nonstate extremists. Another real danger of nuclear deterrence lies in its undermining of international law by its justification of possession of the weapons.

The final portion of the ICJ's opinion on the legality of the use of or threat to use nuclear weapons refers to "an obligation to pursue in good faith and bring to a conclusion negotiations leading to nuclear disarmament in all its aspects." This element of the opinion, which rests upon Article VI of the NPT, goes to possession of the weapons, saying, in essence, that the nuclear weapon states must negotiate to end possession of the weapons, that is, to achieve "nuclear disarmament in all its aspects." It is not possible both to engage in good faith negotiations to achieve nuclear disarmament and to retain nuclear weapons for deterrence. The nuclear weapon states have thus far chosen nuclear deterrence and failed to engage in good faith negotiations for the elimination of their nuclear arsenals. Perhaps this situation is too esoteric to engage the man on the street. That must change. We must drive home, not only to leaders but to the public at large, the dangers of the nuclear status quo based on nuclear deterrence and convey the importance of international law as a way out of the dilemma.

Mobilization and Motivation

Falk: I would situate the failure of mobilization somewhat differently. In my view, the primary failure relates to the inability of antinuclear activists and intellectuals to mobilize those who would support nuclear disarmament, even with enthusiasm, but are unmoved to demand such a result or to engage actively in the struggle to attain antinuclear goals. This shallowness of motivation makes the concern seem to have a low priority. This undoubtedly reflects many different considerations: a sense of despair about challenging such an entrenched national security posture, a false partial acceptance of the relative stability of the present nuclear regime because of the absence of use in sixty-six years, and a rather irrational concern that perhaps giving up nuclear weapons would make the country vulnerable to nuclear terrorism and to a government that "cheated" during the disarming process. As I have stressed throughout these conversations, no rational closure is possible on these issues as the uncertainties are too pervasive. This means that our attitude toward nuclear weapons involves weighing essentially incalculable risks, and when it comes to national security, citizens have a broad willingness to defer to the views of the government, even when they collide with ethical convictions and political preferences. In the end, only competing views of human nature and values count, whether they see human nature as essentially aggressive or only conditionally so. It seems to me that those who say that the path of legality is a dead end when it comes to nuclear weaponry—the Kissingerian mentality—always prefer the risks of nuclear possession to those of nuclear disarmament. In contrast, those who say that nuclearism leads toward the apocalypse—the Kriegerian mentality—always prefer the risks associated with nuclear disarmament and believe that the international order can be transformed ultimately, by stages, from reliance on political violence to peaceful forms of conflict resolution.

Krieger: There is no doubt that a lack of motivation among the general public and policy makers keeps the abolition of nuclear weapons a low priority. In addition to the reasons for this that you suggest, there are also psychological reasons for avoiding the issue, as well as a sense of more pressing day-to-day economic and social concerns. Deference to the authority of government officials' views may prove the greatest obstacle to ridding the world of nuclear weapons. But the people of the United States, the country that most needs to lead, have become too invested in patriotic songs and presidential elections. And they are too removed from critical thinking and conscientious objection to dangerous government policies, including not only nuclear weapons policies but many other policies related to weaponry and war. The widespread passivity of the U.S. citizenry is not a force for change and makes it difficult to create the conditions that would bring about change on issues of war and nuclear disarmament.

I am honored to be placed in your perspective as holding a contrasting viewpoint to "the Kissingerian mentality." But, of course, even Henry Kissinger himself now seems to believe that the risks of nuclear deterrence are too great to be borne indefinitely and favors moving, albeit far too slowly for me, toward a nuclear weapon–free world. You are right about my position. I think it is a foolish manifestation of hubris to continue to tempt fate by relying on nuclear weapons for security. I believe we need to move carefully from where we are today to a world without nuclear weapons, but we need to do so with serious and unwavering commitment. This will require leadership. One tool available to aid in that leadership is international law, including the ICJ's advisory opinion.

I agree with you that the ICJ's opinion is the most authoritative source of international law that exists on the issue of nuclear weapons. The problem is that the law alone does not seem to be sufficient to move the nuclear weapon states to action. I view international law as an element in the "legitimacy war" that needs to be reinforced and is not at present sufficiently powerful to prevent reliance by some states on nuclear weapons. The weakness of the law at present lies in its not directly challenging possession of nuclear weapons. So long as nuclear deterrence justifies possession, nuclear catastrophe is just the push of a button or a mishap away.

I believe the possession of the weapons themselves must be delegitimized and made illegal. This could be done with a negotiated nuclear weapons convention, which would, in effect, supersede the NPT and change the law with regard to nuclear weapons. It must be made illegitimate not only to use or threaten to use the weapons but also to possess them. Any possession of nuclear weapons should be viewed as illegitimate under strengthened provisions of international law and made a global taboo.

Falk: For this type of issue, legality is at best an instrument of persuasion helpful in mobilizing popular support, especially if law is seen as congruent with justice and human well-being, as is the case with nuclear weaponry. But in an atmosphere where political influence is heavily weighted in support of bureaucratic, strategic, and economic interests that favor lawlessness, the tendency will be to dismiss the relevance of law to the shaping of policy. The outcome of the ICJ process should have at least challenged the approach taken by the nuclear weapon states, but they took almost no notice of it after failing in trying to prevent the issue from ever being referred to the World Court. What is more, the non–nuclear weapon states might have seized upon the outcome to challenge the viability of the nonproliferation regime, putting forth a common position demanding that a disarmament process be implemented in good faith and without further delay. But these governments were essentially silent and, in a profound way, became complicit with the damaging view that international law is basically irrelevant in the context of nuclear weaponry.

At the same time, it would be wrong to conclude that in the setting of nuclear weaponry, international law is irrelevant. It should be remembered that the United States used its geopolitical muscle in a failed effort to dissuade the General Assembly from referring the issue to the ICJ. The American judge on the Court wrote a dissent that went along with the view that deterrence plus nonproliferation was the best way to mitigate the harmful effects of nuclear weaponry and that existing international law was incapable of prescribing the conditions under which a use of or threat to use nuclear weaponry might be lawful. In other words, the debate about nuclear weapons has a lawfare dimension, and the ICJ is the most respected arbiter of this debate. For this reason, the U.S. government responded quasi-officially with criticisms of the majority opinion that narrowed the occasions on which it would be lawful to use or threaten to use nuclear weapons and simply claimed, disingenuously in my view, that its arms control initiatives from time to time satisfy its legal obligations under the NPT, which were reaffirmed by the ICJ, including the fundamental legal duty to pursue nuclear disarmament in good faith.

Krieger: The nuclear weapon states approached the ICJ's advisory opinion from the perspective of damage control, seeking to prevent limitations on their freedom to use or threaten to use nuclear weapons. Rather than embracing the opinion as moving toward a safer and more secure world, they fought hard to resist or limit any statements of law that intruded on their ability to use or threaten to use the most powerful weapons yet created by man. This approach has always seemed shortsighted to me in light of the fact that these states and their citizens also remain threatened by these weapons. In many respects, the arms control agreements that the nuclear weapon states have reached are also a form of damage control, achieving incremental steps that disarm public opinion more effectively than they disarm the weapons themselves. The nuclear weapon states have promoted these steps in lieu of the good faith negotiations for nuclear disarmament called for by the NPT and reinforced by the ICJ's advisory opinion.

Falk: Civil society activists and educators who study the ICJ advisory opinion as indicative of the proper approach to nuclearism often go further and single out the long dissent of Judge Weeramantry as the basis of both law and justice—and even political sanity—in the context of nuclear weaponry. For a small number of people, this legal condemnation of nuclear weaponry is reinforced by, and reinforcing of, a preexisting ethical repudiation of the whole idea of weaponry of mass destruction and induces political action of various kinds: civil disobedience at facilities relating to the production and possession of the weaponry, initiatives seeking to terminate the relationship between universities and weapons labs engaged in research and development of the weaponry, and initiation of citizen tribunals (e.g., the London Nuclear Weapons Tribunal) that pronounce upon the criminality of doctrines proposing use of the weaponry. But this is fringe activity.

Krieger: Judge Weeramantry's dissent in the ICJ's advisory opinion is a well-reasoned argument for the illegality of nuclear weapons under any circumstance. Like all good law, it is rooted in justice—and justice not only for those alive on the planet today but for future generations as well. I find it one of the most important statements of the illegality of nuclear weapons to date and all the more valuable for having been made in the official context of the ICJ's advisory opinion. As important as his dissent is, however, it is little known, and its importance little understood, by either the public or by government officials.

Falk: Why, we must ask ourselves, is such an authoritative assessment of nuclear weapons as is contained in Judge Weeramantry's dissent so little known? A superficial explanation would be that the length, density, and complexity of his argument, covering some eighty pages, discourages reading by all except the most devoted antinuclearists. Also, much of his discussion focuses on the historical and cultural context that informs a legal analysis of nuclear weaponry. There is beyond this a Western jurisprudential bias against nonpositivistic styles of analysis, which is further reinforced by a reluctance to give much intellectual traction to viewpoints that question the underlying morality of West-centricism, which, in important respects, is culminated by the advent, use, development, and possession of nuclear weaponry. I am also reminded of the great dissent by Judge Radhabinod Pal, the Indian member of the Tokyo War Crimes Tribunal convened after

World War II to impose criminal accountability on surviving Japanese political and military leaders. The scholarship of international criminal law virtually ignores Pal's dissent, although it questions in a detailed and impressive manner the self-righteous construction of international law to demonstrate that Japan was the aggressor exclusively responsible for the Asian carnage of World War II. Pal's dissent is an exemplary instance of anticolonial jurisprudence, and not only does the Western academic literature ignore it, but it is not published in a text that is readily available in most libraries.

We need to remember that the expansion of Europe at the expense of the non-Western world rested on violence and the superiority of European weaponry and strategic logistics, including naval power. This link between Western militarism and its historical ascendancy is, in my view, one of the deep reasons why there is such a seemingly irrational attachment to nuclear weaponry, making it very difficult to renounce as the supreme expression of political violence. It also suggests that critiques of militarism and what I call "violent geopolitics" need to be an integral part of any movement that mounts an effective challenge to nuclearism. In this regard, I find it encouraging that military approaches to political conflict have had an increasingly poor record in shaping political outcomes, and, particularly since Vietnam, the American reliance on its military superiority, a posture of unprecedented global military dominance, has proven dysfunctional in drawn out conflicts, as well as costly in lives, resources, and reputation. I believe we should call attention to the Weeramantry position in this wider geopolitical setting.

Krieger: You set forth a number of possible reasons why Judge Weeramantry's dissent is not known to the general public or even to political leaders. I would add that there is a general orientation in much of Western society to subordinate international law to geopolitical desire—in other words, not to allow international law to be a limiting factor in seeking geopolitical advantage. International law is thus applied when useful and ignored when self-interest and convenience dictate. This is a striking manifestation of the double standards that have served the interests of the powerful in both the colonial and postcolonial worlds. I think you are right that the West links its military prowess with its historical ascendancy. This may be a psychological factor in the reluctance of the West to give up its nuclear capability and thus put at risk its dominant economic position. The irony, of course, is that by subordinating the universality of international law to the achievement of short-term economic advantage, the West puts itself at risk of nuclear proliferation, nuclear terrorism, and nuclear war. The application of international law to nuclear weapons, nuclear threat, and nuclear war would create conditions that would make all peoples, including the people of the West, more secure.

Falk: What would it take to make the demand for a lawful approach to nuclear weaponry an effective challenge to existing policies? It would seem to require a much greater fear among the public that the weaponry would be used in the near future or a reaction to use that would renew the feeling of urgency that followed immediately upon the use of atomic bombs in 1945. That is, at this point, only a pre- or postcatastrophe surge of public anxiety seems capable of mobilizing enough people to have political weight. Now, possibly an antinuclear Rosa Parks will come along and surprise us. It should be remembered, as has often been pointed out, that Rosa Parks did not act in a vacuum, that a civil rights movement had been growing in the preceding years, and that there was present a Martin Luther King Jr. who knew how to seize an opportunity to move in more peaceful directions.

Krieger: You ask an important question, but one that may not be answerable at present. In essence, you are asking, What conditions would lead to law being given preference over geopolitics with regard to nuclear policies? If we look to the past, one example stands out for me. The nuclear weapon states, at least the United States, United Kingdom, and Soviet Union, agreed initially to the NPT because they believed that international law would keep them safer and relatively more powerful by preventing the spread of nuclear weapons to other countries. They favored international law in this instance because they understood it to be in their geopolitical interests. They even agreed to the clause on pursuing good faith negotiations on nuclear disarmament, but they have never followed the law with regard to this clause. At least in this instance, we can see that the nuclear weapon states have supported, even promoted, the law when they have seen it as undergirding their power but opposed it when perceiving it to limit their power. In this regard, they have played a very dangerous game, moving humanity to the nuclear precipice and putting their own citizens at risk of nuclear annihilation.

An antinuclear Rosa Parks would be a wonderful catalyst for giving the nuclear abolition movement higher prominence, but this is difficult to imagine at the present moment. There are perhaps only two ways in which the movement could be ignited: first, by widespread fear of nuclear annihilation; second, by an awakening to the moral implications of the threat of omnicide posed by nuclear weapons. The former route seems more likely than the latter, but after sixty-six years of the Nuclear Age, most people appear numb to the fear of nuclear annihilation or even a lesser nuclear catastrophe.

An Unequal Treaty

Falk: In retrospect, I believe the NPT was from the outset an example of an unequal treaty that reflected the predominant interests of the rich and powerful. Such treaties have always been viewed with favor by those who benefit and have generally remained effective as long as the power ratio has held up. Throughout the colonial era, unequal treaties formed the basis of many economic relationships that exploited the natural resources of the countries of the global South. I believe it is important to recognize the NPT as an unequal treaty whose lack of mutuality of obligations and benefits casts its validity into doubt. Many nations held in colonial captivity repudiated such unequal treaties in their attempts to couple political independence with economic sovereignty over natural resources. It is questionable whether this effort has succeeded in this present era of economic globalization in which new procedures sustain exploitative economic relationships, most prominently in the resource-rich, yet impoverished, least developed countries of sub-Saharan Africa.

I understand the difficulties that you pointed out earlier with regard to casting doubt on the NPT, and I realize that encouragement of additional nuclear weapons acquisition would be a step backward. Perhaps, a more modest version of my position would be a determined call for the renegotiation of the NPT to ensure that it would be implemented on a more symmetrical basis to include monitoring mechanisms and procedures for mounting legal challenges to noncompliance by nuclear weapon states. Now, only the nuclear weapon states have the will and capabilities to challenge supposed noncompliance by nonnuclear states. The confrontation with Iran that includes UN-backed severe sanctions illustrates this one-sided enforcement regime.

Krieger: I think there is a mutuality of obligations in the NPT, but there has been a lack of mutuality in the implementation of the treaty. The obligation of the non–nuclear weapon states not to develop or acquire nuclear weapons has been largely realized up to this point. On the other hand, the obligation of the nuclear weapon states to pursue good faith negotiations for nuclear disarmament has not been realized. The ICJ advisory opinion made it clear that this was an obligation for nuclear disarmament in all its aspects. The nuclear weapon states have made the NPT an unequal treaty by failing to fulfill their obligations. In doing so, they are devaluing and abrogating a treaty of critical importance to themselves and the world.

I doubt that the NPT can be renegotiated because its amendment process is very difficult, but I believe it is time for a new treaty, a nuclear weapons convention, that would replace the NPT. That treaty should require the elimination of nuclear weapons by a certain date and should set up phases to assess progress along the way. If the nuclear weapon states continue to drag their feet on negotiating such a new treaty, the non–nuclear weapon states should begin the negotiating process without them. The non–nuclear weapon states should make it clear that more than forty years of one-sided implementation of the NPT is far too long, and they should move forward in demanding that the nuclear weapon states achieve new goals and markers. Without such serious commitment on the part of the non–nuclear weapon states, I think there will be drift toward breakdown of the NPT, resulting in nuclear chaos.

Falk: I generally agree with your comment here as applied to the text of the NPT, but I do think the expectations about compliance from the outset were asymmetrical in the sense that the nonproliferation obligations were meant to be taken seriously as duties, whereas the disarmament commitment was always viewed differently, as essentially aspirational rather than obligatory in character. I would argue that this interpretation explains the naming of the treaty as the "Nuclear Non-Proliferation Treaty" rather than the "Nuclear Non-Proliferation and Disarmament Treaty." I do not mean to belabor this issue, but it does bear on my argument that the NPT was, from the time of its drafting, viewed as principally dealing with nonproliferation and only nominally as addressing the imperative of nuclear disarmament.

I would say that the challenge to the antinuclear community of educators and activists is to make international law matter in public attitudes toward nuclear weaponry. Leaders from time to time envision a world without nuclear weapons as a utopia sustained by law that might ultimately be attained but is never credibly pursued. These leaders never acknowledge the dubious legality of current possession of and policies toward the weaponry, and they generally reaffirm, as Barack Obama did at Prague, commitments to rely on a regime of nuclear deterrence until the promised day arrives on wings of unseen angels. In other words, the affirmation is here and now, while the realization is beyond the horizon of feasibility, so far as even the more unconditional repudiations of nuclearism are concerned.

Krieger: Your characterization of the NPT is a fair one. The treaty's predominant focus, particularly from the side of the nuclear weapon states, was nonproliferation. While there was an obligation to pursue good faith negotiations for nuclear disarmament, this has never been met, leading to the conclusion that there has been a decided lack of good faith on the part of the nuclear weapon states. This lack of good faith is causing the treaty to fray and undermining the nonproliferation obligations it imposes.

The Need to Make International Law Visible

Krieger: The great problem that we confront today, which gives rise to public complacency, is the invisibility of both nuclear weapons and the law pertaining to them to most people. Neither appears in the foreground of public consciousness. Our educational systems, even in the most advanced countries, do not concern themselves either with issues of global survival or with critical thinking. Young people are brought up today in a world oriented toward a culture of war rather than peace. Nuclear weapons are often viewed as useful tools in a culture of war. Few people anywhere are even aware of either the ICJ's advisory opinion on nuclear arms or any other aspect of international law pertaining to nuclear weapons. International law is invisible because we do not educate the young or the broader public to know that international law pertaining to nuclear weapons exists and matters. This should not be particularly surprising when the weapons themselves have become invisible.

The challenge for those of us working on these issues in the nuclear abolition movement is to educate the public so that the weapons and their potential for annihilation become visible, as does the international law making the use of or threat to use them illegal. Breaking through the thick walls of public complacency remains our most difficult challenge. The rationality of law, particularly law rooted in justice, is important, but it is not sufficient. If I could wave a magic wand, I would require classes in human survival to be offered in every high school and college throughout the world, and I would make Judge Weeramantry's dissenting opinion required reading and a subject of study. Discussing his dissent in such a course would not only awaken new generations to the importance of the issue of nuclear weapons abolition and the role of international law but also provide for young people a model of critical thinking in action. Of course, establishing such classes would be an extremely difficult task in itself, and it is not sufficient to educate only the young. The most pressing task is to awaken a complacent public and to engage them in transforming public attitudes toward nuclear dangers and the need to fulfill existing legal obligations to achieve nuclear disarmament in all its aspects.

Falk: Basically, I share this perspective. I would only reiterate the point that the invisibility of law is a direct consequence of the geopolitical repudiation of a law-oriented approach to the regulation of hard power. Law is quite visible when it serves geopolitical interests, which explains the relative success of the NPT with respect to countering proliferation impulses. International law, whether in trade or diplomacy or on the oceans, is respected when it serves either the mutual interests of all political actors or facilitates the ambitions and projects of the powerful.

CHAPTER 8

Nuclear Weapons, Culture, and Morality

Falk: We cannot ignore the extent to which American society has trapped itself in a militarist culture that makes it popular for leaders to take bold military action, whereas they pay a price for challenging the defense budget or questioning reliance on a military option. It is ironic at this time to realize that the Pentagon's formal name is the Department of Defense, and its leader is the secretary of defense. This antiseptic labeling completely disregards the nondefensive projection of American power to the far corners of the planet, via a network of bases in foreign countries, navies in every ocean, long-distance delivery vehicles for missiles, the eventual weaponization of both space and the deep ocean, covert operations in countless countries, and repeated instances of military intervention.

A Culture of Militarism

Falk: This portrayal of the United States' reliance on hard power for both its national self-esteem and its continuing claim to be the most righteous of sovereign states has relevance for our consideration of nuclear weaponry and the irrational resistance, spoken and unspoken, to the phased removal of such weaponry of mass destruction from the arsenals of the nuclear weapon states. If positive identity is linked to military dominance, then it is not surprising that the most destructive weaponry ever developed should have this unacknowledged hold on the political imagination of both leaders and citizens.

Krieger: The United States does seem to be trapped in a very encompassing culture of war, and the self-esteem of its citizens is bound up with its military prowess. When U.S. citizens think of themselves as number one, it is generally in terms of military power rather than health, education, or welfare. We spend an enormous amount of our national wealth on our military and think it normal to have our troops, our military bases, and our naval fleets spread throughout the globe. We are the only country on the planet that does this.

The irony you raise about the U.S. Department of Defense reminds me of an insightful observation by the American novelist Joseph Heller, who said, "After World War II, in 1947, the U.S. Department of War, an institution of American government since 1789, was abolished and subsequently reconstituted as the Department of Defense; the Secretary of War was renamed the Secretary of Defense. And from that day to the present, the United States of America was never again in danger of war. It was in danger of defense."[1] Heller uses humor to point to the Orwellian manner in which we delude ourselves about the use of our military forces. After the United Nations Charter prohibited the use of force in international relations but carved out an exception for self-defense, we renamed our Department of War to be consistent with this change of nomenclature without changing our behavior.

What does it say about a culture when its citizens celebrate their military dominance while at the same time rejoicing in their special righteousness? It is a formula for the self-righteous justification of war and, as we have seen, even for the justification of the use of nuclear weapons on civilian populations.

Falk: The cultural norms that celebrate our violence and neglect its impact on others are deeply inscribed in our national narrative. Hollywood movies celebrate the massacre of poorly armed Indian communities that dared to stand in the way of the expansion of settler communities. Only recently, several revisionist historians tried to set the record straight, documenting the cruelty of the American policies of dispossession that compelled one Indian nation after another to abandon sacred ancestral lands to embark on forced marches westward. Best known is *Trail of Tears*, telling of the 1837 forced march of the Cherokee people that led to the depletion of the community from 22,000 to a remnant of 5,000. I raise this historical memory not for further consideration but to underscore the point that the country has a long experience of glorifying indiscriminate and cruel use of force and has very little willingness to engage in an acknowledgment and redress of historic wrongs (against the Indians, African Americans, residents of Hiroshima and Nagasaki, and others) that might finally bring a measure of closure.

Krieger: Our culture is rife with examples of our not only excusing our wars against poorly equipped and unequal opponents but celebrating the slaughter involved as military victory. Examples include the war against Mexico and the Spanish-American War. Both were embarrassingly unequal contests of military might. When the results have been too embarrassing, we have attempted to suppress the information. Thus it was with the secret Pentagon Papers, which Daniel Ellsberg courageously released to the press and the American people.[2] I also recall being shocked and appalled to read that U.S. forces buried Iraqi troops alive during the Gulf War by bulldozing sand over them in their desert trenches. There were a few reports about this, and then the information largely vanished from the media.[3]

It was a particularly sad day for the United States when political pressure forced the cancellation of the planned Smithsonian exhibition on the fiftieth anniversary of the atomic bombings of Hiroshima and Nagasaki.[4] Even after fifty years, the country was not ready to face directly the immense amount of death and suffering those atomic bombings caused. It was, unfortunately, veterans groups and members of Congress that brought pressure to bear on the Smithsonian to reduce its exhibit to display only the *Enola Gay*, the plane that dropped the bomb on Hiroshima. After fifty years, the country was unwilling to confront the moral issues involved in those bombings, and it still is.

Falk: A more recent glaring example involves the killing of Osama bin Laden by Navy SEALs in his Pakistan hideout. There is little doubt that bin Laden associated himself significantly with the 9/11 attacks, which certainly constituted a crime against humanity, but whether he was involved in planning and encouraging the attacks is less certain. To kill an unarmed individual accused of a crime, however heinous, is itself a criminal instance of extrajudicial execution. For the president then to celebrate this feat as an occasion of national pride further illustrates the depth to which this national engagement with political violence has extended. Even more disturbing is the degree to which such a governmental performance increases the popularity of the elected leader, in this instance, Barack Obama, sending a signal from the people to the president that successful uses of force against foreign enemies will be rewarded with increased popularity.

Our cultural justifications draw a dangerous distinction between ourselves as good and the enemy or adversary as evil. George W. Bush invoked this distinction often in the period following the 9/11 attacks, and it was effective as a way to loosen the constraints of law and morality in relation to our recourse to war and violence, while depicting the other as barbaric terrorists—or in the domain of entertainment, as "bad guys" we could abuse for the sake of the common good. The Bush presidency justified torture, claiming its effectiveness in eliciting useful information, attempting futilely to appease the moral sensitivities and objections of liberal lawyers by cloaking torture with the euphemism "enhanced interrogation."

I contend that this cultural/moral atmosphere, even aside from the entrenched bureaucratic position of the nuclear establishment, severely weakens the appropriate response to the emergence of nuclear weapons. It is important to be aware of this and to seek to articulate other cultural/moral realities that would lend support to nonviolent and humane initiatives. These more encouraging realities are also part of the American cultural and moral landscape.

Krieger: The gleeful way in which the killing of Osama bin Laden was received in the United States shows that our culture continues to honor and reward violent solutions. Bin Laden was unarmed; he could have been captured and brought to stand trial for his wrongdoing. I doubt, though, that this was an option for the Navy SEALs who raided his compound. It seems likely that they were under orders to find and kill him. His summary execution and the dumping of his body at sea suggest to me that the terror bin Laden inspired in the United States by demonstrating our vulnerability to attack maintains a strong hold on our political culture and imaginations. If we would come to grips with the reality that we are in fact vulnerable to attack, perhaps we would be more cautious in our behavior and more prone to seek diplomatic and legal solutions to conflicts rather than to rely excessively on military solutions.

Morality as a Justification for Militarism

Krieger: In a culture of war, nuclear weapons may be viewed as another, particularly powerful tool in our arsenal of weaponry. This is a dangerous illusion in terms of national and global security. As long as we continue to view these weapons in a positive light, based on our need to justify our use of them, we will find it more difficult to take appropriate actions to rid the world of them. I think we continue to employ a false and self-deluding syllogism: We are a moral people. We used nuclear weapons. The use of nuclear weapons (by us) is moral. A more appropriate and honest syllogism would be: The use of or threat to use nuclear weapons is immoral. We used nuclear weapons. We acted immorally. Perhaps a still more appropriate syllogism would look forward: The use of or threat to use nuclear weapons is immoral. Any country that uses or threatens to use nuclear weapons is acting immorally. Those countries that are currently using or threatening to use nuclear weapons are acting immorally. I would say that the defense of U.S. morality in using nuclear weapons is an impediment to moving the country in the direction of morality and an obstacle to achieving the global abolition of nuclear weapons, which would provide the country with far greater security than do nuclear arms. A recognition that any use of or threat to use nuclear weapons is an immoral act would clear the way for the United States to assert leadership to achieve a world free of nuclear weapons and to eliminate the threat they pose to all peoples.

Falk: I believe you are overstressing the relevance of morality to the guidelines both leaders and the citizenry rely on in relation to attitudes toward war and peace. It is my impression that for the majority, there is an either explicit or implicit acceptance of the ethos that war is hell, a domain within which morality is either absent or limited to vindicating our side and condemning the enemy. Especially here in America, we like to believe that we are engaged in just wars, but more than this, we like to prevail, to win. If that outcome involves highly immoral acts, they are either rationalized as part of a necessary military strategy, information about them is suppressed, or they are explained away as an aberration.

From this perspective, only the realists, what C. Wright Mills long ago memorably identified as "crackpot realists," could shift public and elite perceptions sufficiently to produce politically significant moves toward nuclear disarmament. In effect, creating an atmosphere in which this weaponry was viewed negatively by the realist elite who shape military doctrine in the Pentagon and elsewhere in the government would require a recognition that nuclear weapons have become a serious burden to the pursuit of American foreign policy goals and grand strategy. Henry Kissinger's Gang of Four opened this debate, basically around the loss of control over proliferation, arguing that the American military edge would be dulled, if not lost, unless nuclear weapons were eliminated.

Perhaps this level of realist questioning did allow Obama the political space within which to make his Prague speech in 2009, although it was carefully delimited to signal an absence of any intent to make nuclear disarmament a political project. This signal was sent in two ways: by reaffirming a commitment to deterrence and by indicating that a world without nuclear weapons is a utopian goal not to be achieved in real time. Of course, Obama's speech did appeal to morality, but because his ideas were not presented or implemented as if intended as a political project, it could be regarded as a statement of moral self-regard that established his credentials for global leadership in the immediate post-Bush diplomatic atmosphere. One can contrast the approach to nuclear weapons with that taken by the Obama administration with regard to the war in Afghanistan or the anti-Qaddafi intervention in Libya. The latter are quintessential political projects that exemplify the fusion of morality and politics on behalf of widely endorsed geopolitical goals that are mainly approached within the realist framework of feasibility, costs, and outcomes.

Returning to the political culture, it seems definitely to bypass the inhibitions of law as well as morality, especially in the context of uses of force where international law, including the UN Charter, converge with a moral consensus that formed after World War II prohibiting aggressive war. This broad prohibition was understood to encompass all international uses of force but was subject to two exceptions. First, if the use of force was authorized by the UN Security Council; and second, in cases of self-defense strictly delimited to a forcible response to a prior armed attack across its borders. When George W. Bush vindicated his 2003 decision to attack Iraq without UN authorization, declaring that the United States would never seek "a permission slip" when its national security interests were at stake, he received a thunderous bipartisan ovation from his congressional audience suggesting the irrelevance of international law.

Krieger: Perhaps you are right that I am overstressing the relevance of morality to U.S. geopolitical behavior. Although we rarely behave morally as a nation, we often wrap our behavior in a moral cloak. We frequently build our case for morality around an opposing leader's immorality, as was the case with both Saddam Hussein and Osama bin Laden. Both were men the United States supported and trained before turning against them. In the case of Hussein, painting him as an "evil doer" was a primary justification for initiating an aggressive war against Iraq. In the case of bin Laden, his leadership of al Qaeda justified a global war on terror. Other leaders of al Qaeda have been held without trial, and many, including bin Laden himself, have been summarily executed. Drones, or unmanned aerial vehicles, maneuvered from great distances have become a new favorite means of assassination in this war on terrorism. Of course, it would be viewed as an extreme moral affront if any other nation attempted attacks on U.S. leaders with missiles fired from drones. In 2011, the U.S. government summarily and purposely executed some of its own citizens with drone attacks in Yemen.

Falk: I find that your own words confirm the view that morality is purely a matter of what might be called "public reason" officially invoked to justify behavior, not to determine whether or not to use force. How else can we explain our embracing of ghastly leaders so long as they serve our geopolitical purposes, then our criminalizing of their behavior as soon as their presence becomes an obstacle to our pursuit of national interests? In an important regard, such manipulations of moral arguments are worse than the failure to offer a moral justification for policy as it gives morality a bad name by converting it into a form of hostile propaganda. It either reflects a sentimental and irrelevant political innocence or cloaks essentially opportunistic and often morally unacceptable behavior. I believe we should not couple our genuine moral repudiation of nuclearism with any expectation that American leaders will follow a meaningfully moral path with respect to nuclear weaponry. The most we can expect reasonably is a prudent path, which is preferable to a reckless path, but it falls far short of a morally acceptable path.

Krieger: It does seem that U.S. leaders use morality more as justification for acts deemed to be in the national interest than as a significant factor in actual decision making. I don't think that Henry Kissinger and his colleagues could ever be accused of basing their arguments for the ultimate abolition of nuclear weapons on moral grounds. In fact, there is no indication that morality enters into their calculations, which all seem to be solidly rooted in national interest. Obama, on the other hand, said in his Prague speech that the United States has a moral responsibility to act and to lead. He said, "As a nuclear power, as the only nuclear power to have used a nuclear weapon, the United States has a moral responsibility to act. We cannot succeed in this endeavor alone, but we can lead it, we can start it."[5] Since he pointed to this moral responsibility, however, his actions have been limited. Even were he to try seriously to do more, any such serious moves in the direction of nuclear disarmament would likely be met with a tsunami of opposition from members of Congress. The U.S. Senate gave only conditional approval to New START, demanding in return the modernization of the U.S. nuclear arsenal and its delivery systems. I doubt that Obama's view of the "moral responsibility to act," assuming its sincerity, is widely shared among U.S. leaders, certainly not among members of Congress.

I agree with you that the George W. Bush administration, and President Bush himself, was particularly contemptuous of international law. In a just world, one that took seriously the hard-earned principles deriving from the Nuremberg Trials, both Bush and Dick Cheney would deserve a place on the docket at the International Criminal Court. Until those Nuremberg principles are taken seriously and applied without favor to the leaders of the most powerful countries, morality will always have a second- or third-tier position in our policy making.

Morality and Civil Society Engagement

Falk: Morality is key to the views of those of us in civil society who challenge reliance on, and even possession of, such weaponry of mass destruction. Our position is one of unconditional repudiation of an option to pursue national policy by such immoral means, and although it may be bolstered by pragmatic arguments to the effect that such weaponry unleashes dangerous forces that make its threat or use an extreme instance of self-destructive behavior, the critical argument is about the immorality of the weaponry and is capable of standing alone.

Given this cultural assessment, two things follow: First, we should direct our principal energy as antinuclear advocates and activists toward reshaping the attitudes of the peoples of the world, especially the young; second, we must align our hopes with a popular mobilization of public opinion that alters the cultural outlook sufficiently to support the adoption of nuclear disarmament as a political project by elected leaders. From this perspective, looking to Congress or the president at this time is a misleading diversion, except possibly for the modest purpose of tweaking initiatives that strengthen arms control managerial initiatives. Without a weakening of the current militarist culture, political leaders will be reluctant to challenge the entrenched nuclearism mentioned above and will never do more than make periodic apolitical statements of moral piety at moments of their choosing.

Krieger: To those who make national security policy, positing the immorality of nuclear weapons may appear a weak argument. Such people tend to base their own arguments and calculations on fear of, rather than concern for, "the other." Of course, once an enemy or potential enemy has been thoroughly dehumanized, killing that enemy is perceived as beyond the boundaries of ordinary morality. Without such a warped perspective, it would seem insane to develop security policies based on killing hundreds of millions of innocent people. For me, this raises questions like, Who are we? What kind of a culture would be content to base its security on threatening to murder hundreds of millions of innocent people? Throughout the Cold War, we lived with the threat of mutual assured destruction, which has the apt acronym of MAD, as in crazy. Now the Cold War has ended, but we still live with multiple assured destruction. "Mutual" morphed into "multiple" as an increasing number of countries joined the nuclear club. I also think that we could replace the word "destruction" with the word "delusions." Those responsible for the policy of maintaining nuclear arsenals on hair-trigger alert are delusional if they think it can be maintained indefinitely without dire consequences. In a sane society, people would feel concern about the consequences of murderous behavior. That was the thrust of Albert Camus's argument in his essay "Neither Victims nor Executioners."[6] Morality would lead us to accept Camus's premise of choosing to be neither victims nor executioners, which also seems pragmatic in a nuclear-armed world.

Ending the Culture of War

Krieger: The question before us is, How do we change a culture of war into a culture of peace? I agree with you that it is unlikely to result from the acts of political leaders, at least not without solid support from the citizenry.

I believe the most important challenge of the Nuclear Age is to awaken people everywhere, particularly young people, and engage them in ending both nuclearism and militarism. If we cannot bring about rapid change toward a culture of peace, at least we can plant the seeds. Sometimes that alone is possible, and in a culture of war, speaking out for peace to try to build a movement for abolishing nuclear weapons and war is a means of planting seeds. Good things happen when people do not give up and instead challenge an unjust and immoral system. It is important to recognize this and to persevere in seeking to encourage the breakthrough of shoots of peace that will eventually become the vines that break down the seemingly unassailable walls of militarism.

Falk: I think it entirely correct to insist that, without a culture of peace, there is neither hope for a morally driven approach to nuclear weapons nor a rational and normative questioning of militarism. And I agree that we must do all we can to produce a culture of peace through educational and activist initiatives. Whether some kind of shock to the system will be needed to transform pursuit of a culture of peace into a political project remains an open question. So far, our efforts entail maintaining a vigil for peace in a militarist setting, that is, waiting for something to happen that gives this advocacy of abolition political relevance.

It is disheartening, although hardly surprising, to read that the most respected institution for the American people is the military, despite its extraordinary waste of resources, lack of success, and discrediting behavior, allegations confirmed by WikiLeaks documents on war crimes in Afghanistan, the Abu Ghraib photos, the treatment of Bradley Manning, and the reliance on "enhanced interrogation" within national security circles. Notably, none of the emerging geopolitical actors such as China, India, and Brazil seem nearly as wedded to militarism as the United States; they seem to view the military's role as limited to genuinely defensive purposes, or at most to resolving border and regional issues involving conflicting territorial claims. China, despite internal repression, shows no appetite for challenging American military dominance and is likely to be a very different superpower than was the Soviet Union during the Cold War. Our addictive relationship to militarism is on the level of popular culture, as well as reflective of the material and bureaucratic interests of segments of government and the private sector.

Krieger: If our military is our most respected institution, that says a lot about who we are as a people. By and large, the military is an institution for carrying out orders to apply violence; in other words, the military largely does what it is told to do. It remains true that civilian leaders control the military, and I think this is as it should be, but it seems apparent that, since the Vietnam War, civilian leadership has been even more militant than military leadership. Perhaps this is because elected leaders are lobbied so hard and effectively by corporations that stand to profit from war and its preparations.

Falk: I view the situation somewhat differently. In my view, the political culture has accepted the idea that America's military successes of the past are associated with its achievements as a country, a source of national pride. The corporate profiteers take advantage of these attitudes, which are generally supported in the media. Oddly, the defeat in Vietnam did not raise enduring questions about relying on military approaches to the pursuit of American security in the world, probably because they occurred against the background of the ongoing Cold War, which tended to make most Americans believe that, without U.S. deterrent capabilities, the Soviet Union would attack and occupy more and more countries, eventually diminishing the influence, prosperity, and security of the United States.

Only after World War I did there emerge a period of widespread public hostility toward war as an institution and its market exploitation by private business. Arms dealers were widely referred to as "merchants of death," disarmament was looked upon with favor, and war was generally seen as dysfunctional and unnecessary. The enormous losses sustained in World War I by both sides, the inconsequential impact of its outcome, and its economic, social, and human costs challenged the earlier (and later) glorification of war and admiration for the military as a profession and institution.

Krieger: To view America's military engagements in the past as a source of national pride requires a very selective reading and understanding of history.

The Mexican-American, Spanish-American, Vietnam, and other more recent wars are certainly examples of aggressive and inequitable applications of force in which history should make clear that the U.S. military played the role of bully and for which neither the United States nor its military forces deserve to be honored. That the people of the United States can view their military forces in a largely positive light suggests that the culture is creative in its ability to fashion its history to support myths of its own goodness and exceptionalism. Perhaps this goes to the very roots of what a culture of militarism does so effectively, that is, paint its militarism as a source of pride, no matter the illegality or immorality of the action or the death and destruction it leaves in its wake. It is in a way an extraordinary feat that the United States could use nuclear weapons to devastate the civilian populations of two Japanese cities and find a way to view this as a positive military achievement. It is one thing to appreciate the soldiers who answer the call to arms but quite another to celebrate the military when it is engaged in illegal acts, including aggressive war and war crimes.

Falk: Citizens have an understandable appreciation of the sacrifice made by those who fight in the military on behalf of the country. Often their social circumstances give young people few other career options. The work of the military is seen as supportive of the security and well-being of the society and carries with it risks of death and injury. In these senses, it is an extraordinary thing for someone to be willing to die on behalf of the foreign policy of his or her country, a willingness that matches the readiness to die to defend one's nation against an attacking enemy. I find hard to grasp, morally or politically, the disposition of the government and society to send its young men and women to distant battlefields to take part in wars between opposed national, religious, ethnic, or geographic factions that have little or no bearing on the global balance of power. Not only do such wars cause widespread death and destruction, but it also involves the United States in roles that have given rise to intense anti-Americanism in many parts of the world, especially in this postcolonial era. At this point, anti-Americanism has eclipsed resentment against the former European colonial powers. This has produced a vicious circle of violence in which military and political intervention overseas generates counterviolence in response, epitomized by the 9/11 attacks, and such provocations in turn stimulate efforts to remove the threats by further foreign interventions.

The global projection of American power and the legitimate grievances of non-Western peoples are never taken into account in shaping these interventionary missions.

Krieger: I agree with you that it is an extraordinary thing for people to be willing to sacrifice their lives for the foreign policy of their country. That is very different from being willing to defend one's country. But, of course, a lot of confusion is sown in this area. In a culture of militarism, young men and women are generally misled by patriotic sentiments and the promise of glory. Or, they may be induced by economic or educational benefits. When it comes to war, political leaders have a duty to act both morally and responsibly to protect the young people in the military who are dependent on their honesty and good judgment. All too often, these leaders fail in both respects. They commit the military to wars based on misrepresentations or outright lies, as was the case with the Vietnam and Iraq wars. These leaders commit the military to wars without constitutional authorization and in violation of international law, as was the case again with both the Vietnam and Iraq wars. Most unfortunately, this is done with little protest from the American people, who are largely silent. Without conscription, the people seem to have lost interest in America's wars. They participate in a culture of militarism that does not question war or the leaders who initiate and sustain it.

Learning the Wrong Lessons from War

Krieger: U.S. presidents appear to have a hard time saying no to war, and they are often rewarded with higher levels of public support when they choose war over peaceful solutions in conflict situations. That support does not seem to hold up over time when we appear to be stalemated and our troops are taking heavy losses, as in the Vietnam and Iraq wars. We seem to have retained very few of the lessons of our loss in Vietnam that might have limited our militarism, though. On the other hand, the political elite have learned numerous tactics that have insulated subsequent wars from public influence. Among the changes in the U.S. approach to militarism that have made it more effective are ending conscription, embedding reporters in military units, and not showing photographs of returning coffins.

You raise an intriguing point when you talk about our having an "addictive relationship to militarism" in both popular culture and at the level of government. Addictive behavior is that to which one continues to return, no matter how unsatisfactory the results. There is a circularity to our addiction to militarism. We prepare for war with vast resources and then find it is our most available tool for dealing with a conflict. After each war, we attempt to strengthen the tool and keep it ready for the next use. All the while, we observe special holidays around our militarism, such as Veterans Day and Memorial Day. National leaders are obsessed with praising the soldiers who fight our wars, the men and women who are the tools of our militarism. The United States needs a support group of friends and allies who will help us break our powerful addiction to war and to nuclear weapons. This could, in fact, be a moral quest with a spiritual base. More likely perhaps, it could be a secular quest led by universities and the media. Of course, this seems a long shot, as nearly all of our institutions, including academia and the media, are influenced by and tend to support our general culture of militarism. The institutions that have escaped this indoctrination into militarism are at present few and not sufficiently influential, but they are capable of planting seeds of peace within the broader culture.

The Role of the Media

Falk: The media is influential as a kind of self-censoring and disciplinary element sustaining the culture of war. Several aspects of this role can be noted: The most respected organs of influence (e.g., *New York Times,* CNN) when debating war/peace issues, including those involving nuclear weaponry, exclude the relevance of international law unless it favors the use of force, focus on feasibility and costs as principally analyzed by retired military officers or conservative think tank national security specialists, and exclude advocates of nuclear disarmament or opponents of violent geopolitics. In effect, pro-military extremists are treated as falling within responsible boundaries of debate, while antimilitary moderates are excluded. Richard Perle and Paul Wolfowitz are good examples of those treated by the media as "credible" commentators, while persons such as yourself or Christopher Weeramantry are regarded as beyond the pale.

It is true that there exist through the Internet and alternative media some outlets for critical views directed at nuclearism and militarism, but even here the more influential public broadcasting and television channels are careful not to go beyond these boundaries of self-censorship. Similarly, books by those of us who clearly situate ourselves within a culture of peace are almost never reviewed and rarely published by mainstream publishers. It is quite remarkable how this country is able to sustain the myth of freedom while policing so effectively the expression of thought seen as hostile to prevailing ideas. As Noam Chomsky has argued for years, indoctrination in a liberal society does not need to prohibit critical ideas because it is so adept at ignoring them.

Krieger: The inability of opponents of militarism and nuclearism to gain access to the most influential media makes the job of bringing about change nearly impossible. When war is on the table, the most important print and electronic media sources make it a point to bring in former military officers as consultants. The discussion turns more to strategy and tactics for pursuing war than to the soundness of the reasons for engaging in it. I don't think I have ever seen a mainstream media consultant brought in to discuss the illegality of aggressive war or the importance of adhering to the Nuremberg principles. A similar critique could be made of the mainstream media's approach to our obligations under international law to achieve the total elimination of nuclear weapons. In these areas, there has never been an adequate national or global dialogue, and such dialogue is badly needed. Some discussion does take place in alternative media, such as on the Internet, and perhaps this will build a base for a movement to end the culture of war. But if the murderous tragedy and fiasco of the Vietnam War was not enough to turn the culture of war toward a culture of peace, we can see how difficult it is to swim against these cultural currents.

The Systemic Nature of Militarism and Nuclearism

Falk: Perhaps this culture of war goes deeper. I'm thinking about the pleasure associated with being a dominant force in history. Somehow, many individuals gain in personal stature by identifying with the strength associated (falsely) with national military capabilities. National "greatness" seems to add meaning to the lives of many ordinary citizens, and not just in America. I recall a poll in Russia not long after the Soviet Union's collapse that asked citizens to name their most favorite and most hated leaders: Mikhail Gorbachev, admired around the world, was by far the most hated in his native country, outpolling even Adolf Hitler and Joseph Stalin; oddly, Stalin was on both lists, ranking just behind Vladimir Lenin on the most favored list. This ranking shows that leaders who uphold the geopolitical status of a country will be admired no matter what horrible crimes they commit, while those associated with its decline will be despised despite consistently honorable behavior.

Where does this lead us? I believe it mainly helps us to see clearly the systemic nature of the problem and to resist false expectations that political democracy or constitutional rights can overcome our national attachment to nuclearism. It also means that we should not dilute our message by thinking we can charm the leadership of the country into accepting a culture of peace. This leadership would be viewed, by many in and out of government who presently exert influence, as treasonous, at this point, if it were to adopt the sorts of antiwar positions that we advocate, or lent consistent support to a principled repudiation of violent geopolitics, or insisted that this country and other leading states should be held accountable under the rule of law in the conduct of foreign policy.

Krieger: The culture of war does go deep. With nuclear weapons, it goes far too deep. It takes us to the precipice of annihilation. While many people in the United States seem to take personal pride in U.S. military strength and nuclear prowess, such prowess does very little to improve our well-being. The celebration of national "greatness" through military might has always benefitted the few at the expense of the many. It has built empires, but while some last longer than others, history teaches us that empires always fall. This has been true for Egypt, Athens, Sparta, Macedonia, Rome, and other empires throughout the ages. In more modern times, it has been true of France, Germany, Britain, and the Soviet Union. It will also be true of the United States. The difference now, in the Nuclear Age, is that the United States has set in motion forces that could take global civilization down with it. That is why nuclearism is so dangerous to all countries without exception. That is why our culture of militarism, in which nuclearism is embedded, must be turned toward peace.

It is also why leadership from below is essential. It is why, in speaking of nuclear weapons, we must advocate clearly and forcefully for abolition rather than arms control, which has been manipulated to fit the culture of militarism. It is also why accountability for wrongdoing under the law remains critical. It is why the rule of law matters and why the Nuremberg principles must be given new life in the twenty-first century. The leaders of all states that commit heinous crimes under international law—crimes against peace, war crimes, and crimes against humanity—must be held to account.

Finally, I would make the point that the dangers of a culture of militarism in the United States are compounded by cultures of complacency and greed. The latter two traits combine to give militarism a free rein in infiltrating our leading institutions and guiding our policies. Complacency and greed are the enemies of democracy and peace, and they reinforce one another. The path to democracy and peace must run through public engagement in the political realm to assure that justice is done and that our imperialistic and militaristic impulses are controlled. President John F. Kennedy, who fought in World War II, said, "War will exist until that distant day when the conscientious objector enjoys the same reputation and prestige that the warrior does today."[7] We need to educate people throughout the world to be conscientious objectors to war and militarism. We need to learn from Gandhi and Martin Luther King Jr. what it means to be nonviolent warriors for peace.

Falk: While I affirm my affinity with these antiwar sentiments and my thankfulness for their existence in our heritage and at the margins of our political culture, I do not take great comfort from them in relation to the challenge of nuclearism or militarism. Is not the primary historical lesson taught by Gandhi and King that change comes only in response to popular mobilization that is sufficiently sustained to cause an established order to give ground? As long as the criticism of British colonialism or racism was limited to moral indictments, nothing much happened that threatened these oppressive circumstances. The unjust arrangements adopted to uphold the status quo, including resorting to repressive violence to discourage popular challenges, continued. The persistence and courage of Gandhi and King paid off in the end but also made martyrs of these two extraordinary individuals.

The Need for Moral Leadership

Krieger: Gandhi and King were indeed extraordinary individuals, leaders of great social movements for change. Both showed exceptional courage and perseverance. Both based their efforts on respect for human dignity without consideration of race or nationality. Each made the moral case that his cause was right, and both were undaunted by the power of the state to oppose them. Both showed that change was possible and paid the ultimate price for their leadership.

It is quite shocking that the United States has produced so few political leaders capable of bringing moral vision and force to their work. Such leaders almost invariably come from outside the power elite, often rising from the ranks of the oppressed. In the United States, most significant moral leadership has come from people of color. In relation to militarism and nuclearism, the situation is more difficult. The injustice is not to an identifiable group from which leaders might emerge. The threat is to all of us, but it is almost imperceptible when viewed against the backdrop of a culture of militarism. The threat is particularly difficult to address because to do so looks like an attack on the patriotic love of country, the mask behind which militarism so often hides and thrives.

Falk: With respect to nuclearism and war, we are addressing a more abstract and remote reality that lacks the immediacy of colonialism or racism, which are felt daily by those they victimize. As mentioned earlier, only a temporary disillusionment with war in 1918 moved the country in a direction that could have led over time to a more peaceful world, but even that initiative was blunted early when the United States refused to join the League of Nations conceived by Woodrow Wilson as a paradigm-changing war-prevention initiative. Worse still was the belief that came to be accepted in many influential circles that the failure of the liberal democracies to maintain strong military establishments had encouraged Nazi Germany and Imperial Japan to embark on a path of aggressive warfare culminating in World War II. This experience was summarized as "the lesson of Munich," the scene of alleged appeasement of Hitler as a result of Western Europe's military weakness. Further, the victory in that war was hailed as just and necessary, and the defeat of fascism and antidemocratic militarism gave rise to a new era dominated by belief in the link between military strength and national security, and even peace. This notion lasted throughout the Cold War, and many even credit it with averting a third world war fought with nuclear weaponry. Over the decades since 1945, the major expansion of the peacetime military budget and governmental infrastructure reinforced this historical experience that seemed to vindicate the belief that military dominance contributes to national security.

That is, the advent of nuclear weapons happened to coincide with a historical moment in which the role of war was viewed in a positive light. This historical conditionality of cultural perceptions of war and military capabilities is clarifying as it suggests that in some settings there could be a turn against war making and related activities. The failure of several recent wars, the shift of competitive economic advantage in world trade and investment to less militaristic countries, and the concern over a growing deficit may induce a new period of skepticism about the value of maintaining a huge and expensive war machine, given the realities of the early twenty-first century. Notably, the BRIC countries (Brazil, Russia, India, and China), with the possible exception of Russia, are basing their rise to global prominence on soft power as expressed by sustained economic development and nonviolent diplomacy. Perhaps part of our job as morally and politically motivated critics of nuclearism and militarism is to encourage this delegitimizing of the war system, both for intrinsic reasons associated with the rejection of violent geopolitics and also for pragmatic reasons arising from the altered nature of world order, especially considering the rise of soft power, the declining efficacy of hard power, and the networked nature of economic globalization.

Awakening the Public to the Real Costs of Militarism and Nuclearism

Krieger: There is no doubt that nuclearism's abstractness and remoteness make it difficult to confront directly. This seems to me to be less the case when it comes to militarism. In recent times, in the aftermath of 9/11, the military has engaged in wars in Afghanistan and Iraq, both of which are highly questionable in terms of what they have accomplished and how much they have cost in lives and treasure. The public support for these wars has been based largely on false arguments of retribution for 9/11 and a generalized fear of future terrorist attacks. But these wars also rely on the silence and docility of the public engendered by a culture of militarism. Awakening the public to the real costs of war and militarism, as well as of nuclearism, is a necessary step in beginning to turn the United States toward a culture of peace.

No other country maintains such expansive and expensive machinery of war as the United States. Economic limitations alone make it seem unlikely that this machinery is sustainable. It is possible that economic circumstances could force the United States to reevaluate its extensive commitment to its military forces, including its nuclear arsenal. I believe that nothing would benefit the United States more than a turn to a culture of peace with a strong preference for the application of soft power based on a foundation of justice, fairness, and morality. As things stand now, the United States, despite its enormous military might, could be destroyed by a country or extremist group with a few nuclear weapons. Could the United States retaliate? Yes, but only if it could identify its assailants and they possessed a territory to retaliate against. Could it prevent such an attack? Probably not. Nuclearism is a recipe for disaster that is a blind spot within a culture of militarism. The only way out of this dilemma is to shift positions on nuclear weapons and seek their universal abolition. By leading in this direction, the United States would be acting both responsibly and morally. It would also be enhancing its own security, while taking an important step toward a culture of peace.

CHAPTER 9

Nuclear Weapons and Democracy

Krieger: Democracy is a broad sharing in the process of political decision making. Representative democracy involves electing representatives to participate in the process of political decision making. In this dialogue, we will address questions concerning the effects nuclear weapons have on democracy and the effects democracy has on nuclear weapons. History reveals that both democracies and totalitarian states have been successful in developing nuclear weapons. Both the United States and the Soviet Union, the first two countries to develop nuclear weapons, did so through programs shrouded in secrecy. The United States, despite its democratic institutions, was able to develop nuclear weapons with a secret wartime budget for the project and minimal knowledge of it in the Congress. While President Franklin D. Roosevelt was well briefed on the atomic bomb project, it was barely known to his vice president, Harry S. Truman, until he acceded to the presidency following Roosevelt's death in April 1945 and was briefed by Secretary of War Henry Stimson. The U.S. public for over three years was unaware of the Manhattan Project to create an atomic bomb and did not find out about it until Hiroshima and Nagasaki were bombed in the final days of World War II.

Secrecy and Disinformation

Krieger: Prior to the U.S. bombing of Hiroshima, the War Department hired a *New York Times* reporter, William L. Laurence, to tell the story of the bomb that the government wanted shared with the public. For his reporting on the bombing of Hiroshima, Laurence was fed misinformation by the U.S. government. He denied, for example, that radiation was killing people. Thus, the creation of the first atomic weapons was initially kept secret from the public, and then the public was misinformed about the bomb by a respected science reporter whose integrity was compromised after he was secretly hired by the War Department to tell the story in positive and heroic terms.[1] The birth of the bomb in secrecy was justified in the name of national security in time of war. The misuse of the press to report on the use of the bomb was perhaps an even greater affront to democratic institutions. Wherever the bomb has been developed, it has happened in secrecy, without the transparency required for healthy democratic debate. There have always been deep concerns that the spread of knowledge about the bomb would increase the dangers of nuclear proliferation and, thus, the risks to national and global security. These concerns, while well founded, have put additional strains on democratic processes and helped to underpin cultures of militarism.

The founders of the United States thought the decision to go to war was far too important to be left in the hands of a single individual; thus, they explicitly gave this power, in the U.S. Constitution, to the Congress rather than the president. Under the Constitution, entry of the United States into war requires a declaration of war by the Congress. While this mandate has been largely ignored since World War II, it was a wise decision on the part of the founders, aimed at making the decision to go to war both more democratic and more difficult. The accretion of power by the president to make war has been unconstitutional and undemocratic, even though, in the post–World War II culture of militarism, Congress has generally been prepared to support any war that a president sought to initiate. The capability of using nuclear weapons concentrates even more power in the hands of the U.S. president and further undermines the possibility of democratic process on decisions that could result in massive human and planetary devastation and even lead to the destruction of the United States itself through retaliation by another country. Nuclear weapons give rise to potentially world-destroying concentrations of power, not only in the United States but in each of the nine countries that currently possess nuclear arsenals, as well as in the countries that may acquire nuclear weapons in the future. Nuclear weapons put world-ending power in the hands of a small number of individuals, power that undermines the very foundations of democracy. These weapons are the capstone of a culture of militarism, and the requirements for their control and use are incompatible with democratic institutions and practices.

Falk: I think you are right to remind us about these two central features of the way in which democracy and nuclear weapons have interacted ever since the first efforts to produce the bomb: first, the reliance on secrecy to preclude debate among citizens as to the morality and prudence of developing, possessing, and using weaponry of mass destruction; and second, the selective release of information in such a manner so as to enhance misleadingly the persuasiveness of arguments justifying the weaponry and minimizing its problematic aspects (e.g., initially suppressing information about the radiation effects).

In my view, secrecy with respect to a matter of such ultimate importance to the well-being of the citizenry is incompatible with democracy in fundamental respects, as seen from the perspective of both citizens and their elected representatives. Removing a decision of such great consequence from the national marketplace of ideas implicitly subscribes to an authoritarian mode of political leadership, although this is regarded as an inevitable feature of wartime and, more generally, of a war system. As you point out, even leaders avoided appropriate disclosure to one another, illustrated by the withholding of information about the Manhattan Project from the vice president, the person constitutionally designated to step in for the president in the event of his or her death or disability. The failure to share this information with Truman, the individual who eventually bore the responsibility for dropping the bombs on Japanese cities, seems to stretch the powers of constitutional government beyond their limits even in the absence of some legal requirement to share such vital information.

There is another point about the veil of secrecy. The decision to develop and possibly use the bomb has multiple ramifications for countries other than those that possess nuclear weaponry, and yet they have no opportunity to engage in a discussion about the permissibility of such weaponry. When it comes to nuclear weaponry, there is not only a democratic deficit when considering the relationship of state and society but also a disenfranchisement of the peoples and their representatives who reside in other countries affected by nuclear weapons policy. This is a radical demonstration that a world of sovereign states can only handle the challenge of nuclearism by either a prohibitory or a permissive rule that applies to all states. But world order is tainted with illegitimacy by the claims of some states to possess and use the weapons and by a nonproliferation regime that privileges the nuclear weapon states (and effectively abandons the treaty obligation to engage in nuclear disarmament).

The Failure of Democracy in the United States

Krieger: The people of the United States cannot be held to account for the failure of democratic practice with regard to the creation of nuclear weapons or the decision to use these weapons in World War II. Since the people had no information at the time about the project to create the bomb, and since the decision to use it was not a matter of public discussion or debate, the people cannot be considered responsible or culpable for the decisions that were made. On the other hand, once the existence and use of the bomb becomes public knowledge, the people in a democracy have a responsibility for what happens next. This is where I think democracy in the United States has failed. It is also where national security concerns, based in large part on the dangers of nuclear weapons and their proliferation, have fashioned a culture of war. This culture of war has become the new norm. In such a culture, sometimes referred to as a national security state, democratic practice contracts and becomes subordinate to national security concerns. For example, the people had an opportunity to make their voices heard with regard to the rapid expansion of the U.S. nuclear arsenal and also with regard to the decision to develop thermonuclear weapons, but they did not choose to engage. In the early 1950s, a time dominated by anticommunist witch hunts, the voices of dissenters were suppressed, and there was widespread deference to national security "experts" who supported ever more extreme forms of militarism and weaponry. Even as prominent an expert as J. Robert Oppenheimer, the wartime scientific director of the Manhattan Project, was stripped of his security clearance for the underlying reason that he opposed the development of thermonuclear weapons.

Falk: You are certainly correct in the narrow sense of stressing the necessary connection between knowledge and responsibility. The American people cannot be held responsible for the development of the bomb, which was brought into being by a narrow governmental elite working with a select group of scientists and engineers. I would still attribute responsibility to the citizenry for creating the expectations that activities undertaken by the leadership for the sake of a war effort or in the name of national security were above public scrutiny if done in good faith. The citizenry had abdicated responsibility for the security of society long before the Manhattan Project was launched, and the subsequent utter absence of public objection seemed to vindicate the work being carried out in secret and the whole notion of introducing such a weaponry under the conditions that existed in 1945. I am claiming that even without explicit knowledge, an implicit acquiescence resulting in complicity has persisted up to the present.

It was possible to justify the secrecy of the developmental phase to avoid informing the German government, which might have responded by making a greater effort, but after the German surrender, there were far fewer grounds for withholding information about the development of such a weapon, given its predictably game-changing effects on future warfare and diplomacy.

Krieger: I think you are right that releasing public information on the Manhattan Project during the war would have motivated Germany to work more intensely on its bomb project and would rightly have been viewed as endangering the Allied war effort. Such information on the new weapon could have been released to the public after Germany's surrender. At that time, however, the scientists on the Manhattan Project had not yet completed and tested the new weapon. It took more than two months after the German surrender on May 8, 1945, to complete the first bomb and test it at Alamogordo, New Mexico, on July 16, 1945. The government could well have been reluctant to release this information with an unfinished and untested weapon. There were also internal discussions within the government and the Manhattan Project about conducting a demonstration of the bomb in a Japanese harbor rather than using it to attack cities. That proposal was rejected. The U.S. government did not see a need for public information and discussion about the new weapon until it was used on Japan. Government leaders deemed decisions concerning the use of nuclear weapons to be rightly placed in their own hands. And, as you say, the public has acquiesced in this position over the years by their complacency. This acquiescence has continued throughout the Nuclear Age and continues today. In many respects, we may view this as a failure of democracy on arguably the most important survival issue in human history.

The First Global Weapons and the Culture of War

Krieger: I agree with your perspective that decisions on nuclear weapons affect people throughout the world and that the world's people are effectively disenfranchised in the decision-making process. Nuclear weapons are the first global weapons. They threaten everyone on the planet. As much as any other factor at work today, these weapons mold us into a global society. In doing so, they help those who are attentive to see the democratic deficits that exist at the international level. State sovereignty stands in the way of a more democratic world order, and the perceived national security of nuclear-armed nations stands in the way of global security. One of the most apparent shortcomings in the international system has been the failure to make the Non-Proliferation Treaty (NPT) universal, despite the fact that all but three countries in the world have ratified it. This vast majority of the world's states cannot impose their democratic will on Israel, India, and Pakistan, which never ratified the treaty, or on North Korea, which has withdrawn from the treaty on the basis of its national security interests. A further shortcoming of the NPT is that the vast majority of the non–nuclear weapon states that are party to the treaty have not been able to impose their democratic will on the five NPT nuclear weapon states to fulfill their treaty obligations to pursue and achieve nuclear disarmament. All of these shortcomings of the NPT make the likelihood of nuclear weapons proliferating to other states and to nonstate extremists more likely.

Falk: In my view, the secrecy surrounding the bomb, as well as its relevance to a triumphalist ending of World War II, has encouraged further passivity among the citizenry of nuclear weapon states, which is a chilling commentary on the failure of a democratic polity to uphold either its right of participation or its expectations that the government will follow international law. If the most important kind of security policy is shrouded in secrecy, including the doctrines surrounding the threat and possible future use of nuclear weapons, then the public is indirectly encouraged to accept their more general irrelevance to policy making with respect to the security domain. It is not surprising from this perspective that the Constitutional role assigned to Congress with respect to war making has been tacitly abandoned in the Nuclear Age without more than an occasional whimper. I find that this deference on security policy and war/peace issues over the decades has had a corrosive effect on the quality of democratic life in this country, and presumably the same is true in other countries that have nuclear weapons programs.

The underlying question is whether the concerns about security were ever of sufficient magnitude to justify these sacrifices of democratic political life. There are two significant historical arguments. The first relates to anxiety that if the United States had not developed the weaponry, there existed a credible risk that Nazi Germany would have done so and then prevailed in the conflict or at least inflicted horrifying levels of destructive harm. We now know that Germany had such a program to develop nuclear weapons, although there is some disagreement about whether its main nuclear scientists were working to develop them with maximum zeal. The question posed is whether, given the knowledge available during World War II, it was a responsible decision to embark on the Manhattan Project despite the practical consequence of encroaching on the guardianship roles of citizens and elected representatives and deliberately fashioning a type of indiscriminate and poisonous weaponry that was intrinsically unlawful and immoral.

The second historically rooted question is whether, given the strategic calculations in 1945, it was reasonable to drop atomic bombs on Japanese cities to save American lives that would otherwise be lost in an invasion of the Japanese homeland or to scare the Soviet Union out of contesting American ambitions in the Pacific region after the war. Here again, the decision was made as if it were a normal battlefield calculation, although later revisionist history has cast doubt on whether the same strategic results could not have been achieved by diplomacy rather than through the atomic incineration of Hiroshima and Nagasaki. But suppose Japan was perceived at the time as not being prepared to surrender, would this have made the attacks less unlawful or immoral? Of course, strategic bombing with conventional explosives had already taken place in Germany and Japan on a massive scale, making the use of the atomic bomb seem like less of a rupture with past behavior or with the law of war.

Krieger: It seems to me that nuclear weapons, by their nature and the threat posed by their spread to other countries, demand a high level of secrecy, which may simply be incompatible with democratic practice. For the most part, the scientists engaged in the Manhattan Project thought they were developing a powerful new weapon to use as a deterrent in the event that Germany succeeded in developing such a weapon. This turned out not to be the view of the political leaders who ultimately decided to use the atomic bombs on Hiroshima and Nagasaki, and their views carried far more weight than those of the scientists. Of course, the views of the people, who did not even know of the project to create the bomb, were not taken into consideration, except to surmise that they would be angry if they found out this weapon, developed at great wartime expense, had not been used as soon as it was available.

The National Security State and Democracy

Krieger: I think there may be a more general principle at work here, which is that in times of war, democratic processes contract, while in times of peace, they at least have the potential to expand. In a sense, nuclear weapons have put the countries that possess them and their allies on a permanent war footing. We even refer to the four decades of nuclear standoff between the United States and Soviet Union as the Cold War. Although the Cold War has ended, nuclear weapons still have a corrosive effect on democratic practices. I think it is fair to say that national security policies controlled by a relatively small group of individuals and not subject to broad public debate, particularly nuclear weapons policies, diminish democracy. The secrecy surrounding these policies also creates greater uncertainty and distrust in the international system. While there are still places for the public to enter the discussion, few members of the public choose to do so. Examples of places where public concern could make a difference include the debates on military expenditures and the deployment of missile defense systems that Russia so strongly opposes.

Falk: These reflections of ours on the Nuclear Age raise broad and profound issues of security and survival in relation to the proper functioning of a democratic society. How important is the survival of any particular state, including our own, as compared to adhering to basic norms of morality and law and as compared to the survival of civilization or even the species? What social forces should decide such issues? Is the grand strategy of a state beyond the domain of democratic decision making and legal or moral accountability? Is national security policy inherently authoritarian, an exception to the potentialities of democratic and law-abiding governance? Part of the decline of democracy in our time arises, in my view, because we do not even ask such questions, much less attempt to answer them. The reality of democracy is most insidiously diminished by invisible encroachments that society hardly even notices, which should remind us of Thomas Jefferson's insistence that sustaining democracy depends on the vigilance of its citizenry. Yet, we have drifted so far in the direction of normalizing this reliance on nuclear weaponry as to make it feel utopian, or even slightly subversive, to raise such doubts or even to pose questions.

Krieger: You pose the question, How important is the survival of any particular state? It is an important question because of the International Court of Justice's inability to say in its advisory opinion whether, under the current state of international law, it would be legal or illegal to use or threaten to use nuclear weapons when the very survival of a state was at stake. It must be remembered, though, that the Court also said that any use of nuclear weapons that violates international humanitarian law would be illegal. This leads me to the conclusion that any use of or threat to use nuclear weapons would be illegal, regardless of whether the very survival of a state were at stake. I think the answer to your question depends upon where one sits. The survival of a particular state will always be of critical importance to the people within that state, certainly more so than to the people of some other state. This does not, however, give them the right to use nuclear weapons in defense of that state. It does give them the opportunity now, before it is too late, to take steps to demand that all the nuclear weapon states fulfill their obligations under international law to pursue negotiations in good faith for nuclear disarmament in all its aspects.

The other questions that you pose go to the heart of the tension between the national security state and democracy. The national security state tends toward secrecy, restriction of information, closed decision making, and authoritarian practices. Democracy requires shared information, openness, and the ability to participate in key decision making. Key decisions, such as to go to war or to develop new nuclear weapons systems, often have the potential to result in large scale loss of life. The absence of widespread dialogue and debate in democratic societies on these questions suggests a level of complacency that is deeply detrimental to both democracy and national security. That this broader dialogue is missing in our democracy demonstrates that it does not stand on firm ground. Initiating such a dialogue in the United States, the country that must at least help lead the way out of the nuclear weapons era, is one of the most important tasks of those who are committed to a safer and saner future, free of nuclear threat. But developing such a dialogue in the United States alone is not sufficient. It must be a global dialogue that begins with an acknowledgment of the risks that nuclear weapons pose to civilization and to all people everywhere.

A New Global Dialogue on Nuclearism

Krieger: If normalizing nuclear weapons within the context of the national security state has lulled people into complacency, we must find a way to break through to new levels of democratic concern for life rooted in compassion, morality, and more effective international law. Nuclear weapons make it necessary to bring human compassion and morality into the public marketplace of ideas, leading an awakened global citizenry to challenge the national security state and its reliance on nuclear weapons. Opening a serious and spirited global dialogue on nuclear dangers and the corrosive effects of nuclear weapons on democracy may be one of the most important steps that citizens in democracies can take in acting for their own security as well as that of humanity as a whole, including future generations.

Falk: I agree with you that initiating a global dialogue on nuclear weapons policy in relation to law, morality, and prudence could have a powerful consciousness-raising and even mobilizing effect, encouraging the formation of a political movement challenging nuclearism and making the goal of denuclearization a realistic political project. That seems to me more likely to be effective than the top-down antinuclear realism of Henry Kissinger's Gang of Four because it would pose a political challenge, not just advance a rational argument. At the same time, it seems difficult to stimulate such a dialogue without some catastrophic historical event first puncturing the balloon of public apathy. Such an event might be a use of or deadly accident involving nuclear weapons or the acquisition of such weaponry by an extremist nonstate actor.

Krieger: You identify a serious dilemma: how to stimulate public discussion of and engagement in this issue of human survival, absent making the issue more tangible by some use of or threat to use a nuclear weapon. We are tasked with awakening the public imagination before a nuclear war or accident takes its toll, and I think there needs to be a political challenge coming from below, but it would be helpful and maybe necessary also to have political leaders espousing nuclear dangers. Interplay between political leaders among themselves and with the public in a democracy would help in stimulating public engagement. Rational arguments do not seem to be sufficient to awaken the public imagination. Various forms of art must also be brought to bear on the issue in order to bring human emotions and instincts into the mix. Another problem is that this issue seems to require broad and long-term thinking by a public that has become accustomed to narrow and short-term thinking.

The Death of Democracy and Ethics

Falk: I think another consideration deserves reflection. What if democracy has itself been superseded by the realities of the Nuclear Age? It seems too easy to deceive or manipulate the public or to encourage postures of apathy and denial with respect to certain risks and threats that are abstract and remote. From this point of view, only a guardian elite government would have the understanding and capacity to opt for denuclearization. In effect, democracy dies with the advent of nuclearism, and it is only a question of whether its death is acknowledged or not.

With an outlook not so different from that attributed by Plato to his ideal rulers, I suggest that only benevolent authoritarians would have the will and capability to renounce the nuclear option on behalf of a sovereign state. This is an abstract and hypothetical argument, as it seems highly unlikely that such a leadership will emerge in any of the nuclear weapon states, and certainly not within the United States. Even theoretically, there are problems with an authoritarian scenario, including the possibility that an entrenched nuclear establishment would assassinate such rulers rather than allow itself to be deprived of nuclear weaponry. It does give this way of thinking some plausibility, however, that the countries that have backed away from nuclear weapons have been governed by authoritarian leaders. Muammar Qaddafi's Libya was possibly the best example.

Krieger: I think you perhaps go too far to say that "democracy dies with the advent of nuclearism." Clearly, nuclearism, with its strong tendencies toward secrecy and authoritarianism, diminishes democracy, but only insofar as the people acquiesce and are content to remain complacent bystanders. I continue to believe that the potential of democracy, but only of an active and engaged democracy, offers a way out.

Benevolent authoritarians are not so easy to find and are probably contradictions in terms. At any rate, such leaders are highly likely to be more authoritarian than benevolent. We surely cannot count on the rise any time soon of philosopher kings or magicians who will bring wisdom to bear on nuclear issues or wave away the threats posed by militarism and nuclearism. Solving these problems will require engaged citizens and effective democracy, at least as a starting point. I can't see any other way.

Falk: We are dealing with at least three sets of issues, I believe. First, can the moral and legal sensitivities of democratic societies be aroused sufficiently to turn belatedly against nuclear weaponry? Second, is it more likely that an authoritarian leadership can reverse direction at this stage and work more effectively toward a world without nuclear weapons? And finally, are the answers to such questions more difficult for the United States than other countries such as Russia and China?

Krieger: It is not only moral and legal issues that can awaken and engage the public. Issues of personal, as well as national, security related to nuclear weapons can as well. If the public actually felt threatened, that would be a cause for engagement, awakening the sleeping tiger of democratic dissent. While authoritarian leaders can potentially fast-track nuclear disarmament measures, I suspect that they are neither more nor less likely to do so than democratic leaders. In viewing the situation as it exists vis-à-vis the United States, Russia, and China, I don't think that democratic processes are currently impacting disarmament activities. The United States and

Russia, which have the vast majority of the world's nuclear weapons, are reducing their arsenals slowly, but they are also modernizing them. China is maintaining a minimum nuclear deterrent force, while keeping its nuclear warheads separated from their delivery vehicles. It is also modernizing its nuclear forces.

I would say that the major obstacles to more rapid nuclear disarmament are the slow pace of the United States and its insistence on deployment of missile defenses, which Russia views as a threat. Thus, perceptions of national security, not issues of immorality or illegality, are driving nuclearism and impeding nuclear disarmament. Somehow, such considerations of national security must be taken out of the exclusive province of political elites and become a focus of democratic concern. I feel that is the principal challenge of civil society organizations such as the Nuclear Age Peace Foundation—that is, finding a way to awaken and engage a slumbering and far too complacent public on this issue of supreme importance to humanity's future.

Shocking the Public Awake

Falk: But David, with all due respect, the Nuclear Age Peace Foundation has made this effort for more than twenty-five years, including during periods of the Cold War when substantial portions of the citizenry were alarmed about the dangers of nuclear war. I do not see much hope if reliance is placed solely on an educational and consciousness-raising process, even with a measure of sympathy in higher echelons of political leadership, without some type of "shock" to the system that arouses the public sufficiently to give rise to militant activism. Of course, there is always the possibility that a crusading and charismatic personality will emerge to take on the challenge of nuclearism, generating a movement from below that reinforces doubts that have been growing about the strategic value of nuclear weaponry, given the dangers of further proliferation, use by nonstate actors, and transnational black markets in nuclear materials and knowhow. Martin Luther King Jr. did this for civil rights in the United States, as did Gandhi in India when he led a movement to challenge British colonial rule, but no such personality has emerged in relation to nuclear weaponry. Linus Pauling did wage a successful crusade against nuclear testing in the atmosphere, and

Helen Caldicott was effective in the 1980s in raising fears about a range of dangers arising from nuclearism. These individuals had an impact because they were crusaders who were able to make the threat of nuclear weaponry seem real and tangible. Unlike with racism or British colonialism, especially in the absence of severe global conflict between dominant political actors as was the case during the Cold War, it is difficult to overcome the abstraction of the threat and the extent to which governmental claims of competence in relation to national security quell criticism. This returns us to a focus on the ineptitude of democracies in dealing with an issue of this kind, given the underlying political culture that is trustful of the military, respectful of the bureaucratic guardians of national security, and easily manipulated by claims of secrecy or the selective use of leaked information. Part of the mix of resistant elements includes a corporatized media that does not often raise challenging questions in the realm of national security, especially to the extent that private-sector interests are at stake.

Krieger: Perhaps you are right to be skeptical of the degree of success that civil society organizations are having in awakening the public to the necessity of abolishing nuclear weapons, but I think you are overly so. When you view history over a long stretch of time, no great movement for social change has happened quickly. The abolition of slavery, women's suffrage, human rights, civil rights, ending apartheid—in each case progress emerged slowly, over decades, sometimes over centuries. When success does come, it is usually hard won and occurs after many people have tilled in the fields of change without recognition or reward. After change is achieved, it seems self-evident that it is right, but until it comes, it seems impossibly distant. Right now, despite decades of effort by organizations like the Nuclear Age Peace Foundation, the goal of a world without nuclear weapons still seems impossibly distant, but I think the groundwork is being laid for the change that is needed.

You talk about a central role for a charismatic leader, a Gandhi or King. That would be welcome and may come to pass. In the meantime, I view nothing as more critical than speaking truth to power and making the case that these weapons of mass annihilation continue to pose an untenable risk. The truth is that we don't know exactly whom we reach when we speak out, and so the act of speaking out is, in a sense, an act of faith that there will be an impact. Pauling brought his fame and respect as a scientist and his energy as an activist to the public forum on the issue of ceasing atmospheric testing of nuclear weapons. What he accomplished was significant, but what he left unaccomplished was even more so. Helen Caldicott brought her knowledge and compassion as a physician and her emotional power and passion to the public arena. She awakened many people to an issue they had not seriously considered, but she also left much to be accomplished. You say that both Pauling and Caldicott made the threat of nuclear weapons "real and tangible." It seems clear that making the issue real and tangible is a key to success in stimulating public engagement, but there is also a danger of concern fatigue. When the boy yells out that the sky is falling and it doesn't fall, people lose interest after awhile and revert to complacency.

It would be useful to compare the nuclear weapons abolition movement to the movement to abolish slavery. For a long time, the people of the United Kingdom and the United States expressed no clear democratic preference on the need to abolish slavery. In the United States, maintaining the institution of slavery precipitated the South's seceding from the Union, which resulted in a bloody and devastating civil war. In other words, the abolition of slavery was a long and costly struggle. The people who engaged in seeking the abolition of slavery were at one time considered radicals. But they did the right thing; they took a stand for humanity. They persevered and ultimately prevailed. That is how I view the effort to abolish nuclear weapons. It may be a long and difficult struggle. The people may be complacent. But in seeking abolition, we are doing the right thing, and we will prevail. As Martin Luther King Jr. pointed out, the arc of history bends toward justice.[2] We should take heart from the movement to abolish slavery. Democracies may be easily influenced by entrenched and moneyed interests, but even these interests have much to gain from abolishing nuclear weapons, which are equal opportunity destroyers.

Democracies certainly have their limitations, particularly when undergirded by a culture of militarism and overly trustful of a national security establishment, as is the case in the United States. Despite these distressing limitations, however, democracies often do the right thing in the end. In the United States, citizens ultimately turned against the Vietnam War. They also turned against the Iraq War and are turning against the Afghanistan War. The U.S. population has been far too docile about these wars for far too long, but they are making their voices heard, and they are doing so finally because a few persistent opponents of war have continued to speak out against these conflicts, refusing to be silenced. U.S. citizens cannot overlook indefinitely the immorality and ugly reality of these wars. I think there will come a time when the immorality, illegality, impracticality, and excessive dangers of nuclear weapons will also be impossible to ignore any longer, and the people will demand action from their leaders. In the meantime, those of us who understand the dangers nuclear weapons pose to humanity must keep speaking out and challenging policies reliant upon nuclear arsenals.

Falk: On these issues you raise, we both agree and disagree. I think you are right to feel that engagement with the issue is worthwhile even if the end is not in sight, and such a dedication has led many social movements in history from seeming futility to eventual success. We must never lose the belief that change happens even when the play of entrenched forces appears to block it. The abolition of slavery, the collapse of apartheid, the liberation of Eastern Europe, and the struggle against colonialism all achieved success due to the resolve of the few prevailing over the interests of the powerful and the passivity of the many. The key to the eventual achievement of unlikely political goals seems to depend on arousing the many. This happened in 2011 in the Arab world, especially in the extraordinary movements that took shape in Tunisia and Egypt, successfully and unexpectedly challenging entrenched dictatorial and oppressive regimes.

At the same time, eliminating nuclear weaponry is different in some crucial respects, most notably because the outbreak of nuclear war would be such a catastrophe for the peoples of the world. Slavery, colonialism, and apartheid were each ordeals, causing great suffering, but without apocalyptic implications. With nuclear weapons we are edging toward a precipice, and if we do not back away, at some point we will experience a tragedy of unprecedented magnitude. We need to work toward that never happening, but how can we, given the political realities? Time is not on our side. Patience is not a political virtue, although perseverance is. I think we must confront this apocalyptic challenge and acknowledge its uniqueness in the annals of profound challenges to human destiny.

Krieger: In all the struggles you mention and in others, the key has been moving public opinion to a position of active support for change. Generally, this has happened through an emotional appeal to human decency and fairness and the creation of sympathy for the plight of the oppressed or identification with the mistreated. The genius of Gandhi and King lay in accomplishing this in the service of their respective goals. The Arab Spring unleashed pent-up emotional desire for change. I fear that, on the whole, we have fought the battle for nuclear weapons abolition too much on the fields of rationality rather than seeking emotional connection with the people. Helen Caldicott has brought emotional force to the table for nuclear weapons abolition, and that is perhaps the reason for her relatively strong success. I think we will succeed in moving the masses to the side of abolition when we find the key to opening wider the doors of emotion. After all, we are engaged in a struggle that could destroy everything that each person on the planet holds dear. That should be grounds for action. It makes nuclear weapons abolition the overriding cause of our time.

I agree with you that time is not on our side, given the apocalyptic implications of nuclear weapons. I also agree that we are very close to the precipice. We need to bring the implications of our present dangerous situation to the people more effectively and with greater emotional force. Perhaps one way to open that door is to draw on the implications of the nuclear power disaster at Fukushima.

From Hiroshima to Fukushima

Falk: We might have hoped that a disaster in the nuclear energy domain would raise questions about military nuclearism. The Japanese disaster at Fukushima would seem to have had those features that might have led to a cultural shock sufficient to overcome nuclear complacency, especially given the symbolism of Japan as the country so catastrophically victimized at the dawn of the Nuclear Age. Arguably Fukushima has had some transnational effects. Germany and Switzerland now seem committed to phasing out nuclear power, Italy has put the future of nuclear energy to a vote of citizenry, and several other countries are giving this option more careful thought by reexamining the risks of nuclear energy and the problems associated with alternatives. But even in those most responsive societies, with strong ecologically minded movements opposed to nuclear power, there seems to be a reluctance to question reliance on nuclear weaponry.

Krieger: People don't always see the connections between nuclear weapons and nuclear power. The nuclear industry and governments have been strong in asserting a role for the "peaceful" atom in generating electricity. But I think a lot of people, as well as countries, have reassessed their support for nuclear energy in light of the Fukushima accident. I see Fukushima as an important wake-up call for both nuclear energy and nuclear weapons, and as you say, many countries are now committed to ending their reliance on nuclear power plants. I think this is a positive step forward. One of our colleagues, Steven Starr, has pointed out that each of the 440 commercial nuclear reactors in the world contains "at least 100 times more long-lived radioactivity than was produced by the bombs which destroyed Hiroshima and Nagasaki."[3] Consequently, Starr points out, "a catastrophic accident at just one of these reactors has the potential to release as much radioactive fallout as would a nuclear war fought with 100 atomic bombs."[4] He goes on to describe a nuclear reactor as "a sort of nuclear-war-in-a-can."[5] Most people don't know this, and they need to know.

Yes, there is resistance to change, but disasters like Fukushima are raising awareness throughout the world. They provide an opportunity to make new connections in the minds of the people. For example, one nuclear power plant may have the capacity to release as much radioactivity as one hundred Hiroshima-size nuclear weapons, but the same number of nuclear weapons, if actually used on cities in South Asia or elsewhere, could result in a nuclear winter—a blockage of sunlight reaching the earth and subsequent lowering of temperatures, causing widespread drought and crop failures, resulting in the deaths of 1 billion people worldwide.[6] This is surely not trivial and makes government indifference and public complacency in the face of it all the more appalling.

Falk: I agree with this important observation. Every disaster presents a hidden opportunity, an invitation to change direction. The initiatives in European countries relating to nuclear power disclose a public worried about the dangers of nuclear power and exhibiting a readiness to learn from Fukushima, even if it imposes extra costs on energy and indirectly creates burdens for business and consumers. In the years ahead, I believe we will witness a struggle for hearts and minds between those who insist on a materialist calculus of values and those who are fighting to recover a spiritual, ethical, and ecological calculus of value. The outcome of this struggle will go a long way toward determining whether the lives of our grandchildren will be fraught with danger and despair or blessed with hope and progress.

I believe there is a continuing role for educational attempts to inform and activate the American people, but I feel that at the present time, these efforts do not constitute a political project. Rather, they are a bearing of witness to the failure of the public and the government to act responsibly, and I feel this failure should be highlighted, not obscured out of gratitude for small crumbs of recognition. That is why I believe our credibility rests on maintaining a critical posture toward governmental conduct and not succumbing to the lures of co-option. In a democracy, we should be able to insist that our elected government uphold the law and behave ethically in relation to an issue as important as the role of nuclear weaponry. And when that insistence is met with evasion and silence for decades, we are obliged to expose these deficiencies of national governance and, perhaps, extend the discussion to the deficiencies of a world order built on geopolitical premises of hard-power capabilities and the nonaccountability of nuclear weapon states to international law or the UN Charter. We have to ask, What does it mean to be a democracy in the early twenty-first century with specific reference to our principal concern about nuclearism? Or is the game over and lost? If not, how can we best proceed, given the utter insensitivity at the centers of governmental authority? Maybe insensitivity is too strong an indictment. There have been rhetorical acknowledgments of the sort contained in Barack Obama's speech or the antinuclear positions urged by Dennis Kucinich, although his isolation in Congress reinforces the point that the preconditions for a political project are not present.

Krieger: I hope you are right that we will see in the years ahead a struggle between a materialistic calculus of values and a calculus based upon spiritual and ethical principles. This would mean that spiritual and ethical principles will remain viable in our materialistic culture. I would say, though, that even in a materialistic world, nuclear weapons would have no place. They are capable of destroying not only life and all that is sacred but also all the material possessions that are so prized. Nuclear weapons fail to meet spiritual, ethical, or materialistic standards. They fail on all grounds, and only by twisting the truth about their utility have they maintained their place in national security programs (which really should be renamed, due to nuclear weapons, national insecurity programs).

Obama Incrementalism?

Krieger: I agree with you that the conditions for a political project on abolishing nuclear weapons are not yet present. A bearing of witness to the failure of the public and the government to act responsibly needs to be highlighted. The Nuclear Age Peace Foundation and other civil society organizations are attempting to do just that. The U.S. government, led now by President Obama, makes the case that it is acting responsibly by taking incremental steps toward the goal of a world free of nuclear weapons. But, of course, the government is caught up in hard power and its own inertia and continues to move at a glacial pace toward the goal of a world free of nuclear weapons. There can be no doubt that national security concerns, exacerbated by a culture of militarism, are having a strong dampening effect on democracy. Nonetheless, I don't think the game is over. Democracy may be weak, but it continues to have life, and where there is life, there is hope. There also remains the possibility that the United States may be influenced from beyond its borders. If enough of its allies are ready to forego the U.S. nuclear umbrella and to make this clear to the United States, then the United States may have little choice but to close the umbrella, rethink its own nuclear policies in terms of its own interests in survival, and take serious steps toward nuclear weapons abolition.

Falk: I would make only a single observation in response. I do not believe that Obama is taking incremental steps toward a world without nuclear weapons or that such a goal is being approached at a glacial pace. I believe the world is no closer to those goals than it was in 1945 and is more likely moving in the opposite direction. There is not the public fear or the semiserious commitment to nuclear disarmament that existed fifty years ago. I think you do a disservice to the real nature of the challenge if you treat arms control measures as other than managerial steps designed to stabilize nuclearism. The more stable the nuclear regime is perceived to be, the less incentive and political will are present to move toward the elimination of the weaponry. Whenever an arms control measure is agreed upon, as with New START, there is a subsequent falling off of any larger effort, a reinforcement of complacency, and confusion about the fundamental difference between disarmament and denuclearization and arms control and nuclearism.

Krieger: I understand your concerns, but I continue to think that we should take Obama at his word that he seeks a world without nuclear weapons. He may see it, as he has stated, as a long-term project that will not occur within his lifetime, but he has nonetheless made an affirmative statement that he seeks the goal. We may not be closer to a world free of nuclear weapons now than we were in 1945, but we are closer than we were in 1986, when there were some 70,000 nuclear weapons in the world. Today we are down to some 20,000, with about 6,000 of these deployed. This is still far too many, and the threat remains intolerable. However, we are moving in the right direction, and while this is not enough, it at least indicates some recognition that the value of the weapons is diminishing. There are still supporters of nuclear weapons in the national security apparatuses of the nuclear weapon states, but I would say their influence is diminishing, as reflected in the calls for abolition from Henry Kissinger, George Shultz, William Perry, and Sam Nunn. If arms control successes tend to have a mollifying effect on the population, it is up to concerned civil society groups, like the Nuclear Age Peace Foundation, to keep their efforts focused on the goal of abolition and to keep attempting to shake democratic majorities from their far-too-comfortable complacency.

Falk: I think we disagree on tactics and perceptions here. I judge Obama by his performance and not by his words. And that performance is dismal, with respect not only to nuclear weapons but also to closely related issues involving constitutional restraints on war making, governmental policies on national security, and the vindictive approach to secrecy as illustrated by the abusive treatment of Bradley Manning. Also, I disagree that quantitative reductions are necessarily moves toward nuclear disarmament or even indicate a reduced willingness to deploy, use, or threaten to use the weapons. These reductions were offset by promises to modernize the arsenal and refusals to adopt more restrictive policies toward threats and use. I see no evidence for a growth of antinuclear sentiment in the nuclear weapon states except as it relates to the undercutting of the United States' dominant posture due to further proliferation or access by nonstate actors (and the availability of near-nuclear conventional capabilities making the impact of denuclearization very minor, if it has any at all, on overall U.S. military capabilities).

The broader issue between us here concerns, I believe, the source of hope about change. I think we both endorse the idea of speaking truth to power, but I believe you are overly ready, despite decades of evidence to the contrary, to give the benefit of the doubt to governmental statements of good intention. I may be jaded by my years of disillusionment with the sort of rhetorical misdirection given over and over again in relation to the Israel–Palestine so-called peace process, which has turned into a cover for transforming occupation into de facto annexation and ethnic cleansing. Robert Gates, in his final days as secretary of defense, testified before the Senate Appropriations Committee as follows: "I would say based on 27 years in C.I.A. and four-and-a-half years in this job, most governments lie to each other. That's the way business gets done."[7] And of course, they lie to their own citizens, which is also how business gets done. Our government avoids lying to the extent possible by keeping secret the information needed by citizens to judge policies and punishing those brave individuals who inform the public of what they should know (Daniel Ellsberg, Bradley Manning).

Krieger: I believe our disagreement is based on tactics, not perceptions. I share your perceptions of the dismal nature of Obama's performance in upholding and even strengthening the national security state with its democratic deficits in transparency and participation. He has made the war in Afghanistan his own by greatly increasing the number of troops there. He excluded Congress from its Constitutional role with regard to the U.S. and NATO attacks against Libya. The treatment of Bradley Manning and Obama's prejudicial comments about Manning's guilt have undermined the basic right of a citizen to be presumed innocent until proven guilty. He has also made unprecedented use of drone aircraft that has resulted in large numbers of civilian casualties in a variety of countries. And clearly Obama has not taken bold action toward achieving a world free of nuclear weapons. He has had rhetorical flourishes, particularly in Prague, but the New START agreement he reached with Russia is not a major step forward. If the price to be paid for the treaty is the modernization of the U.S. nuclear arsenal, New START may turn out to be a significant step backward.

Still, tactically, I think it is helpful to look to some of the more positive statements President Obama has made and use these to stimulate and enliven the public discourse on the dangers of nuclear weapons and the need to abolish them. When he said at Prague, "I state clearly and with conviction America's commitment to seek the peace and security of a world without nuclear weapons," and stated that we have "a moral responsibility to act," those words were a call to action. I don't say that we should accept them as a substitute for action or as sufficient without action, but we should use them as a stimulus for engaging the public and as a measure of the success or failure of U.S. leaders in general and of Obama himself in particular. I see Obama's words at Prague less as a source of hope than as a stimulus to action from below. They form one of many tools that may be used in trying to awaken and engage the public in this issue of such paramount importance.

CHAPTER 10

The Path to Zero

Falk: As we approach the end of this conversational journey, the most haunting question is what can be done to advance this struggle to rid humanity of the threats posed by the existence of nuclear weaponry. In my view, part of this struggle is facing the obstacles while remaining dedicated to the goals. This is not easy because, as we have acknowledged throughout, the passivity of the public gives entrenched pro-nuclear interests and attitudes great leverage. Political leaders, even assuming dedicated good will, seem unable, and perhaps unwilling, to challenge the nuclear establishment absent strong societal support, which has not been forthcoming, especially in the period since the end of the Cold War. True, when a public figure such as the American president makes a speech, such as that given by President Barack Obama in Prague, there is a surge of hope and enthusiasm that raises expectations temporarily, but they seem to subside quickly, perhaps because they are not backed by a social movement that will exert continuing pressure.

Obstacles to Achieving a World Free of Nuclear Weapons

Falk: Even when an American leader seems to call for steps toward a world without nuclear weapons and affirms such a vision, three further discouraging features are normal accompaniments, although not initially completely appreciated: first, clear signals that the goal is "ultimate," which is a way of saying that it is an aspiration, not a political project that entails a commitment to achieve realization by way of a plan; second, various indications that, until the world is without serious conflicts of a strategic nature, deterrence will be maintained and even reinforced by further weapons development; and third, a lack of clear distinction drawn between arms control initiatives that essentially stabilize nuclearism and disarmament plans that contemplate a process of denuclearization ending in zero. Carefully analyzed, Obama's speech exhibited all three of these disabling dimensions.

Krieger: It is true that the obstacles to achieving a world without nuclear weapons are formidable. As we've discussed, a great deal of public complacency surrounds the issue. For the most part, the dangers of the weapons remain beyond the public imagination. There is also a general public perception that nuclear weapons have a protective function—that is, that they deter the use of nuclear weapons against their possessors. We've discussed at some length nuclear deterrence and its flaws. I believe that, going forward, an important part of the abolition effort must be aimed at effectively communicating the flaws of nuclear deterrence theory—for example, its reliance on rationality in a world where irrational behavior is commonplace. Perhaps an even better example is the inapplicability of nuclear deterrence to a nonstate extremist organization in possession of a nuclear weapon. States cannot deter those who have no territory to retaliate against or who are suicidal. The point I want to make here is that a key to gaining traction on nuclear abolition is moving the public out of its comfort zone by education that nuclear deterrence is a flawed theory rather than an immutable law. No one, I think, would want to wake up to discover that one or many cities had been destroyed because deterrence theory was unreliable and ineffective.

I agree with you that an American leader could lead the way toward nuclear abolition were he or she prepared to do so. So far, we've heard a lot of statements of aspiration from American leaders, but no clear plan that would create a political project to achieve the goal. President Obama gave perhaps the best statement of aspiration of any U.S. president, but his vision appears far ahead of his actions toward the goal. While expressing the need for U.S. leadership, he reaffirmed his commitment to nuclear deterrence and has pledged significant sums of money, over $200 billion over the next decade, toward modernizing the U.S. nuclear weapons complex and the U.S. nuclear arsenal and its delivery systems. His actions simply are not aligned with a U.S. commitment to provide leadership toward a world without nuclear weapons. This must be clear to anyone who follows this issue closely, but it is likely not clear to the general public.

Falk: I would agree with all that you say here, even including your assertion that Obama's statement is "perhaps the best statement of aspiration." I can, with an effort, accept this, but when you go on to say that "his vision appears far ahead of his actions toward the goal," we part company.

I realize that I am probably belaboring this concern, but it seems to me important if we are to understand that the way forward depends, at least in the present climate of congressional and public opinion, on developing a politics from below and no longer being enticed by wishful thinking relating to politics from above. Liberals tend to believe that public elites solve by incremental steps the problems confronting society, and they are distrustful of and uncomfortable with direct action, or what I am calling politics from below. In my view, our struggle resembles the early stages of the civil rights movement—that is, before Martin Luther King Jr. came onto the scene and long before the presidencies of John F. Kennedy and Lyndon B. Johnson were able to turn racial grievances into emancipatory laws. Thinking operationally in the present political atmosphere, we will get nowhere writing letters to Congress or imploring our elected leaders to move toward nuclear disarmament. Maybe imploring is okay, provided we are not deceived into thinking that doing so can budge the giant boulder that nuclearism has become.

The Need for U.S. Leadership

Falk: Perhaps, we have been too American-centric in our assessments of how to proceed. We need to recognize that Americans think that all of the world's problems derive from what the United States does and doesn't do and that it alone has the capacity to promote solutions. While trying to be sensitive to this form of critical chauvinism, I do think it seems justified with respect to nuclear weapons. The Nuclear Age has been from the outset an American-led undertaking, dramatized by U.S. development and use of this weaponry at the end of World War II, and the U.S. government possesses the decisive leverage to initiate disarmament negotiations, especially since the collapse of the Soviet Union. Indeed, every serious disarmament initiative has been born or died in Washington, although there are some grounds for believing that Mikhail Gorbachev would have joined in a process dedicated to total nuclear disarmament had he found willing partners in the West, especially the United States. In this sense, the United States seems to have both the main responsibility and the correlated principal opportunity. This is not to say that initiatives from the other nuclear weapon states would not be welcome; indeed, they might awaken both societal and governmental support in this country. It may also be that a revolt against the nonproliferation regime by nonnuclear states could stimulate constructive moves to consider nuclear disarmament as a preferred policy option.

I believe we should approach the momentous challenge of what can be done, given current realities, against this background. I would say that as of now, the vision of a world without nuclear weapons is an important ingredient in our private and public political and moral imaginations, but it remains prepolitical as far as prospects for realization are concerned. We need to keep asking ourselves what must happen to allow nuclear disarmament to become a political project, which links means to foreseeable ends. It seems that at times during the Cold War, as after the Cuban Missile Crisis of 1962, societal fears of nuclear war lent support to antinuclear activists. This happened even more fervently in Europe, where acute anxieties surfaced from time to time about a war between the Soviet Union and the United States waged on European soil—in effect, a third world war in Europe fought with nuclear weapons. Thankfully this never happened, but the fears associated with this possible catastrophe did illustrate the degree to which citizen involvement with nuclear issues does reflect the level of perceived anxieties. At the other extreme of public arousal exists a wide variety of educational efforts to convince people that nuclear weapons are dangerous, and their mere possession is intolerable. Although education along these lines is significant, it lacks mobilizing potential unless other conditions are present in the societal atmosphere. Somehow, we need to avoid manipulating fear as a source of mobilization while bringing to bear sufficient passion to reach people in an enduring manner. It may be that cultural approaches are most effective at this stage, showing the apocalyptic potential of nuclear weapons in a manner that does not attempt to inform in any direct way but keeps the reality of nuclear weapons alive in our consciousness. We also require the virtues of patience and vigilance: persistence in striving for our goal of a world without nuclear weapons, readiness to take advantage of opportunities to move in this direction, receptiveness to coalitions with like-minded groups, and doing our best to avoid confusing the public with the make-believe of arms control.

What Would the United States Do if It Were Serious?

Krieger: Perhaps we have been too American-centric, but it is difficult to imagine getting out of the Nuclear Age without U.S. leadership. If the United States chooses not to be a leader in this effort, then it will likely be viewed as an obstacle, at least to other nuclear weapon states. It is an interesting exercise to pose the question, What would the United States do if it were serious about abolishing nuclear weapons? I can think of several actions the United States could take. First, it could convene a meeting of the world's nuclear weapon states to begin negotiations on eliminating their nuclear arsenals. This is actually required by Article VI of the Non-Proliferation Treaty, that is, good faith negotiations for total nuclear disarmament. Second, the United States could reach agreement with Russia to take the nuclear arsenals on both sides off high-alert status and change their policies from Launch on Warning to No Launch before Detonation in order to minimize the possibilities of an accidental or unintentional launch based on human or technological error that could trigger a nuclear war. Third, the United States could pledge No First Use of nuclear weapons and encourage other nuclear weapon states to join it in this commitment. Fourth, the United States, as the only country to keep nuclear weapons on foreign soil, could remove its approximately two hundred nuclear weapons from Europe.

Yet another step the United States could take, if it chose to lead, would be to conduct an environmental and human impact study on its nuclear arsenal and release the results to the public. Shouldn't the public be aware of what the use of the U.S. nuclear arsenal would do to the environment and to human well-being? Such an exploration would estimate how many people, including Americans, would be expected to die in a nuclear exchange with a nuclear-armed foe or in the event of a nuclear accident. Actually, I think that the citizens of every nuclear weapon state should demand such studies, just as environmental impact statements are now required for municipal building projects. It seems certain that the results would be shocking to the public and likely to policy makers as well.

Another reasonable expectation of all nuclear weapon states would be to develop roadmaps for how they envision getting to zero nuclear weapons. Such roadmaps would reveal and make public visions of the path to a nuclear weapon–free world. These visions could be compared and contrasted. The nuclear weapon states could commence a dialogue on the best way forward, and this could take place under public scrutiny. An unwillingness to engage in such visioning and discussion of a world free of nuclear weapons would signal to the world who is leading and who is putting up barriers to achieving the goal.

I hope you agree that actions such as I am suggesting would go beyond managing nuclear dangers and would actually be significant steps toward achieving a world without nuclear weapons. I suppose that the most important missing element underlying all of these possible actions is political will. Generally speaking, where there is political will, there is a way ahead, and where there is no political will, only rhetoric remains. The failure to achieve a political project suggests that very little political will exists to move from aspiration to action. I actually think the prospects for U.S. leadership to achieve the abolition of nuclear weapons is becoming increasingly remote and that the leadership will need to come from other countries. You have suggested a political project in which the non–nuclear weapon states give warning of their intention to withdraw from the Non-Proliferation Treaty if the nuclear weapon states do not take serious actions within a designated time frame. I'm not sure, though, that this could be converted to a political project. It would require an unprecedented level of courage by the non–nuclear weapon states and would signify a departure from their general dependence on the richest countries in the world, which include many of the nuclear weapon states and their allies.

It is not easy to think of patience and vigilance as virtues when the need for progress on nuclear disarmament is so urgent. Yet, patience and vigilance are necessary when the alternative is giving up in despair. The commitment of those seeking to end the nuclear weapons threat to humanity must be to stay the course and bring their utmost passion and creativity to the effort. Soon the baton of leadership will be passed to a new generation. One of the most important tasks of those of us committed to a nuclear weapons–free world must be to help educate a new generation of leaders about the need to abolish nuclear weapons, disturbing their comfort level in living with continuing nuclear threats hanging over their countries and their futures.

Falk: I agree that U.S. leadership would seem indispensable if a nuclear disarmament process is to proceed very far, or even proceed at all. But I am not sure that the United States is currently best situated to initiate a nuclear disarmament process. I think it is relatively comfortable with the present engagement with nuclearism, retaining and developing its nuclear weapons arsenal while doing its best to weaken acquisition and development by others. To shake this status quo outlook will require, in my judgment, a challenge from without that makes American leadership recalculate the relative dangers, risks, and uncertainties associated with the possession of nuclear weaponry as compared to those arising from a disarming process. From this standpoint, I have suggested an ultimatum from non–nuclear weapon states that are parties to the NPT: Implement Article VI within two years or we will exercise our right of withdrawal under Article X.

I think your proposal is sound regarding the steps that the U.S. government would take if there did exist within it a consensus favorable to the implementation of nuclear disarmament and the endorsement of a blueprint for moving to a world without nuclear weapons. But the persisting unwillingness to take any of these steps, which are prudent even without a commitment at the outset to full-fledged nuclear disarmament, is indicative of the deep roots of the nuclearist consensus, which actually seems to go beyond the declared goals of keeping deterrence invigorated. It also seeks to retain an option to introduce nuclear weaponry into threat diplomacy and battlefield situations as possibly needed in future pursuits of strategic nuclear interests.

A No First Use Pledge

Falk: Otherwise, why would the U.S. government not willingly declare adherence to a No First Use pledge? What conceivable justification, consistent with a deterrence rationale for retention of the weaponry, is there for not assuring other governments that the United States will only use such weaponry in retaliation against a prior attack with nuclear weaponry? It is rather clear that such a declaration, especially if backed up by non-nuclear deployments, would both give the United States some new claim to leadership with respect to the weaponry and exert enormous psychological pressure on other nuclear weapon states to follow the American lead. I have long felt that the issuance of such a declaration, accompanied by reinforcing language and adjustments in military planning, offers the public here and abroad a litmus test as to governmental sincerity about the endorsement of nuclear disarmament. In this spirit, I feel it is an important antinuclear priority. It both exposes the attachment to nuclearism of the existing political leadership and provides a way for this government, or any government, to demonstrate its commitment to the vision of a world without nuclear weaponry.

There are technical issues on the fringe. What about other weapons of mass destruction—biological, chemical, radiological? Should the No First Use pledge not refer to all these categories? Some argue that a democratic government, such as our own, would take such a pledge seriously, while an authoritarian government would either make the pledge for propaganda purposes without feeling bound or break the pledge if its strategic interests so dictated. Of course, there are no ironclad assurances in this domain. But the No First Use approach, hopefully as part of a comprehensive framework, is an attractive initiative because it would clear the air of the long history of ambivalence about renouncing the supposed strategic benefits of nuclear weapons, recalling threats to use these weapons that were made on several occasions during the Cold War and in relation to debates over strategic doctrine. It was clear that the use of nuclear weapons was often contemplated by American leaders in response to nonnuclear challenges mounted by adversaries. In conclusion, I would welcome a focused campaign to advocate a No First Use policy as a sign of political life in the antinuclear global civil society movement.

Krieger: You have emphasized a No First Use policy as an indication of governmental sincerity about achieving nuclear disarmament. Right now China has such a policy, as does India. China's policy is reinforced by the minimal nature of its nuclear deterrent force. It has never developed a large nuclear arsenal in competition with the United States and Russia; rather, it has maintained an arsenal of about two hundred nuclear weapons. In regard to a No First Use policy, among the nuclear weapon states, China has led the way, but only India has followed. I think the parties to the NPT should apply pressure for all nuclear weapon states that are signatories to the treaty to adopt No First Use policies by the time the parties convene in 2015 for the next NPT Review Conference. I would say, though, that this should be but one of many demands from the non–nuclear weapon states for movement toward nuclear disarmament by the nuclear weapon states. I would encourage them also to demand that the nuclear weapon states take all of their nuclear weapons off high-alert status and adopt No Launch before Detonation policies. I would also call upon the non–nuclear weapon states to demand that each nuclear weapon state make public its roadmap to zero as well as its prerequisites for reaching this goal. Finally, and most importantly, I would urge the non–nuclear weapon states to demand the onset of negotiations by 2015 on a nuclear weapons convention for the phased, verifiable, irreversible, and transparent elimination of nuclear weapons. This would require all states to begin a process of reconceptualizing security for a world without nuclear weapons. I am saying here that No First Use policies would be a step ahead and a sign of life in the nuclear disarmament arena, but such policies are not sufficient. To achieve a world with zero nuclear weapons will require far more.

Summarizing Our Consensus

Krieger: Let me try to summarize where we have arrived. First, we agree that U.S. leadership may be needed but is not there at present and is unlikely to be forthcoming without considerable pressure from the people. Second, such pressure from below is not currently on the horizon, but we should not give up in our educational efforts to awaken the American people and engage them in a movement to achieve a world free of nuclear weapons. Third, absent U.S. leadership, we will have to look elsewhere for leadership to achieve progress toward zero nuclear weapons. Fourth, such leadership could come from the non–nuclear weapon states that are parties to the Non-Proliferation Treaty. To assert such leadership, they would have to band together and make strong demands on the nuclear weapon states that are parties to the NPT. To be taken seriously, those demands might have to be in the form of non–nuclear weapon states delivering an ultimatum to withdraw from the NPT in their "supreme interests," under Article X of the treaty. Fifth, an initial demand on the nuclear weapon states should be a policy of No First Use. While this is important in demonstrating sincerity in seeking to achieve the goal of zero, it is not sufficient. Sixth, the strongest litmus test of sincerity by the nuclear weapon states would be convening negotiations on a nuclear weapons convention, demonstrating the good faith negotiations required by Article VI of the NPT and by the advisory opinion of the International Court of Justice (ICJ).

In the steps summarized above, I have focused on the parties to the Non-Proliferation Treaty. In doing so, I have left out the three nuclear weapon states that never joined the NPT—Israel, India, and Pakistan—and the one country that withdrew from it, North Korea. These countries would have to be brought into the negotiations for a nuclear weapons convention at some point. It would be preferable at the outset of negotiations, but they could be brought in later if necessary. Each country with nuclear weapons would need to reveal the prerequisites for its own security in a world without nuclear weapons. These issues would need to be dealt with in the negotiations on a nuclear weapons convention.

In many respects, I think it would be even more appropriate for the non–nuclear weapon states to lead in the effort to eliminate nuclear weapons than for any nuclear weapon state to do so. Among the non–nuclear weapon states, many have chosen to forego the option of acquiring nuclear weapons. They have found ways to achieve security without them. Some, of course, have agreed to put themselves under the umbrella of a nuclear weapon state, and these countries will need to rethink their security policies for a world without nuclear weapons. They will have to choose between remaining reliant on another country's nuclear weapons and living in a world without nuclear threats. I think most of these will opt for the security of a world free of nuclear weapons.

The Black Swan

Falk: I think your summary of our consensus is helpful in crystallizing how to think about moving into the future. I would raise two further points beyond those you have mentioned. First, I would mention "the black swan" phenomenon to the effect that the main shifts in historical reality have been unanticipated and even seemed implausible or irrelevant until after they occurred. To explain the metaphor, only white swans were thought to exist because no one had reported seeing a black swan; then black swans were identified in Australia, and the impossible suddenly became a fact of existence. For a full elaboration of this hypothesis about change, see Nassim Nicholas Taleb's *The Black Swan: The Impact of the Highly Improbable*.[1]

The application of the black swan phenomenon to our concerns is this: We cannot begin to know or understand what the future will bring, positively or negatively. For this reason, whatever the apparent limits of seemingly feasible political change, we should struggle as hard as we can for what we believe to be right—although, to avoid fanaticism in the name of a supposedly benign end, we should renounce violence unconditionally as a means, but not militant tactics of opposition and resistance. In effect, we need to embrace what I have called in the past "a politics of impossibility," not in some utopian quest for what seems beyond reach but to attain a prudent and rationally desirable end. Politics, as we are taught, is generally regarded as "the art of the possible," and such a perspective with respect to nuclearism either induces despair or irrelevant moralism. Instead, I am proposing dedication to the goals of a world without nuclear weapons, although our understanding of the political setting at present seems to make this an impossible undertaking. When it becomes possible, it will be as a result of the intervention in our history of some totally unanticipated happening: a shock of some sort to the system, a charismatic leader who mobilizes a new public consciousness, a new cultural turn toward spirituality and universal humanism, even a repudiation of war as a legitimate institution.

Highlighting No First Use

Falk: My other response is on a more tactical level. I would favor highlighting the No First Use proposal as the priority of the moment, precisely because it is so simple, so seemingly persuasive morally and politically, and because it would create a momentum and sense of direction leading rather naturally, and maybe even inevitably, toward complete denuclearization. To have multiple policy objectives tends to depoliticize the effort to move forward on an unambiguous disarmament track without moving sideways via arms control measures. It is, of course, good to take the other steps that you mention, but I would like to see the nuclear weapon states, especially the United States, explicitly and unequivocally repudiate any right to use or threaten to use nuclear weapons except conceivably in response to a prior nuclear attack. Such a position seems to me implicit in the majority opinion in the ICJ case addressing the legality of nuclear weapons. Adopting such a No First Use posture would be the kind of step back from the nuclear precipice that would give the world a sense that denuclearizing language from American leaders could be trusted as something more than a rhetorical flash in the pan.

Once such a pledge was made in a formal and binding fashion, ideally in unconditional language, the next step would be the imperative of seeking a negotiable plan for ridding the nuclear weapon states of their arsenals in a phased and verified process, solemnized by a treaty framework that included verification and compliance mechanisms. I think insisting on these two steps is simple and strategic and can be made to encompass other, more technical adjustments that reduce risks along the path leading to nuclear disarmament.

We must, in my view, not completely neglect issues of expenditures on the military, arms sales, nonnuclear weaponry of mass destruction, and the related, possibly overlapping challenge of demilitarization.

Krieger: "The black swan" phenomenon suggests that more is possible than we can understand or foresee, and we cannot view the future as a straight-line projection from the past. We can look at this phenomenon as a source of hope in a world where it is necessary to make the seemingly impossible possible. I might say it more simply: We fight for a world free of nuclear weapons because the future of humanity depends on achieving this goal. It is the right course of action, and regardless of how improbable success may seem, we must proceed in our efforts without faltering. We don't know what actions we may take that may change the dynamics of the system, bringing about an unlikely and improbable new reality. Always inherent in the present is a range of possible futures, some more and some less likely. Those of us who fight for a world free of nuclear weapons must find the places of leverage in the global system at which the improbable may become the more likely. This is the challenge of all who seek to create a more decent world. It is the particular challenge of those who, by word and action, seek to transform the present into a safer and saner future.

I have no difficulty in joining you in seeking No First Use policies by the nuclear weapon states. I believe such policies would signify and reflect a willingness to limit the political and military uses of the weapons. This would provide a foundation to move on to negotiations for a nuclear weapons convention. If nuclear weapons were limited to responding to a nuclear attack, and all nuclear weapon states established policies that they would not initiate one, there would be, in effect, a standard by which no use could occur, absent a violation of the policy. This would be a major step forward, but many analysts and policy makers would argue that policies alone are not sufficient, since they can be violated. This is why such policies, to be believable, must be backed up by actions on the ground, such as China's keeping its nuclear warheads separated from their delivery vehicles. This means that China would have to take the detectable actions of moving its warheads and attaching them to delivery vehicles before it could use its nuclear weapons.

So far, the United States has been resistant to adopting a No First Use policy, not wanting to relinquish the edge of power that its nuclear weapons are perceived to provide. This is perhaps an area of government vulnerability in its current nuclear policy. I doubt very much that American citizens would favor the United States' current First Use policy if they understood what it was. Such a policy—the threat to strike first in annihilating potentially hundreds of millions of innocent people—seems at best extraordinarily cowardly. If the United States could be pressed to adopt a No First Use policy, this would quite likely change the present dynamics of the global system, leading other countries to join it in adopting such a policy. As I mentioned earlier, both China and India already have No First Use policies. Another possibility would be for Russia, France, and the United Kingdom, or some combination of these three, to agree among themselves to adopt No First Use policies and to put pressure on the United States to join them. The most difficult countries to influence to adopt No First Use policies would likely be Israel and Pakistan, but immense international pressure would be on them if the other nuclear weapon states adopted such policies.

Beyond No First Use

Krieger: I still think, though, that other issues need to be addressed with regard to nuclear weapons—for example, taking them off high-alert status. This is necessary to reduce the likelihood of an accidental or inadvertent launch. This would undoubtedly become easier to accomplish with No First Use policies in place. You also mention other areas outside the nuclear realm, such as military expenditures, arms sales, nonnuclear weaponry of mass destruction, and demilitarization. These are all important issues, and all relate to the national security concerns of states in the international system. They would need to be taken up, at least in part, in parallel negotiations, along the lines of the McCloy-Zorin Accords, in conjunction with a nuclear weapons convention. In other words, successful negotiation of a nuclear weapons convention would require that the security concerns of all countries, not only the nuclear weapon states, be considered in the process of eliminating nuclear weapons. The goal of a nuclear weapons convention is to create a more secure world for all, not a world made safe for conventional warfare and continued lopsided military budgets. There can be no doubt, though, that the current world security system, based on nuclear threats, puts people everywhere at risk of annihilation, and this is simply unacceptable.

The main outline of a plan for moving forward would be No First Use campaigns, coupled with de-alerting campaigns, leading to negotiations for a nuclear weapons convention to achieve the total elimination of nuclear weapons. The leadership for advancing this plan would need to come from civil society groups working in conjunction with allies in governments when possible. I think that this plan should put a heavy emphasis on bringing young people into these campaigns, awakening them to the importance of existing nuclear dangers to their future and engaging them in action. Young people throughout the world could and should become new and fresh leaders in the global effort to eliminate nuclear weapons. They could also be the triggers to bring "the black swan" phenomenon into play.

Falk: A small point: The black swan phenomenon, by its nature, is not susceptible to inducement into being as it consists of those parts of reality that shape historical change but are currently hidden from our perception or understanding, and to the extent they are put forward, they are dismissed as utopian or implausible. This domain of the unknown does, however, as you earlier suggest, give grounds for hope, as well as invalidating pessimism and cynicism as justifications for not acting on behalf of what we believe. As most social movements in our lifetime have demonstrated, the mainstream saw early adherents as fools dedicated to achieving the unattainable. Since we are not intelligent enough to know what is impossible, it is imperative to pursue what we believe to be right, even if its realization seems, according to conventional wisdom, to be highly unlikely.

I am comfortable with your views on No First Use and de-alerting. I agree that for No First Use to be credible as a step, it must be accompanied by shifts in doctrine and views about defensive postures in relation to threats directed at national security. It may be tactically sensible to couple these two proposals and call prominent attention to the positions adopted by China and India.

Regional Approaches to Nuclear Disarmament

Falk: I think we should also mention the regional approach to nuclear disarmament and to threat reduction. I have long felt that a nuclear-free zone in the Middle East would represent a very significant enhancement in the security of the region and would be mutually beneficial for all states, including Israel, the only state currently possessing nuclear weapons. It has long disturbed me that the United States has not used its diplomatic leverage in relation to the politics of the region to initiate negotiations along these lines. Of course, in this most volatile region, a series of steps would make maximum sense: nuclear weapons–free zone, a mutual nonaggression agreement, and an Israel–Palestine agreement establishing a just and sustainable peace.

I think that the nuclear weapons issue should be dealt with initially and separately from the other two components of this broader program for the Middle East and would make the attainment of these goals more likely. And due to the threat diplomacy, covert operations (including sabotage), and sanctions that have been employed in reaction to Iran's supposed illicit nuclear weapons program, an urgency attaches to this particular region.

Of course, this regional approach has application elsewhere in the world, especially in South Asia and Northeast Asia. It has already proved beneficial in inhibiting the development of nuclear weapons in other regions.

Krieger: I find regional approaches to nuclear disarmament useful for threat reduction and nonproliferation, but far from sufficient. They can reduce dangers within a region, and they can also set standards that can then be applied more broadly in a universal nuclear weapons prohibition, a nuclear weapons convention. Thus, I favor existing regional nuclear weapon–free zones and would certainly join you in supporting new regional nuclear-free zones in the Middle East, South Asia, and Northeast Asia. Success in establishing these zones would constitute important gains toward a world free of nuclear weapons. I do think, though, that these regions all have deep-seated conflicts and security concerns that will make breakthroughs quite difficult and may require a global rather than regional framework.

The black swan phenomenon may not be susceptible to inducement and may be a hidden current of history. I would say, though, that although the projection of history is not predetermined, it has its currents, both visible and hidden, that are subject to change by means of forces brought to bear on them. These may be forces of nature, of human spirit, and of technological innovation. Generally, all of these forces will be at work and interacting. In the case of nuclear weapons, a great battle of forces is taking place between technological innovation and the human spirit, and the outcome remains uncertain. Humanity as a whole is challenged as never before to maintain control of its most dangerous and deadly technological innovation, thermonuclear weapons.

Any particular moment of the present is pregnant with the future, but the future is always undetermined and subject to change. The currents of history can be redirected by committed individuals and the formation of new institutions. In this regard, I believe that creativity and persistence, rooted in hope, can change the world. That is why I believe it is so important to educate and inspire young leaders to join the effort to achieve a world free of nuclear weapons. They not only can, but will, change the world. I think we should do all we can to awaken youth to the importance of combating nuclear dangers and to engage them in this effort to move history past the threat that nuclear weapons pose to their future far more than ours.

Falk: I had not intended to suggest that regional approaches to denuclearization would be sufficient to satisfy our goals, only that in the setting of the present conflict configurations, regional steps seem so sensible to reduce risks of catastrophic war and prudent from the outlook of the United States and the other major nuclear weapons states. It might also be the case, as with No First Use, that the political process involved in establishing a nuclear weapon–free zone in a war-prone region would generate some pro-disarmament momentum.

Youth as Critical Actors

Falk: As we come to the end of these conversations, it is appropriate to express our hopes for the future as you have done by singling out youth as critical actors in plotting an escape from nuclearism. I think we should do all we can to inform and stimulate the young to recognize how important it is to achieve a world without nuclear weapons, and what an empowering journey it would be along the path to such a benevolent outcome.

Beyond this, we need to keep our ethical and political sensibilities oriented toward broader and deeper structural changes in world order that might make the advocacy of nuclear disarmament more effective. I am thinking particularly of steps to democratize the manner in which world politics are conducted, perhaps starting with the establishment of a global parliament shaped in light of the experience with the European Parliament or imposing "compulsory jurisdiction" on all sovereign states with respect to the referral of disputes among states to the ICJ. Another useful change would be to strengthen the global rule of law so that it applied to the strong and weak alike and gave the International Criminal Court authority to assess allegations of criminality responsibly brought against governments and individuals acting on behalf of sovereign states. In effect, I am urging a series of steps that do two main things: (1) increase the role of people in the formulation of global policy and enhance the relevance of international law to the resolution of disputes among states, and (2) impose agreed standards of accountability on those who act on behalf of states.

Revolutions of the Mind

Falk: In this spirit, also, I think the time has come to insist on the pursuit of nonviolent geopolitics, to renounce once and for all the option to wage "wars of choice." Outgoing Secretary of Defense Robert Gates indicated that the United States has lost its appetite for such wars, given the unanticipated high costs of its conflicts in Iraq and Afghanistan. Ever since

Vietnam, reliance on military solutions for political conflicts has proved extremely costly and rarely successful. Heeding this record of the decline of hard power, the rise of soft power requires adjustment in the strategic pursuit of global objectives. Added to this for the United States and Europe are serious financial crises that give rise to demands to shift resources from the military to the needs of society. From these perspectives, the promotion and acceptance of a nonviolent geopolitics as a matter of national policy would be an enormous move in the direction of closing the gap between international law and foreign policy. It should not be overlooked that the UN Charter back in 1945 outlawed wars of choice and strictly limited the lawful right of a state to use force in situations of self-defense against a prior armed attack. This legal repudiation of aggressive war had been the basis for holding German and Japanese leaders criminally responsible for committing what were called "crimes against peace" in the London Charter that laid the foundations for the Nuremberg and Tokyo tribunals. Given this background, it is time now to take the political and psychological step of basing foreign policy on law, backed up by experience and the prudent conservation of scarce resources.

Yet, can we not still ask, What have these proposed global reforms to do with achieving a world without nuclear weapons? I would answer my own question with a single word: everything. I have argued all along, and for many years, that nuclear weaponry is the crown jewel of the war system, and unless that system is discredited and dissolved (in substance and in our minds), we will never get very far with nuclear disarmament. All profound changes in social conditions have started as "revolutions of the mind," including the motto of the World Social Forum, "There are alternatives." I think there are many reasons to believe that we are in a prerevolutionary phase with respect to war and that the rising powers in the non-West are likely to be quite receptive to a peace-oriented world order if the West can be persuaded to join in the process. This is where a revival of American leadership would have the greatest potential purchase on the future!

Krieger: I appreciate that, as we bring our conversation to an end, you raise these important issues of global reform. I am very much in favor of these changes that would democratize the international system and make international law the accepted measure of conduct with appropriate accountability for national leaders who violate this law. I have always favored the accountability imposed at the Nuremberg Trials and deeply regretted the failure of the victorious Allied powers in World War II to apply the same standards to their own leaders subsequent to the tribunals. It has been my position, though, that the urgency of the need to achieve a world without nuclear weapons gave this issue priority, as a pragmatic matter, over these other needed systemic changes. I am less sure of this now—less sure, that is, of the capability to achieve nuclear weapons abolition within the framework of a war-centric international system.

If it is essential to change the war-centric system to a peace-centric system in order to eliminate the nuclear weapons threat to humanity, then I doubt very much that the United States can be counted on to lead this revolution in human thought and behavior. The United States has been the leader of the war-centric world, and its warlike behavior has intensified in the decade since 9/11. The leadership toward peace, the needed nonviolent revolution, will need to come from other countries that embrace soft power as the path to a more secure, prosperous, and decent future. The United States will require an intervention from its friends based on the principle that friends don't let friends drive drunk. The United States has been driving drunk with power for far too long.

The future well-being of the planet and its inhabitants requires solving some large-scale problems that are not susceptible to war-centric solutions. The abolition of nuclear weapons is one of these, but there are many others, including global warming, the pollution of the oceans and atmosphere, massive poverty, and epidemic diseases. All these share a common factor—success in solving them will require global cooperation. Anything short of global cooperation will doom the system to failure. The war-centric system is rooted in insecurity and greed, and nuclear weapons are wrongly viewed as the ultimate means of achieving security. In today's terminology, the war-centric system is unsustainable, and it makes life itself unsustainable.

I agree with you that "revolutions of the mind" have become necessary. We must change our thinking if we are to change our unsustainable patterns of behavior. In our present world, we are all hostage to unconscionable inequities, war, and, ultimately, nuclear annihilation. We owe it to ourselves and to life itself to break free of the bonds of war-centric geopolitics. The only way to do this is to insist that the war-centric system be transformed into a peace-centric system that embraces a nonviolent geopolitics. It is, indeed, a revolutionary vision, but one that has worked on a smaller but significant scale with leadership from Gandhi to King to Nelson Mandela. It is a vision that must be conveyed to today's youth with an appropriate sense of urgency. We can attempt to convey the vision and help to educate them, but I doubt that we can fully empower the next generation. This they will have to do themselves, in the realization that life is sacred and they, like all of us, are on this planet to contribute to a better world and act as trustees for future generations.

Notes

Chapter 1

1. Barack Obama, "Remarks by President Barack Obama, Hradčany Square, Prague, Czech Republic," White House, April 5, 2009, www.whitehouse.gov/ the_press_office/Remarks-By-President-Barack-Obama-In-Prague-As-Delivered.
2. Ibid.
3. George P. Shultz, William J. Perry, Henry A. Kissinger, and Sam Nunn, "A World Free of Nuclear Weapons," *Wall Street Journal,* January 4, 2007, www .pugwash.org/reports/nw/nuclear-weapons-free-statements/NWFW_statements_ USA.htm#anchorWallSt1; "Toward a Nuclear-Free World," *Wall Street Journal,* January 15, 2008, www.pugwash.org/reports/nw/nuclear-weapons-free-statements/ NWFW_statements_USA.htm#anchorWallSt1; "How to Protect Our Nuclear Deterrent," *Wall Street Journal,* January 19, 2010, www.pugwash.org/reports/nw/ nuclear-weapons-free-statements/NWFW_statements_USA.htm#anchorWallSt1; "Deterrence in the Age of Nuclear Proliferation," *Wall Street Journal,* March 7, 2011, http://online.wsj.com/article/SB10001424052748703300904576178760530169414 .html.
4. Dwight D. Eisenhower, "Farewell Radio and Television Address to the American People, January 17, 1961," Dwight D. Eisenhower Presidential Library and Museum, www.eisenhower.archives.gov/all_about_ike/speeches/farewell_address .pdf.
5. Ibid., 2.
6. Ibid., 4.
7. Ibid.
8. Gareth Porter, "From Military-Industrial Complex to Permanent War State," Common Dreams, January 17, 2011, www.commondreams.org/view/2011/01/17-6.

Chapter 2

1. Ronald Reagan, "Address before a Joint Session of the Congress Reporting on the State of the Union," Reagan 2020, January 25, 1984, http://reagan2020.us/ speeches/state_of_the_union_1984.asp.

Chapter 3

1. "Treaty on the Non-Proliferation of Nuclear Weapons," entered into force on March 5, 1970, U.S. Department of State, www.state.gov/www/global/arms/treaties/npt1.html#2.
2. *Advisory Opinion of the International Court of Justice on the Legality of the Threat or Use of Nuclear Weapons,* United Nations General Assembly, A/51/218, October 15, 1996, 37.
3. Ibid.
4. Richard J. Barnet, *Who Wants Disarmament?* (Boston: Beacon Press, 1960).

Chapter 4

1. The McCloy-Zorin Accords can be found on the website of the Nuclear Age Peace Foundation at http://nuclearfiles.org/menu/key-issues/nuclear-weapons/issues/arms-control-disarmament/mccloy-zorin-accords_1961-09-20.htm.
2. Ibid.
3. Ibid.
4. Ban Ki-moon, "The United Nations and Security in a Nuclear-Weapon-Free World," Address to the East-West Institute, United Nations, October 24, 2008, www.un.org/apps/news/infocus/sgspeeches/search_full.asp?statID=351.
5. The Model Nuclear Weapons Convention can be found on the website of the International Network of Engineers and Scientists against Proliferation at http://inesap.org/sites/default/files/inesap_old/mNWC_2007_Unversion_English_N0821377.pdf.
6. David Krieger, *Nuclear Non-Proliferation and Disarmament: Shifting the Mindset, a Briefing Booklet for the 2010 Non-Proliferation Treaty Review Conference* (Santa Barbara, CA: Nuclear Age Peace Foundation, 2010).

Chapter 5

1. Martin Luther King Jr., *The Trumpet of Conscience* (San Francisco: Harper & Row, 1967), 23.
2. Ibid., 31.
3. Ibid., 34.
4. Glenn Paige, *Nonkilling Global Political Science* (Bloomington, IN: Xlibris Corporation, 2007).
5. David Krieger and Daisaku Ikeda, *Choose Hope: Your Role in Waging Peace in the Nuclear Age* (Santa Monica, CA: Middleway Press, 2002).
6. E. P. Thompson, *Exterminism and Cold War* (London: Verso, 1982).

Chapter 6

1. *Global Fissile Material Report 2009: A Path to Nuclear Disarmament,* Fourth Annual Report of the International Panel on Fissile Materials, 2009, 103. This report can be found on the website of the International Panel on Fissile Materials at www .fissilematerials.org/ipfm/site_down/gfmr09.pdf.

2. *Global Fissile Material Report 2010: Balancing the Books: Production and Stocks,* Fifth Annual Report of the International Panel on Fissile Materials, 2010, 9. This report can be found on the website of the International Panel on Fissile Materials at www.fissilematerials.org/ipfm/site_down/gfmr10.pdf.

3. Ibid.

4. *Global Fissile Material Report 2009,* 113.

5. Mikhail Gorbachev, "Before Fukushima," *Hindustan Times,* April 3, 2011, www.hindustantimes.com/Before-Fukushima/Article1-680937.aspx.

6. H. Patricia Hynes, "25 Years after Chernobyl: Lessons Learned," Common Dreams, www.commondreams.org/view/2011/04/12-11.

7. Robert Jay Lifton, "Fukushima and Hiroshima," *New York Times,* April 15, 2011, www.nytimes.com/2011/04/16/opinion/16iht-edlifton16.html.

Chapter 7

1. Robert Jackson, "Nuremberg Trials: Opening Address for the United States," *A Teacher's Guide to the Holocaust,* Florida Center for Instructional Technology, http://fcit.usf.edu/holocaust/resource/document/DocJac17.htm.

2. "Treaty on the Non-Proliferation of Nuclear Weapons," entered into force on March 5, 1970, United Nations, www.un.org/disarmament/WMD/Nuclear/NPT .shtml.

3. *Advisory Opinion of the International Court of Justice,* 36.

4. Ibid.

5. Ibid.

6. Ibid.

7. Ibid., 37.

8. Ibid., 170 (emphasis in original).

9. Ibid., 37.

10. Ibid., 42 (emphasis in original).

11. Ibid., 42–43.

Chapter 8

1. Joseph Heller, *Picture This* (New York: Simon & Schuster, 1988), 270.

2. Daniel Ellsberg, *Secrets: A Memoir of Vietnam and the Pentagon Papers* (New York: Viking Penguin, 2002).

3. See, for example, Patrick J. Sloyan, "Iraqis Buried Alive—U.S. Attacked with Bulldozers during Gulf War Ground Attack," *Newsday*, September 12, 1991.

4. See, for example, Kai Bird and Martin J. Sherwin, "The Myths of Hiroshima," Common Dreams, August 5, 2005, www.commondreams.org/views05/0805-24.htm.

5. Barack Obama, "Remarks by President Barack Obama, Hradčany Square, Prague, Czech Republic," White House, April 5, 2009, www.whitehouse.gov/the_press_office/Remarks-By-President-Barack-Obama-In-Prague-As-Delivered.

6. Albert Camus, "Neither Victims nor Executioners," trans. Dwight MacDonald, *Politics* (July–August 1947).

7. "John F. Kennedy Quotations," John F. Kennedy Presidential Library and Museum, www.jfklibrary.org/Research/Ready-Reference/JFK-Quotations.aspx.

Chapter 9

1. Amy Goodman and David Goodman, "The Hiroshima Cover-Up," *Baltimore Sun*, August 5, 2005, www.commondreams.org/views05/0805-20.htm.

2. Martin Luther King Jr., "Where Do We Go from Here," speech given on August 16, 1967, in Atlanta, Georgia, and available on the website of the Martin Luther King Jr. Research and Education Institute at http://mlk-kpp01.stanford.edu/index.php/kingpapers/article/where_do_we_go_from_here.

3. Steven Starr, "'Safe' and 'Clean' Nuclear Power," Nuclear Age Peace Foundation, www.wagingpeace.org/articles/db_article.php?article_id=255.

4. Ibid.

5. Ibid.

6. Alan Robock and Owen Brian Toon, "Local Nuclear War, Global Suffering," *Scientific American*, January 2010, http://climate.envsci.rutgers.edu/pdf/RobockToonSciAmJan2010.pdf.

7. Robert Gates, "Exit Near, Gates Speaks Bluntly of U.S. Allies," *New York Times*, June 15, 2011, www.nytimes.com/2011/06/16/world/16pentagon.html.

Chapter 10

1. Nassim Nicholas Taleb, *The Black Swan: The Impact of the Highly Improbable* (New York: Random House, 2007).

Index

About the Authors

Richard Falk is Albert G. Milbank Professor of International Law and Practice Emeritus at Princeton where he was a member of the faculty for 40 years. Since 2002 he has been a research professor at the University of California–Santa Barbara. He has been Special Rapporteur on Occupied Palestine for the UN Human Rights Council since 2008, and served on a panel of experts appointed by the President of the UN General Assembly, 2008–2009. He is the author or editor of numerous books including the forthcoming *Legality and Legitimacy in Global Affairs* (Oxford 2012).

David Krieger is a founder of the Nuclear Age Peace Foundation, and has served as President of the Foundation since 1982. Under his leadership the Foundation has initiated many innovative projects for building peace, strengthening international law, abolishing nuclear weapons, and empowering peace leaders. Among other leadership positions, he is one of 50 Councilors from around the world on the World Future Council. He is the author and editor of numerous books and articles related to achieving peace in the Nuclear Age. A graduate of Occidental College, he holds MA and PhD degrees in political science from the University of Hawaii.